FINAL

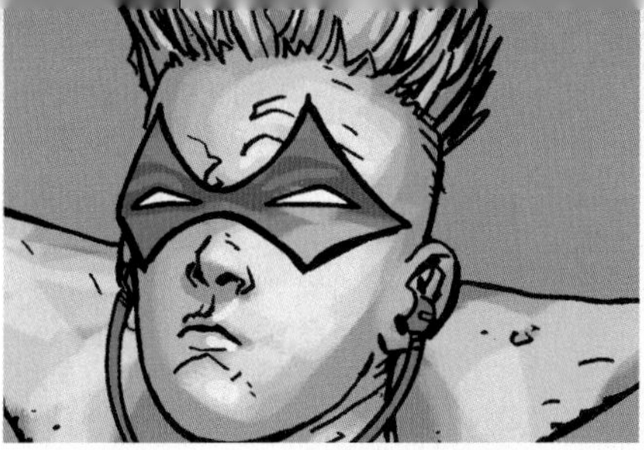

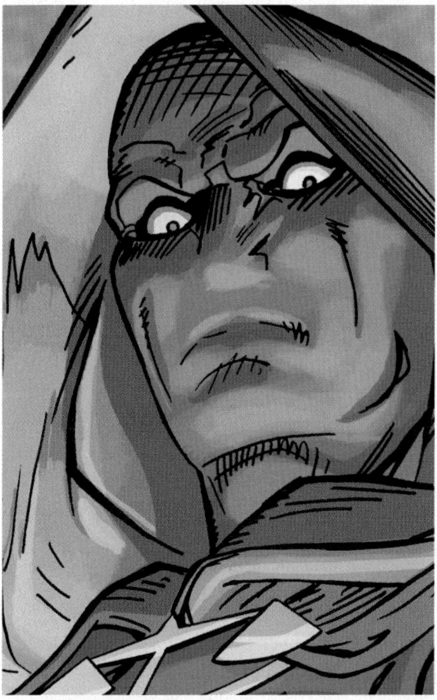

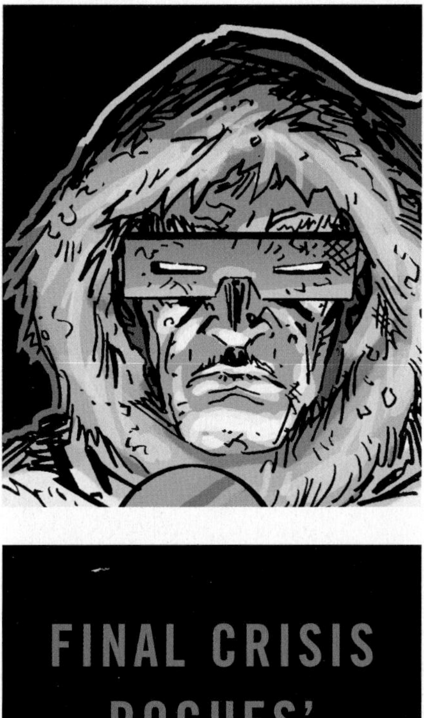

FINAL CRISIS ROGUES' REVENGE

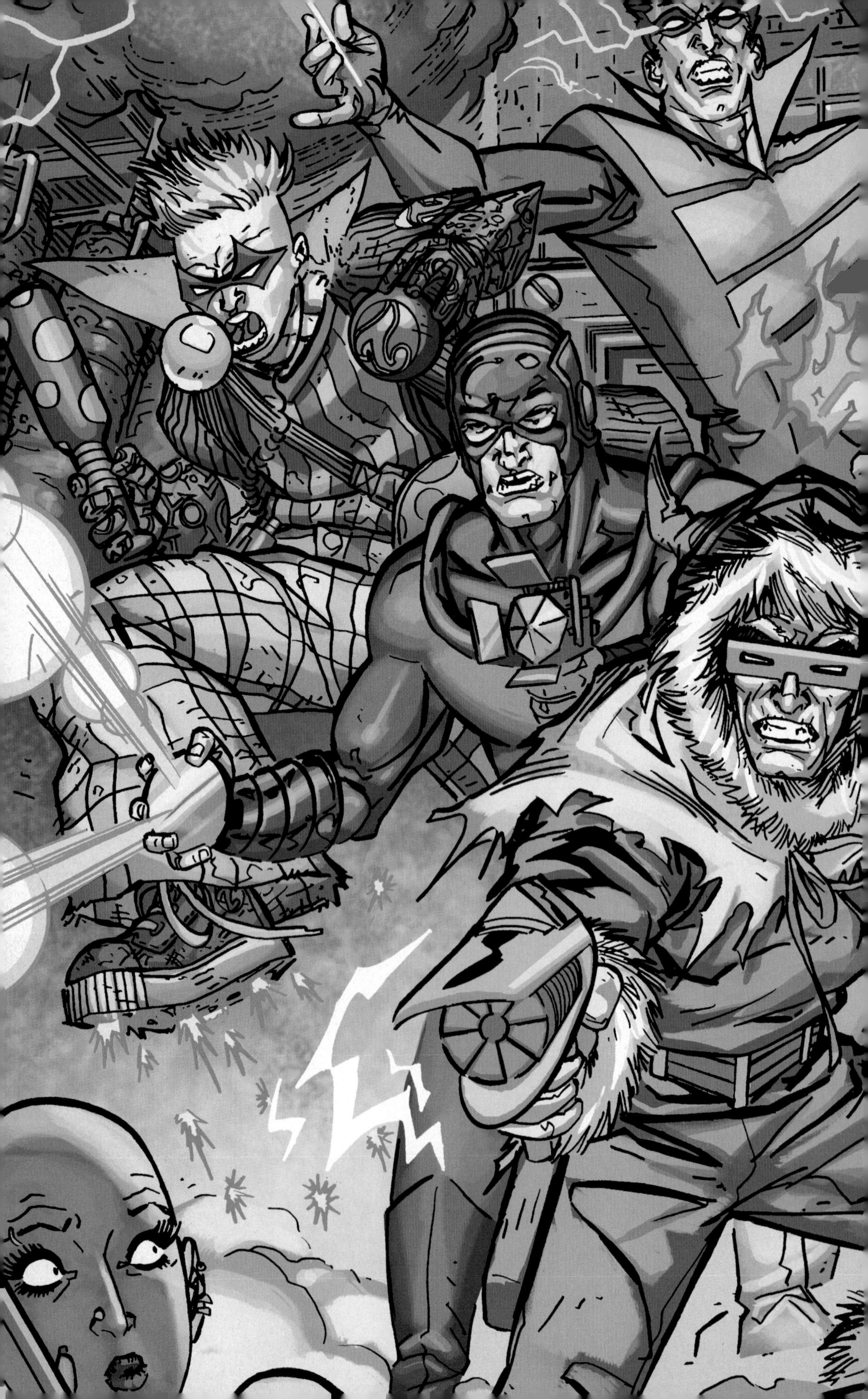

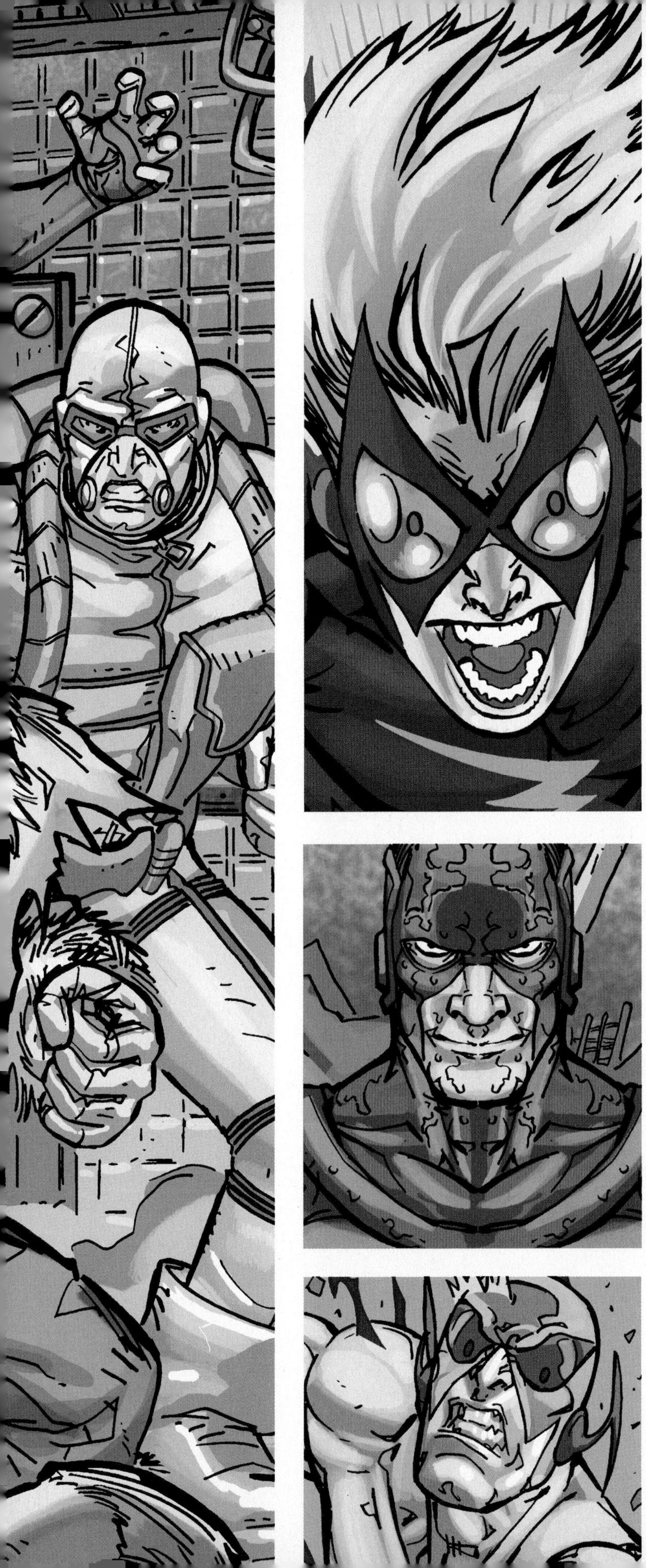

FINAL CRISIS ROGUES' REVENGE

Geoff Johns
Writer

ROGUES' REVENGE
Scott Kolins
Artist and Covers

Dave McCaig
Colorist

Nick J. Napolitano
Letterer

ABSOLUTE ZERO
Scott Kolins
Penciller

Dan Panosian
Inker

James Sinclair
Colorist

Digtal Chameleon
Separator

Gaspar
Letterer

ROGUE PROFILE: ZOOM
Scott Kolins
Penciller

Doug Hazlewood
Inker

James Sinclair
Colorist & Separator

Kurt Hathaway
Letterer

Dan DiDio   Senior VP-Executive Editor
Joey Cavalieri   Editor-original series
Chris Conroy   Assistant Editor-original series
Sean Mackiewicz   Editor-collected edition
Robbin Brosterman   Senior Art Director
Paul Levitz   President & Publisher
Georg Brewer   VP-Design & DC Direct Creative
Richard Bruning   Senior VP-Creative Director
Patrick Caldon   Executive VP-Finance & Operations
Chris Caramalis   VP-Finance
John Cunningham   VP-Marketing
Terri Cunningham   VP-Managing Editor
Amy Genkins   Senior VP-Business & Legal Affairs
Alison Gill   VP-Manufacturing
David Hyde   VP-Publicity
Hank Kanalz   VP-General Manager, WildStorm
Jim Lee   Editorial Director-WildStorm
Gregory Noveck   Senior VP-Creative Affairs
Sue Pohja   VP-Book Trade Sales
Steve Rotterdam   Senior VP-Sales & Marketing
Cheryl Rubin   Senior VP-Brand Management
Alysse Soll   VP-Advertising & Custom Publishing
Jeff Trojan   VP-Business Development, DC Direct
Bob Wayne   VP-Sales

Cover by Scott Kolins

FINAL CRISIS: ROGUES' REVENGE

DC Comics, 1700 Broadway, New York, NY 10019
A Warner Bros. Entertainment Company
Printed in the USA. First Printing.

ISBN: 978-1-4012-2333-5
SC ISBN: 978-1-4012-2334-2

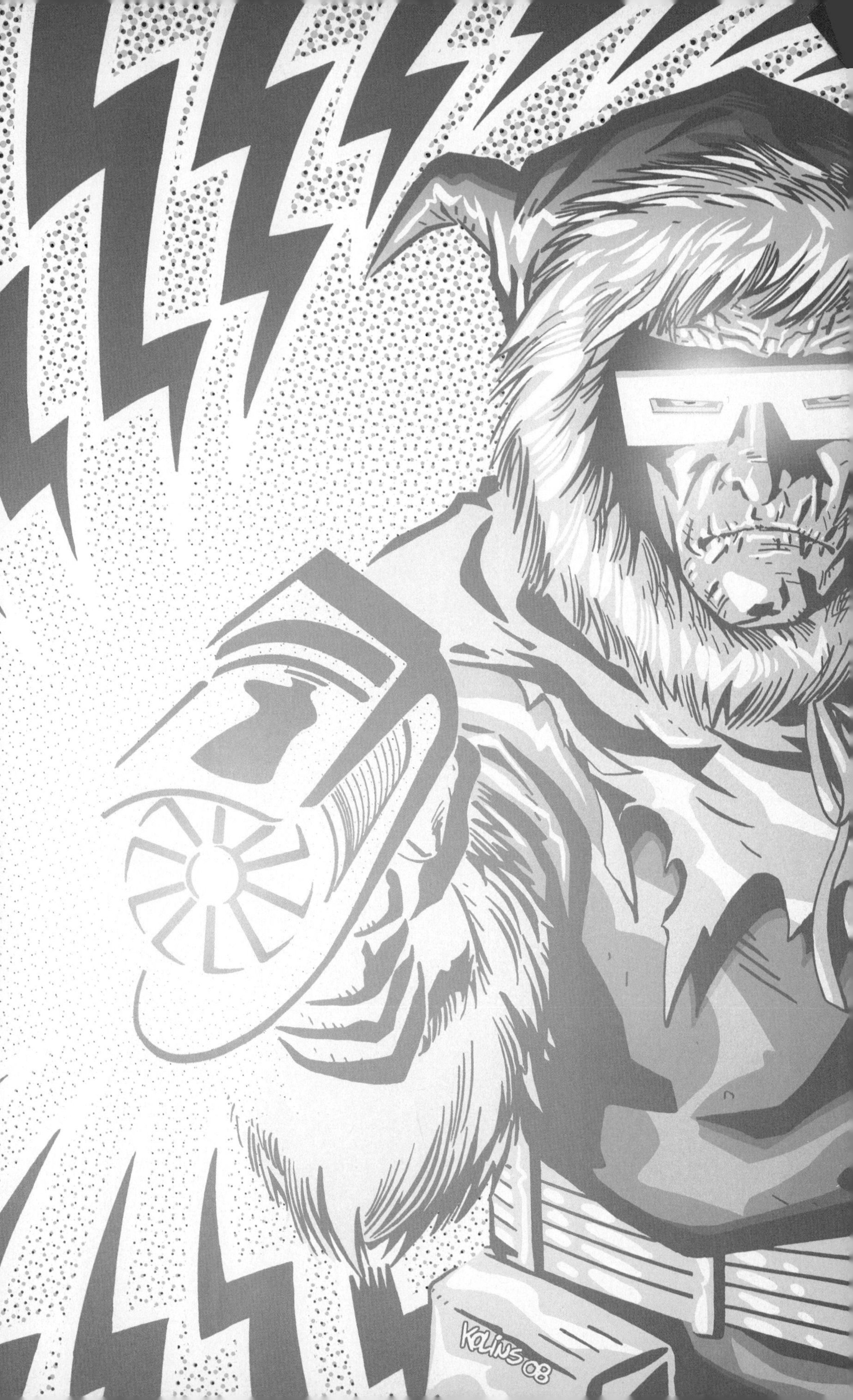
KOLINS '08

Cover to FINAL CRISIS: ROGUES' REVENGE #1

Sliver cover to FINAL CRISIS: ROGUES' REVENGE #1

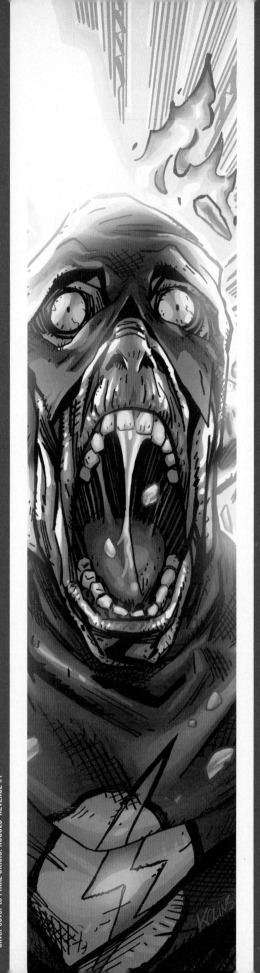

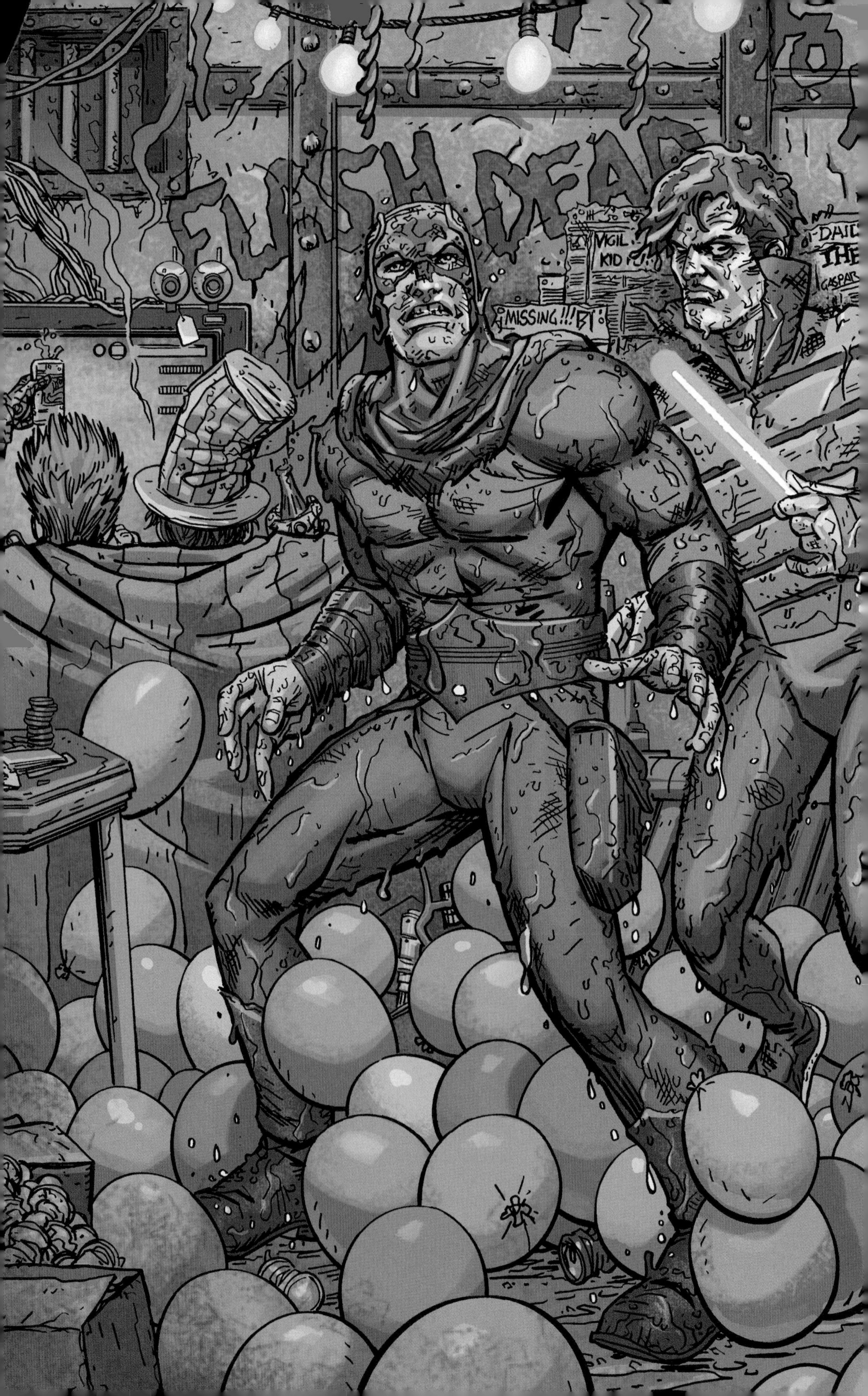
VIGIL
KID
MISSING!!!
GASPAR

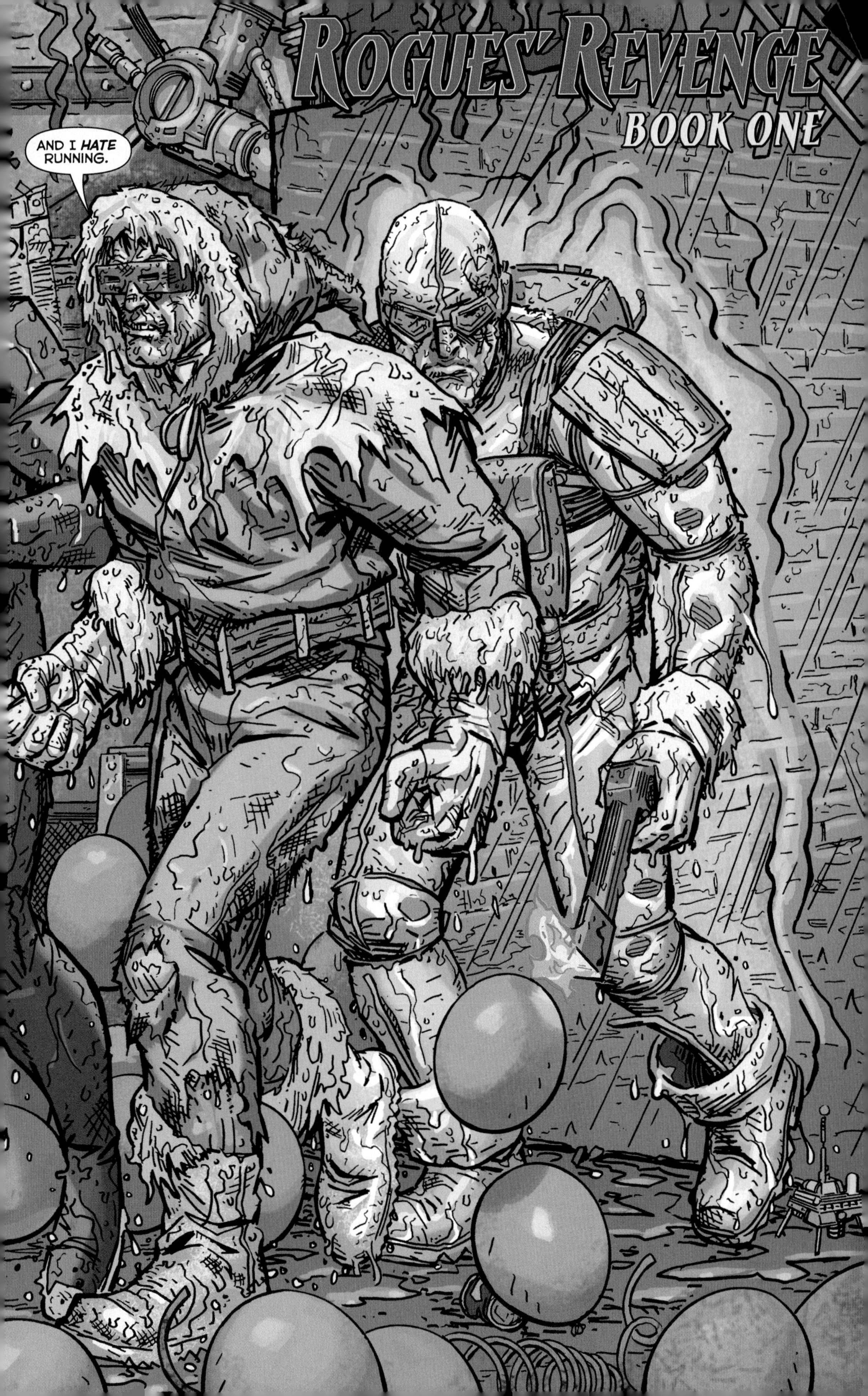
ROGUES' REVENGE
BOOK ONE
AND I *HATE* RUNNING.

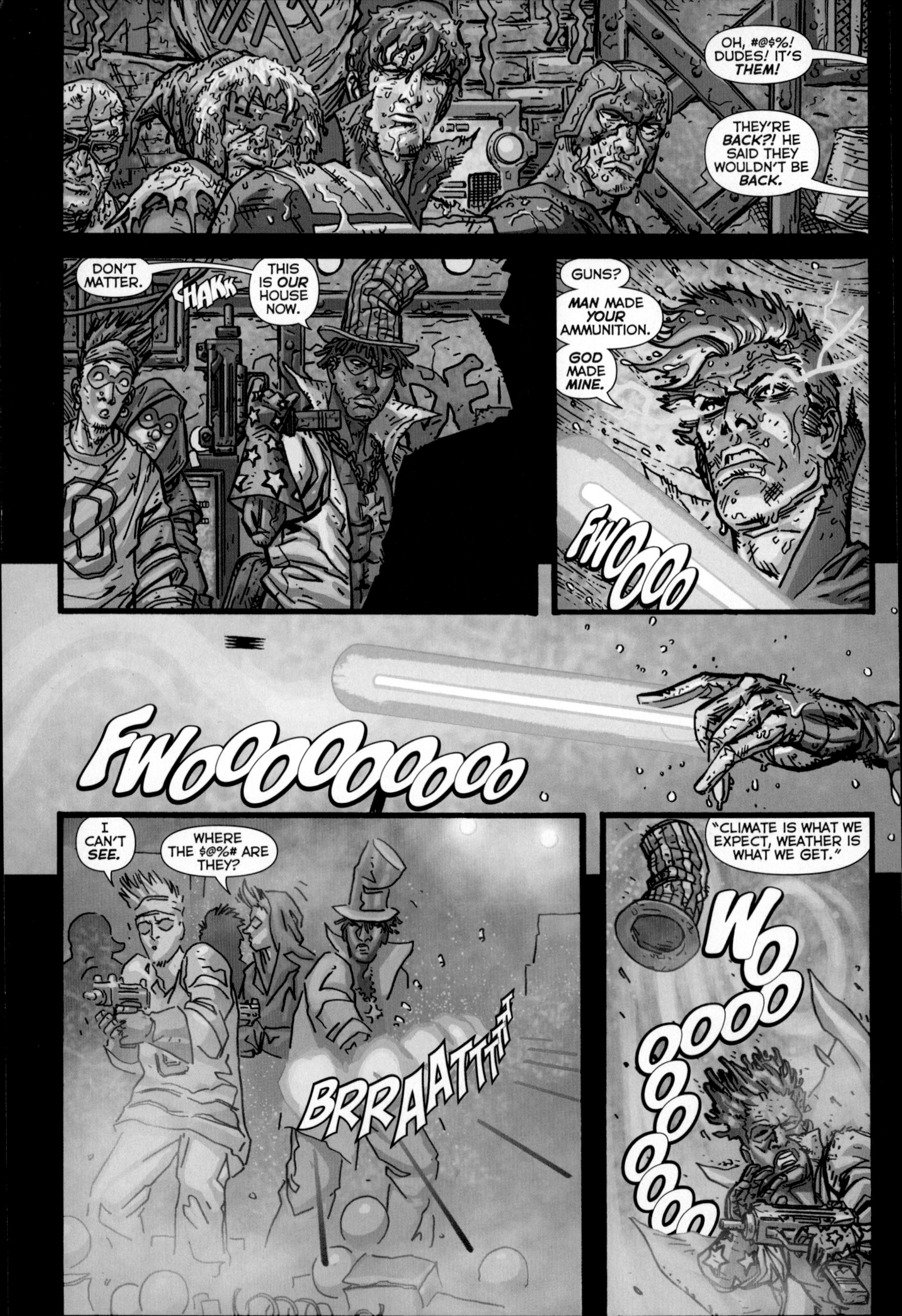
OH, #@$%! DUDES! IT'S THEM!
THEY'RE BACK?! HE SAID THEY WOULDN'T BE BACK.
DON'T MATTER.
CHAKK
THIS IS OUR HOUSE NOW.
GUNS?
MAN MADE YOUR AMMUNITION.
GOD MADE MINE.
FWOOOO
FWOOOOOOOOOO
I CAN'T SEE.
WHERE THE $@%# ARE THEY?
BRRAATTTT
"CLIMATE IS WHAT WE EXPECT, WEATHER IS WHAT WE GET."
WOOOOOOOOOOOO

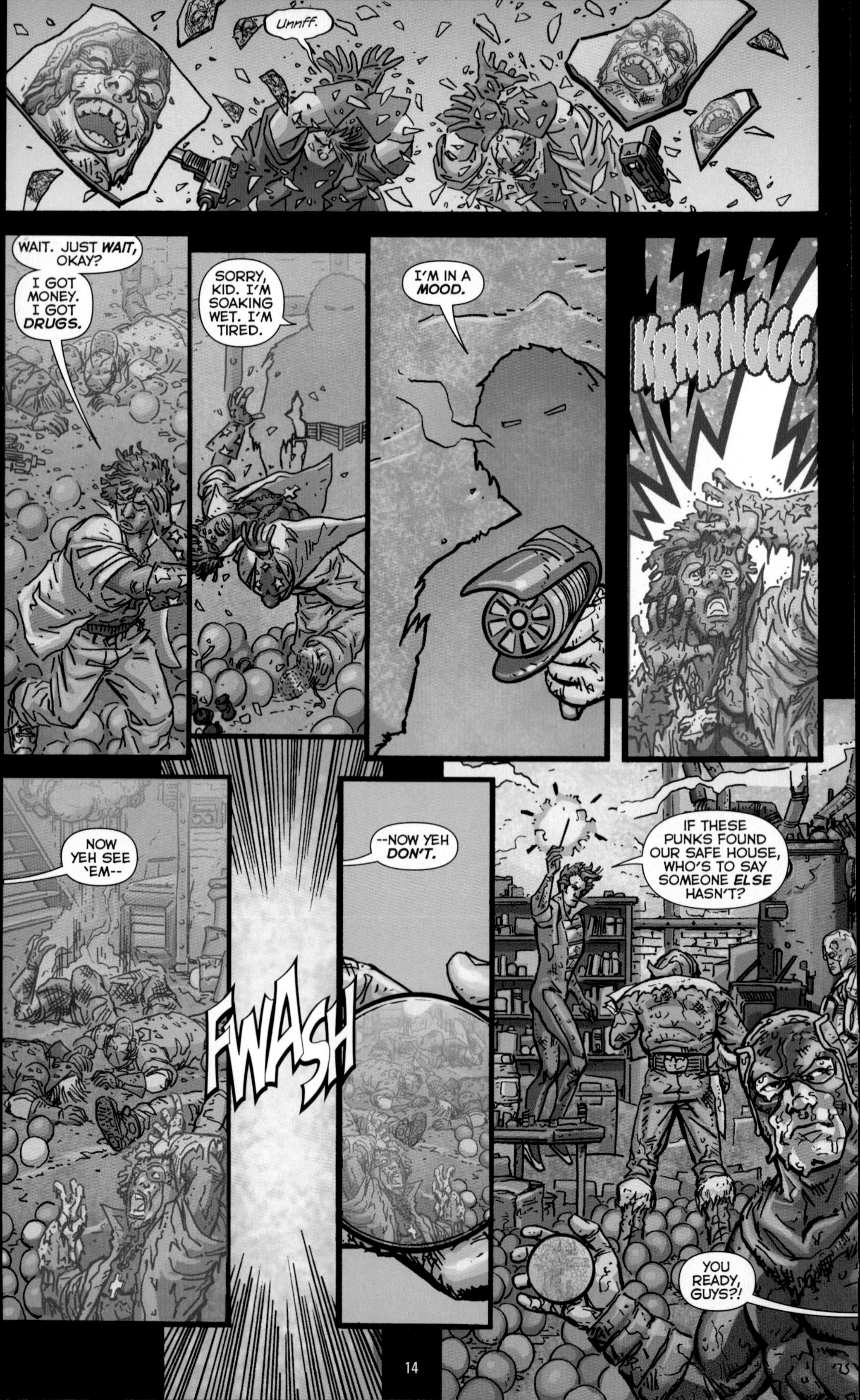
Unnff.
WAIT. JUST WAIT, OKAY?
I GOT MONEY. I GOT DRUGS.
SORRY, KID. I'M SOAKING WET. I'M TIRED.
I'M IN A MOOD.
KRRRNGGG
NOW YEH SEE 'EM--
FWASH
--NOW YEH DON'T.
IF THESE PUNKS FOUND OUR SAFE HOUSE, WHO'S TO SAY SOMEONE ELSE HASN'T?
YOU READY, GUYS?!

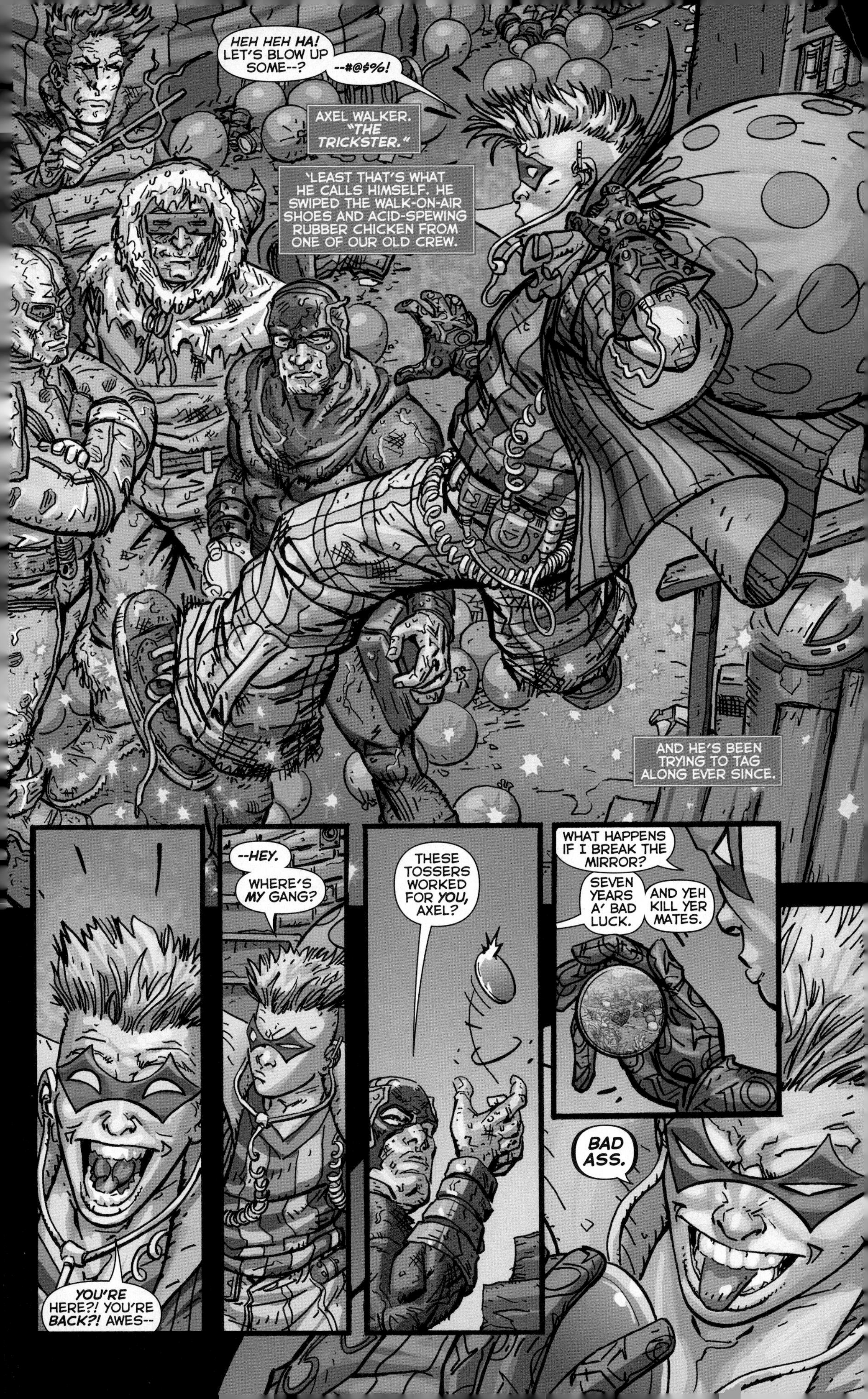
HEH HEH HA! LET'S BLOW UP SOME--?
--#@$%!
AXEL WALKER. "THE TRICKSTER."
'LEAST THAT'S WHAT HE CALLS HIMSELF. HE SWIPED THE WALK-ON-AIR SHOES AND ACID-SPEWING RUBBER CHICKEN FROM ONE OF OUR OLD CREW.
AND HE'S BEEN TRYING TO TAG ALONG EVER SINCE.
YOU'RE HERE?! YOU'RE BACK?! AWES--
--HEY.
WHERE'S MY GANG?
THESE TOSSERS WORKED FOR YOU, AXEL?
WHAT HAPPENS IF I BREAK THE MIRROR?
SEVEN YEARS A' BAD LUCK.
AND YEH KILL YER MATES.
BAD ASS.

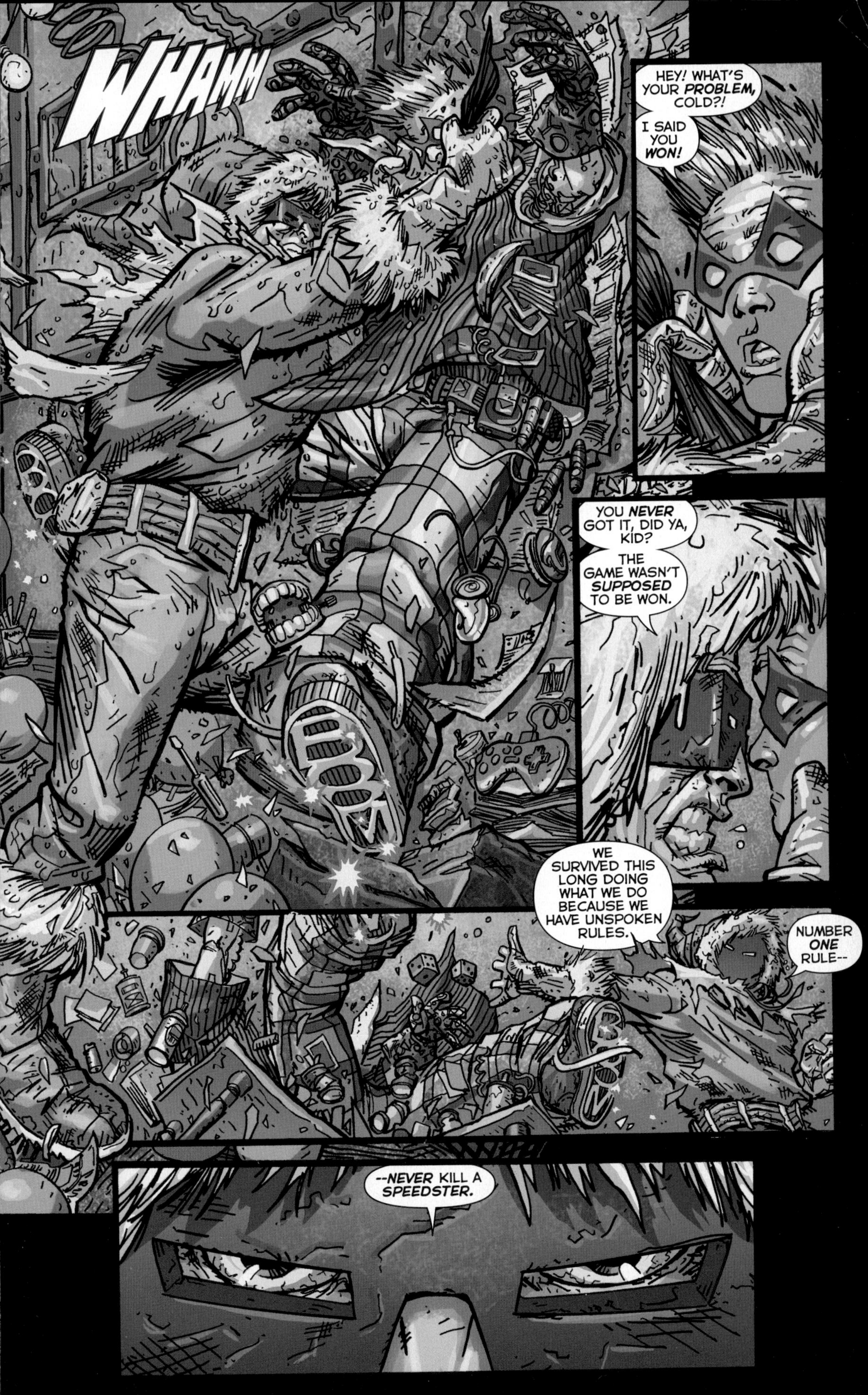
WHAMM
HEY! WHAT'S YOUR PROBLEM, COLD?!
I SAID YOU WON!
YOU NEVER GOT IT, DID YA, KID?
THE GAME WASN'T SUPPOSED TO BE WON.
WE SURVIVED THIS LONG DOING WHAT WE DO BECAUSE WE HAVE UNSPOKEN RULES.
NUMBER ONE RULE--
--NEVER KILL A SPEEDSTER.

I thought I could handle it. I'd been through one passing of the torch already. Unlike the rest of them--

SQUEEEE

--I was better for it.

IT'S AN **OPEN** AND **SHUT** CASE, MORILLO! SO **CLOSE** IT, ALREADY.

When Barry Allen died, he gave those golden boots to Wally West.

That's when I started singing a different tune. And Wally was the first to stand up for me.

To tell everyone the Pied Piper was the Rogue that reformed.

THE ROGUES **MURDERED** KID FLASH!

But I was so worried about Bart being in over his head--

THE **DEATH** OF **KID FLASH** WAS A **MISTAKE**.

--I didn't realize how much I was in over mine.

I KNOW YOU GET **HEADACHES** WHEN YOU **THINK** TOO HARD, CHYRE, BUT YOU NEED TO LOOK **DEEPER** HERE.

When Wally went off to raise his twins (who've apparently redefined the word "Impulse")--

SQUEEEE SQUEEEE

--I took it upon myself to make sure Bart Allen would be safe.

19

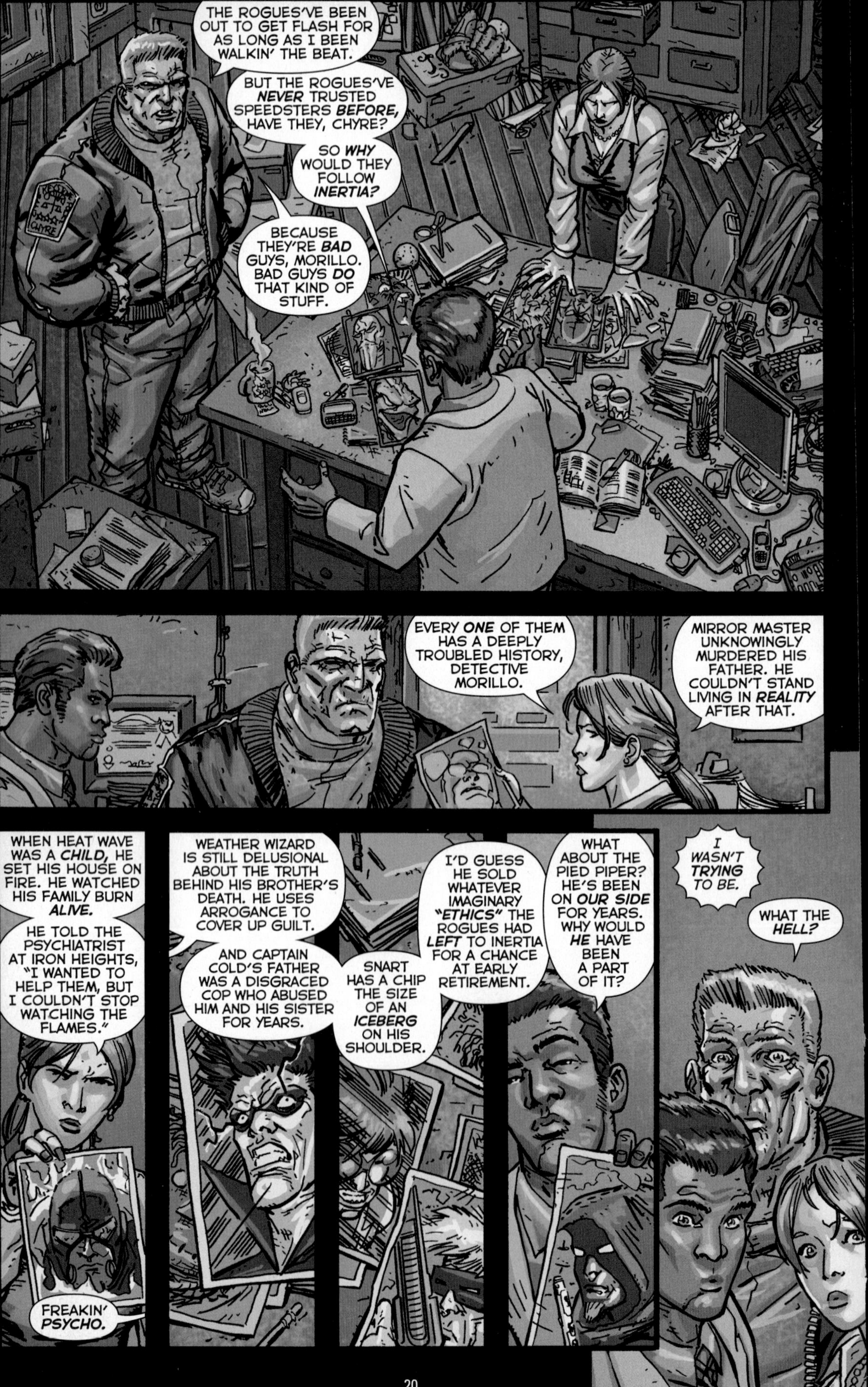

THE ROGUES'VE BEEN OUT TO GET FLASH FOR AS LONG AS I BEEN WALKIN' THE BEAT.
BUT THE ROGUES'VE NEVER TRUSTED SPEEDSTERS BEFORE, HAVE THEY, CHYRE?
SO WHY WOULD THEY FOLLOW INERTIA?
BECAUSE THEY'RE BAD GUYS, MORILLO. BAD GUYS DO THAT KIND OF STUFF.
EVERY ONE OF THEM HAS A DEEPLY TROUBLED HISTORY, DETECTIVE MORILLO.
MIRROR MASTER UNKNOWINGLY MURDERED HIS FATHER. HE COULDN'T STAND LIVING IN REALITY AFTER THAT.
WHEN HEAT WAVE WAS A CHILD, HE SET HIS HOUSE ON FIRE. HE WATCHED HIS FAMILY BURN ALIVE.
HE TOLD THE PSYCHIATRIST AT IRON HEIGHTS, "I WANTED TO HELP THEM, BUT I COULDN'T STOP WATCHING THE FLAMES."
FREAKIN' PSYCHO.
WEATHER WIZARD IS STILL DELUSIONAL ABOUT THE TRUTH BEHIND HIS BROTHER'S DEATH. HE USES ARROGANCE TO COVER UP GUILT.
AND CAPTAIN COLD'S FATHER WAS A DISGRACED COP WHO ABUSED HIM AND HIS SISTER FOR YEARS.
SNART HAS A CHIP THE SIZE OF AN ICEBERG ON HIS SHOULDER.
I'D GUESS HE SOLD WHATEVER IMAGINARY "ETHICS" THE ROGUES HAD LEFT TO INERTIA FOR A CHANCE AT EARLY RETIREMENT.
WHAT ABOUT THE PIED PIPER? HE'S BEEN ON OUR SIDE FOR YEARS. WHY WOULD HE HAVE BEEN A PART OF IT?
I WASN'T TRYING TO BE.
WHAT THE HELL?

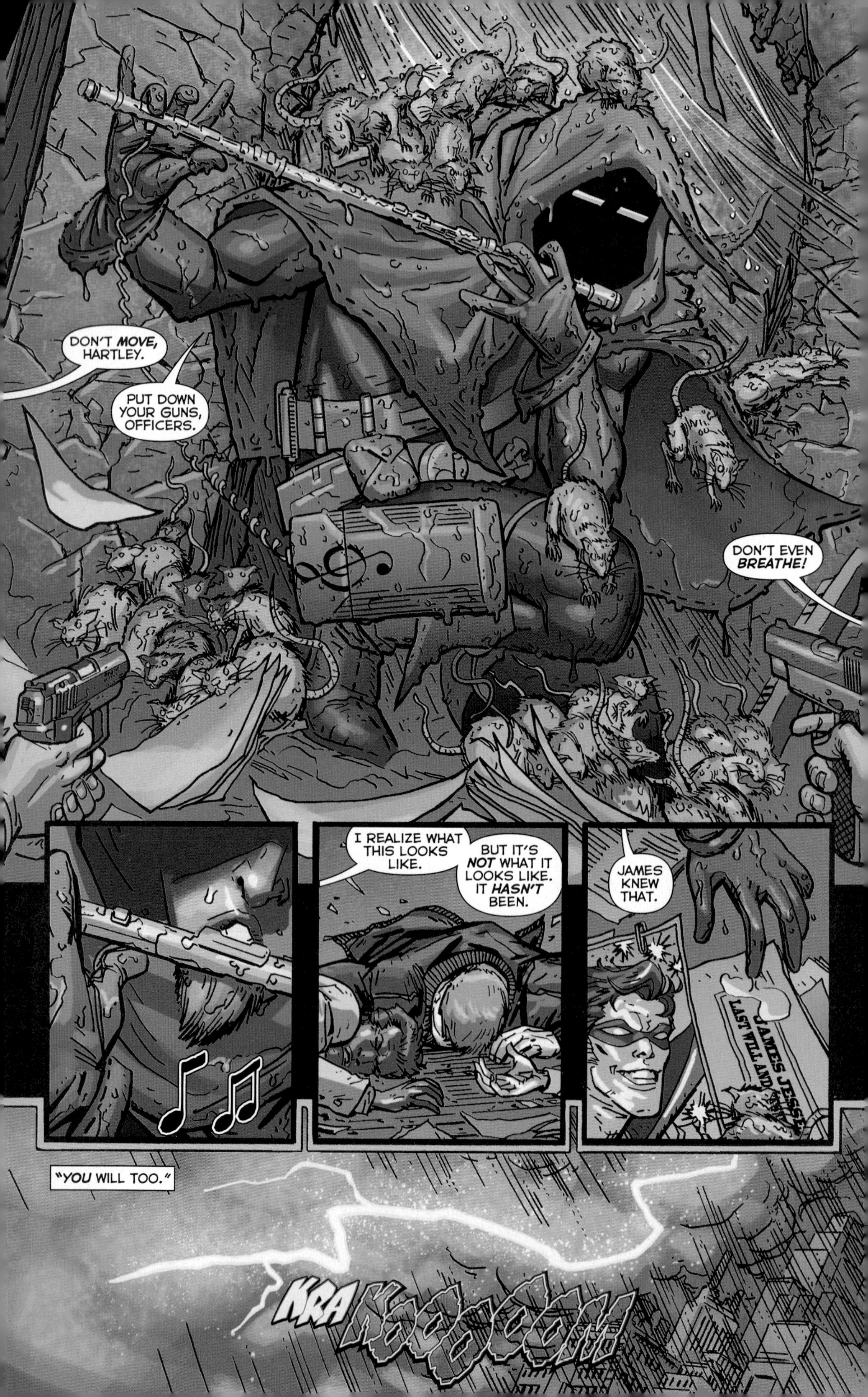

DON'T *MOVE,* HARTLEY.
PUT DOWN YOUR GUNS, OFFICERS.
DON'T EVEN *BREATHE!*
I REALIZE WHAT THIS LOOKS LIKE.
BUT IT'S *NOT* WHAT IT LOOKS LIKE. IT *HASN'T* BEEN.
JAMES KNEW THAT.
JAMES JESSE
LAST WILL AND
"*YOU* WILL TOO."
KRAKOOOOOM

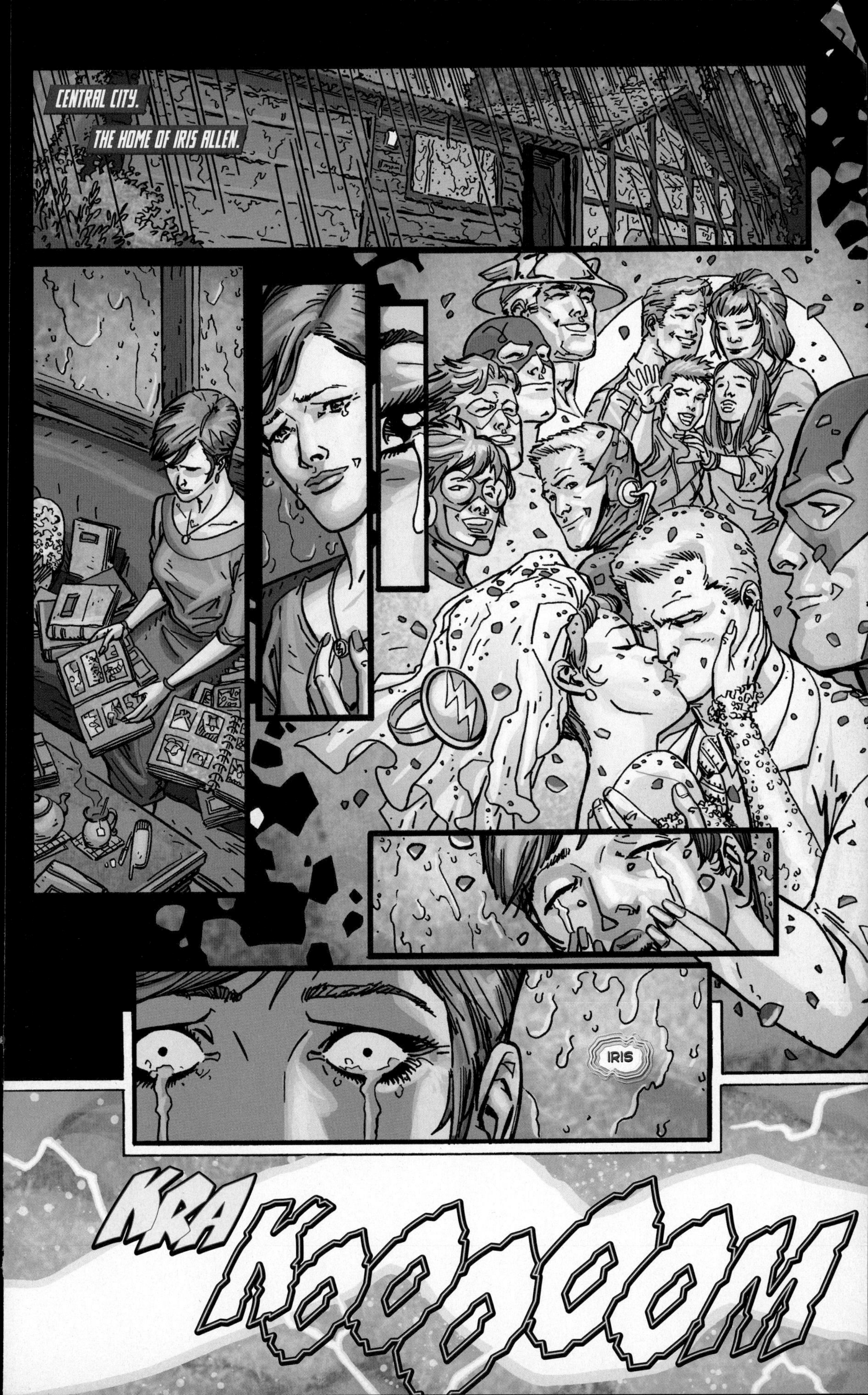
CENTRAL CITY.
THE HOME OF IRIS ALLEN.
IRIS
KRA
KOOOOOM

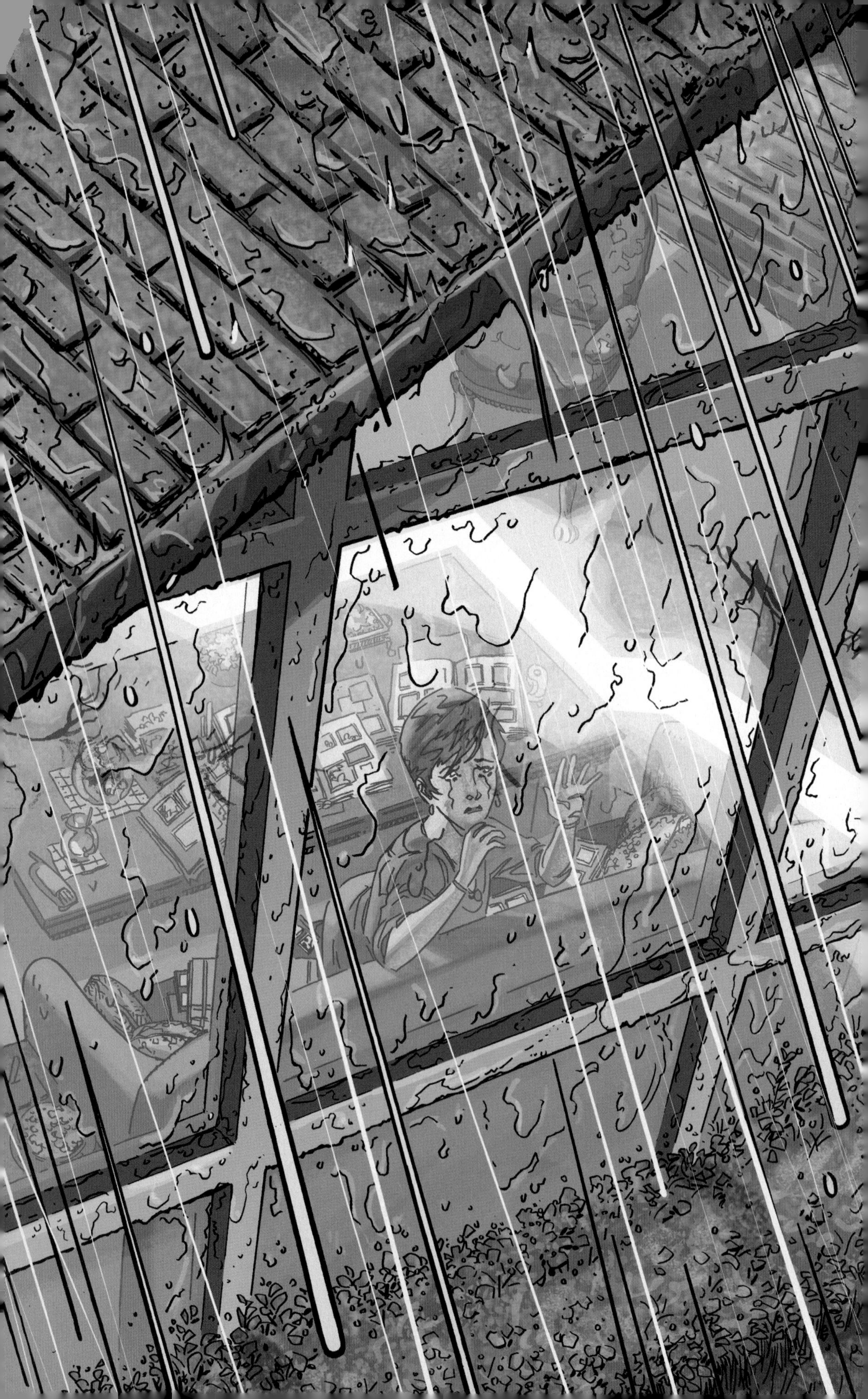

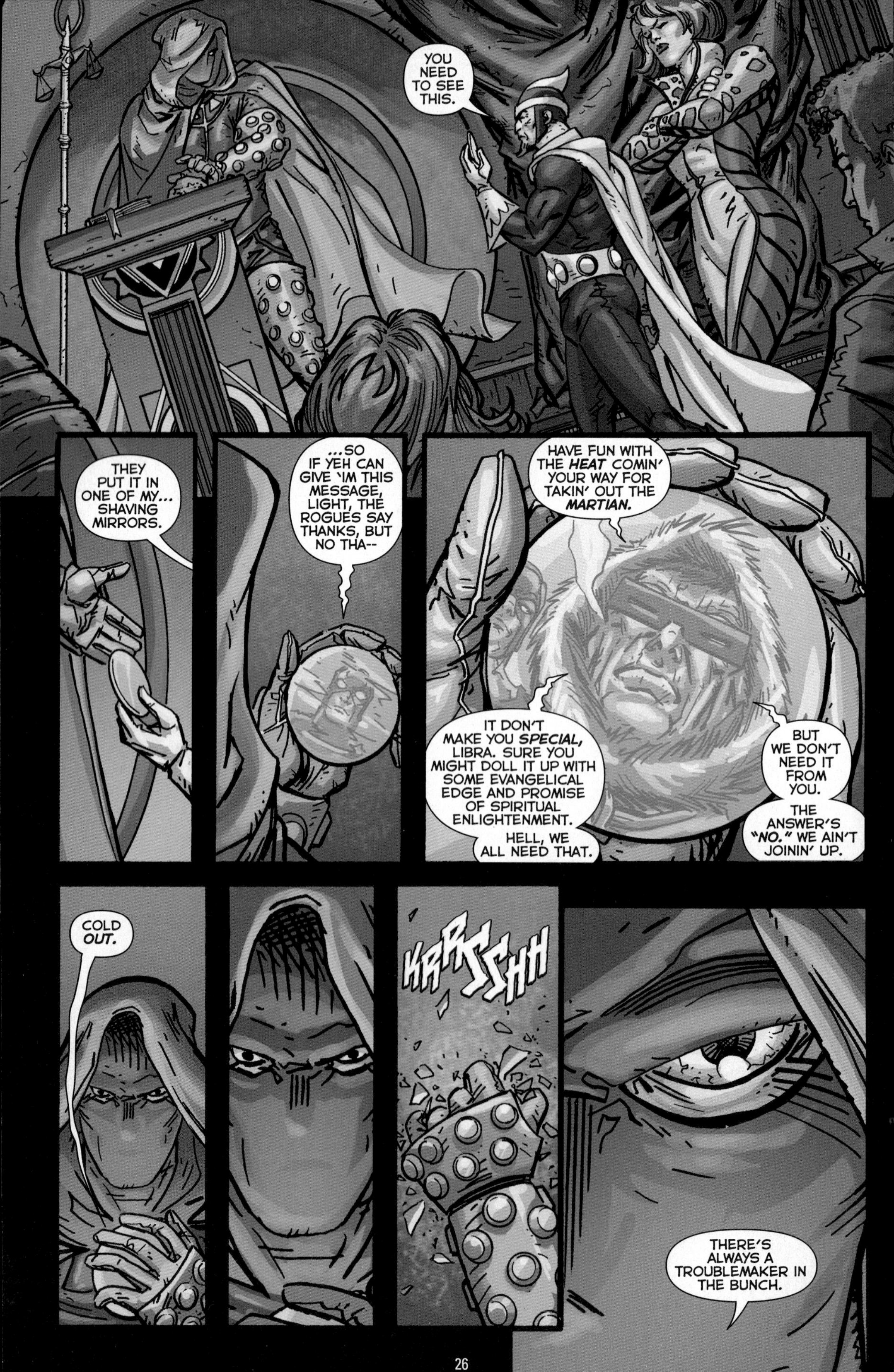
YOU NEED TO SEE THIS.
THEY PUT IT IN ONE OF MY... SHAVING MIRRORS.
...SO IF YEH CAN GIVE 'IM THIS MESSAGE, LIGHT, THE ROGUES SAY THANKS, BUT NO THA--
HAVE FUN WITH THE HEAT COMIN' YOUR WAY FOR TAKIN' OUT THE MARTIAN.
IT DON'T MAKE YOU SPECIAL, LIBRA. SURE YOU MIGHT DOLL IT UP WITH SOME EVANGELICAL EDGE AND PROMISE OF SPIRITUAL ENLIGHTENMENT.
HELL, WE ALL NEED THAT.
BUT WE DON'T NEED IT FROM YOU.
THE ANSWER'S "NO." WE AIN'T JOININ' UP.
COLD OUT.
KRRSSHH
THERE'S ALWAYS A TROUBLEMAKER IN THE BUNCH.

WHO IS HE?

PLAQUE SAYS HE WAS KID FLASH'S RIVAL FROM THE FAR FUTURE.

HEY, CHECK IT OUT. IT'S LIKE HE'S *LOOKING* AT SOMETHING.

WHAT DO YOU THINK IT IS?

IF YOU BELIEVE THAT KIND OF THING.

YEAH. IF YOU BELIEVE THAT.

THADDEUS THAWNE INERTIA

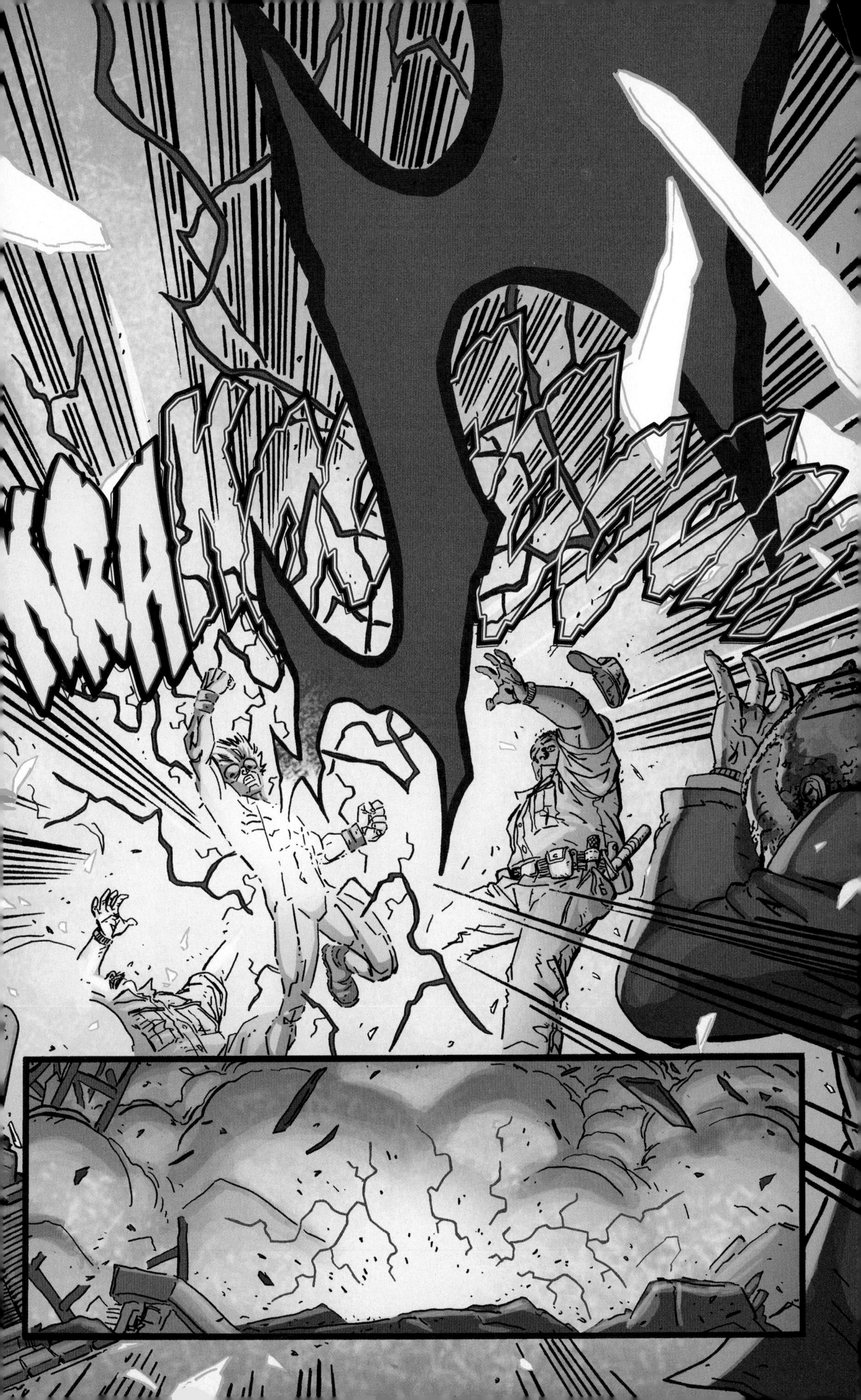

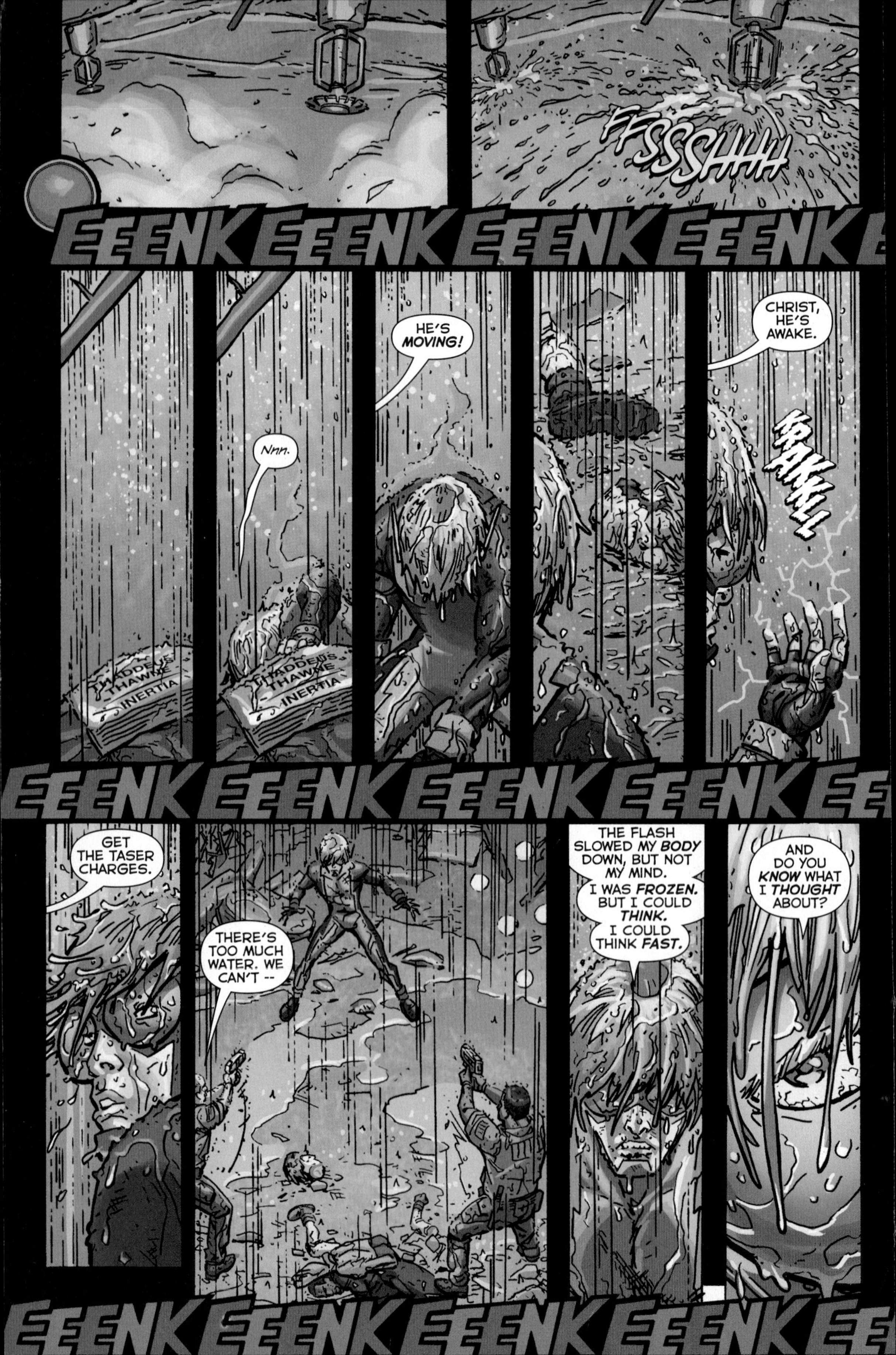
FFSSSHHH
EEENK EEENK EEENK EEENK
THADDEUS THAWNE INERTIA
Nnn.
THADDEUS THAWNE INERTIA
HE'S *MOVING!*
CHRIST, HE'S AWAKE.
EEENK EEENK EEENK EEENK
GET THE TASER CHARGES.
THERE'S TOO MUCH WATER. WE CAN'T --
THE FLASH SLOWED *MY BODY* DOWN, BUT NOT *MY* MIND.
I WAS *FROZEN.* BUT I COULD *THINK.* I COULD THINK *FAST.*
AND DO YOU *KNOW* WHAT I *THOUGHT* ABOUT?
EEENK EEENK EEENK EEENK

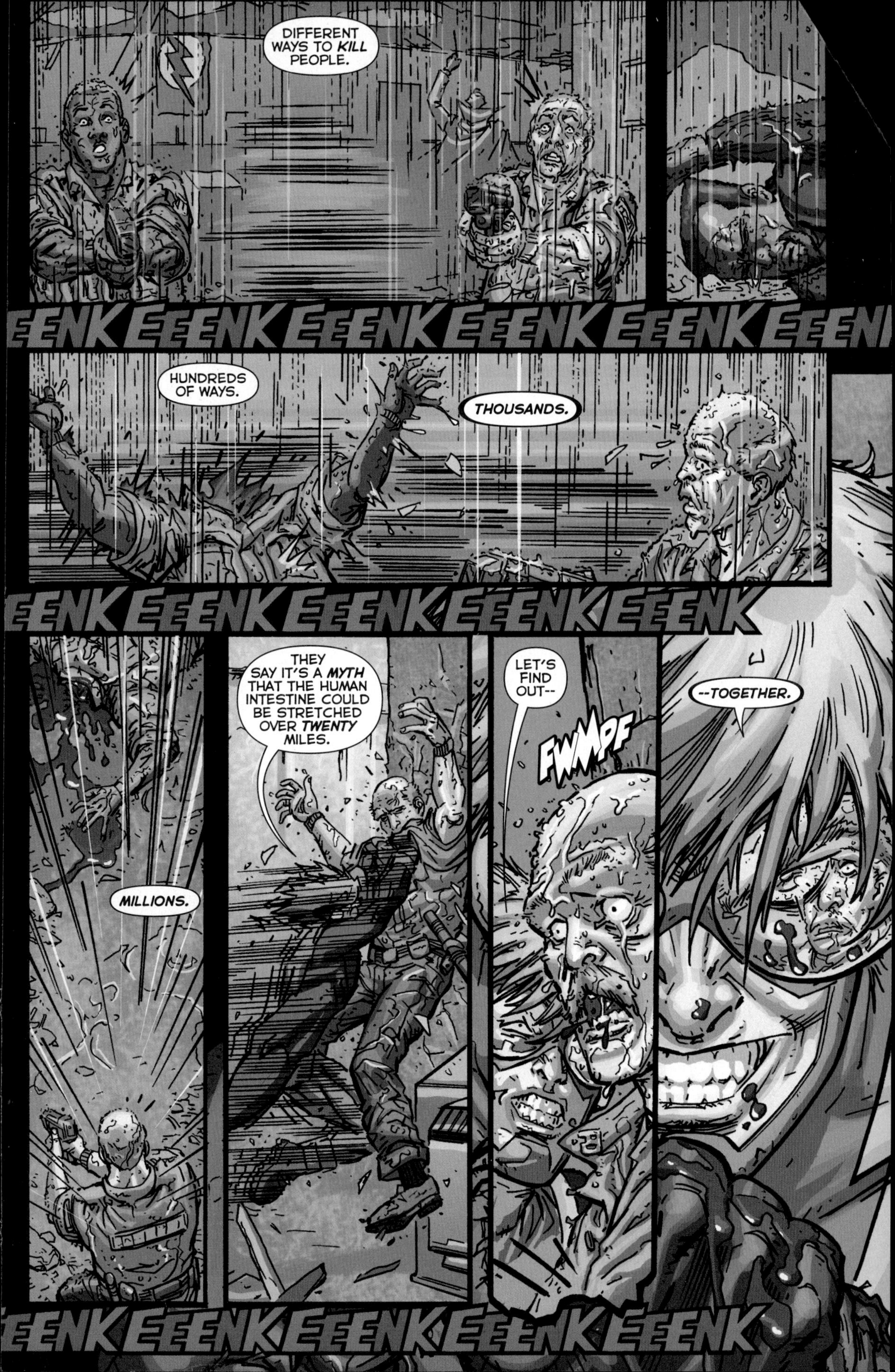
DIFFERENT WAYS TO KILL PEOPLE.
EEENK EEENK EEENK EEENK EEENK EEENK
HUNDREDS OF WAYS.
THOUSANDS.
EEENK EEENK EEENK EEENK EEENK
MILLIONS.
THEY SAY IT'S A MYTH THAT THE HUMAN INTESTINE COULD BE STRETCHED OVER TWENTY MILES.
LET'S FIND OUT--
FWMPF
--TOGETHER.
EEENK EEENK EEENK EEENK EEENK

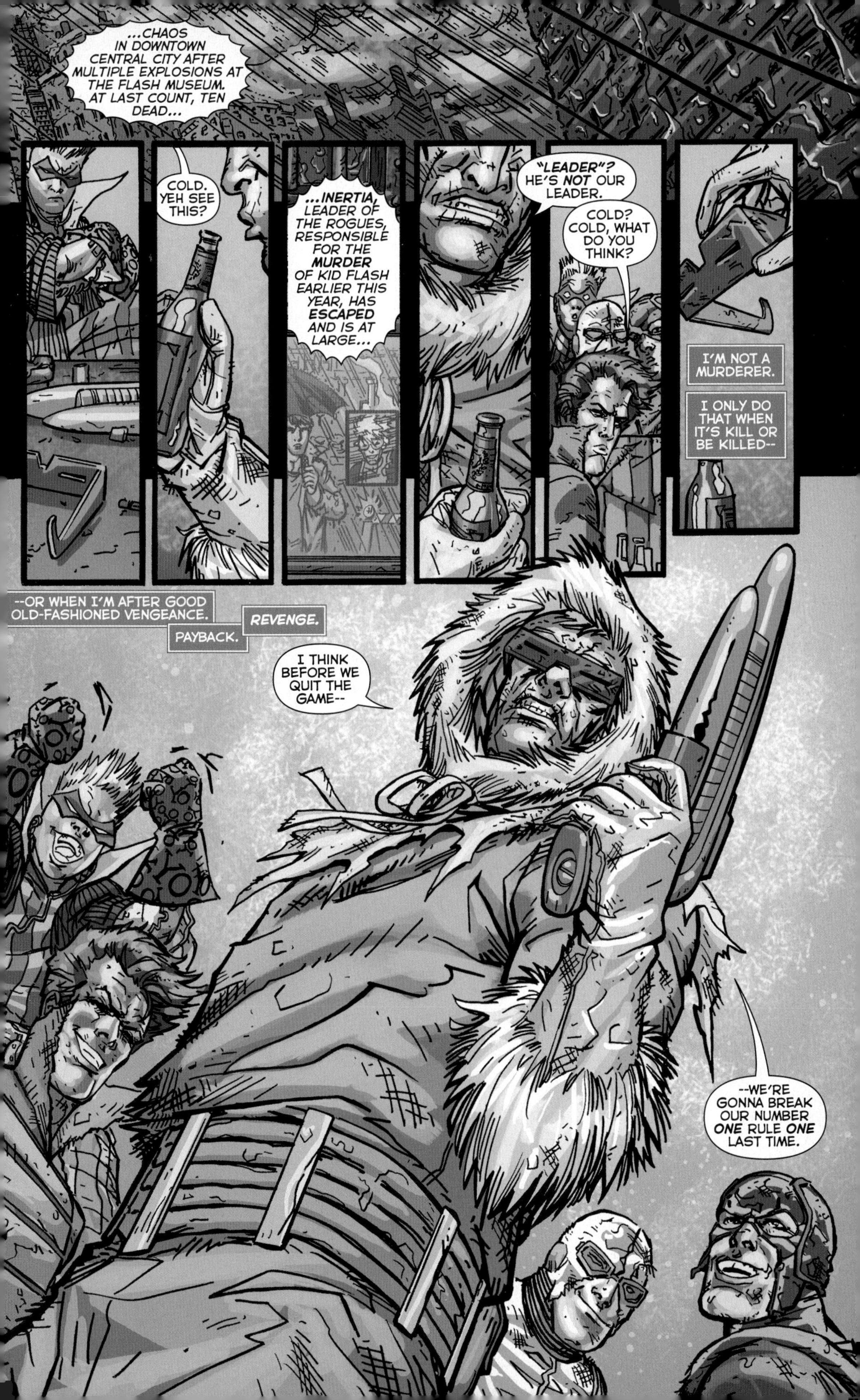
...CHAOS IN DOWNTOWN CENTRAL CITY AFTER MULTIPLE EXPLOSIONS AT THE FLASH MUSEUM. AT LAST COUNT, TEN DEAD...
COLD. YEH SEE THIS?
...INERTIA, LEADER OF THE ROGUES, RESPONSIBLE FOR THE MURDER OF KID FLASH EARLIER THIS YEAR, HAS ESCAPED AND IS AT LARGE...
"LEADER"? HE'S NOT OUR LEADER.
COLD? COLD, WHAT DO YOU THINK?
I'M NOT A MURDERER.
I ONLY DO THAT WHEN IT'S KILL OR BE KILLED--
--OR WHEN I'M AFTER GOOD OLD-FASHIONED VENGEANCE.
PAYBACK.
REVENGE.
I THINK BEFORE WE QUIT THE GAME--
--WE'RE GONNA BREAK OUR NUMBER ONE RULE ONE LAST TIME.

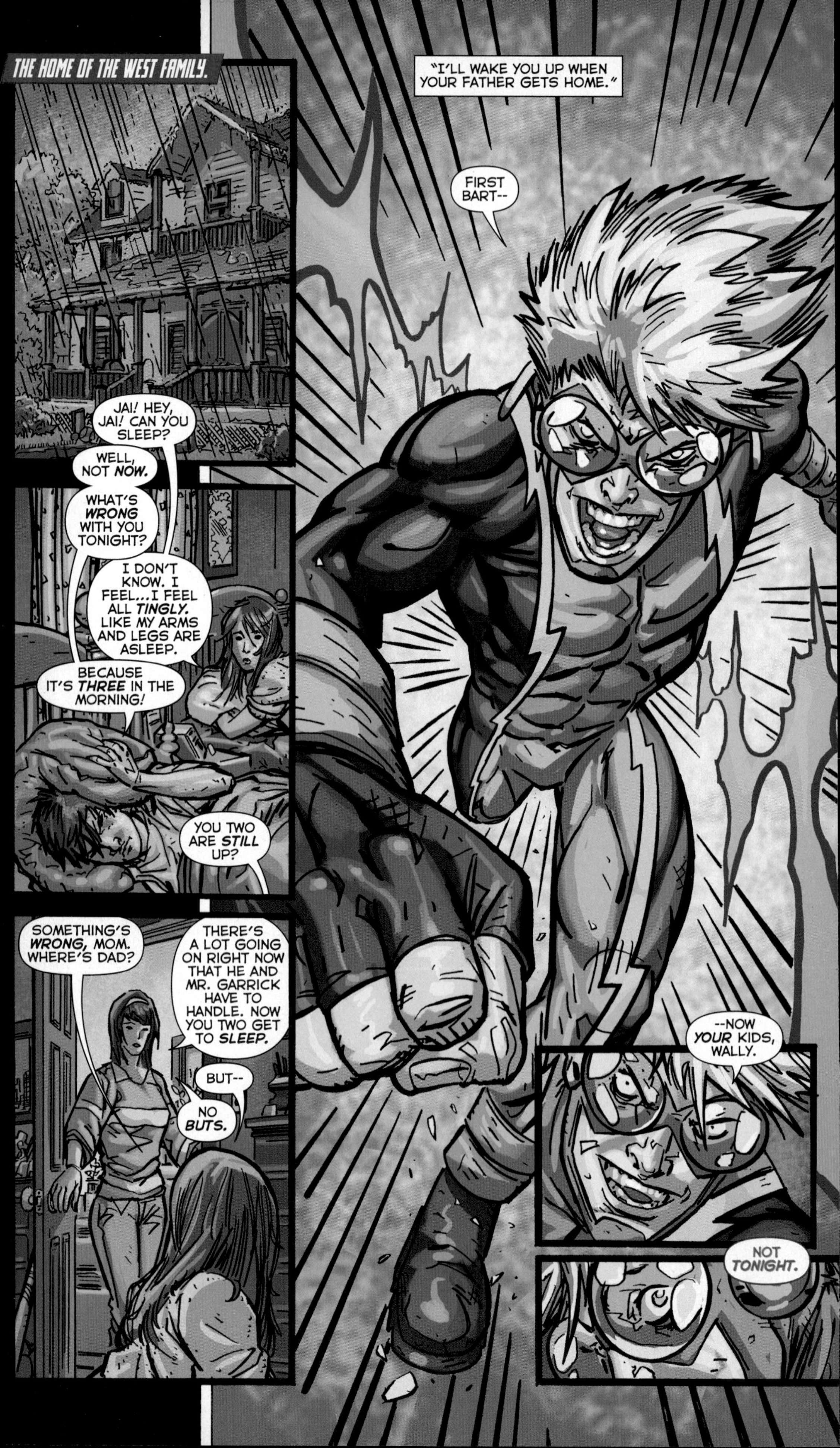
THE HOME OF THE WEST FAMILY.
JAI! HEY, JAI! CAN YOU SLEEP?
WELL, NOT NOW.
WHAT'S WRONG WITH YOU TONIGHT?
I DON'T KNOW. I FEEL...I FEEL ALL TINGLY. LIKE MY ARMS AND LEGS ARE ASLEEP.
BECAUSE IT'S THREE IN THE MORNING!
YOU TWO ARE STILL UP?
SOMETHING'S WRONG, MOM. WHERE'S DAD?
THERE'S A LOT GOING ON RIGHT NOW THAT HE AND MR. GARRICK HAVE TO HANDLE. NOW YOU TWO GET TO SLEEP.
BUT--
NO BUTS.
"I'LL WAKE YOU UP WHEN YOUR FATHER GETS HOME."
FIRST BART--
--NOW YOUR KIDS, WALLY.
NOT TONIGHT.

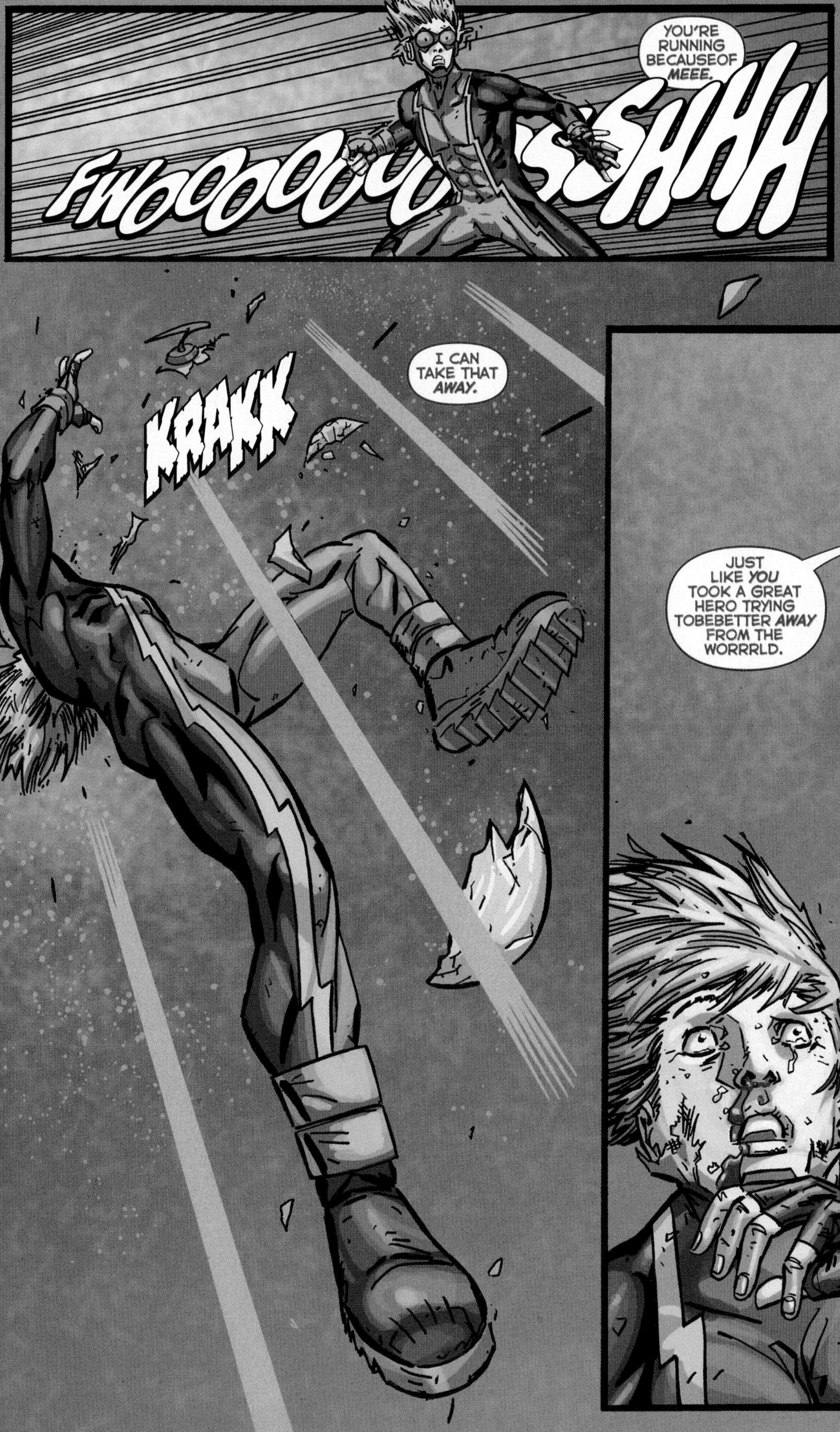
YOU'RE RUNNING BECAUSEOF MEEE.
FWOOOOUUUSSHHH
I CAN TAKE THAT AWAY.
KRAKK
JUST LIKE YOU TOOK A GREAT HERO TRYING TOBEBETTER AWAY FROM THE WORRRLD.

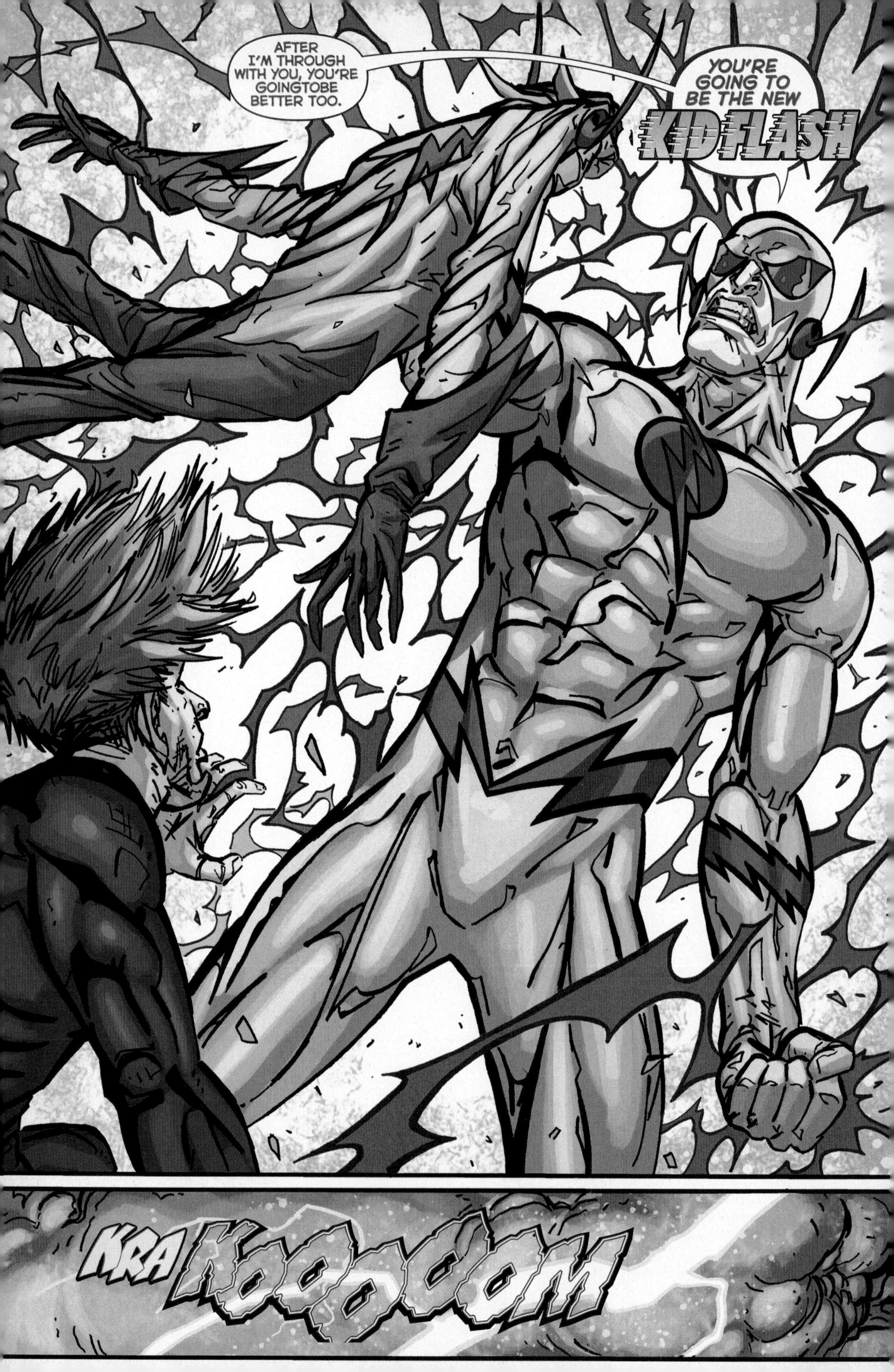
AFTER I'M THROUGH WITH YOU, YOU'RE GOINGTOBE BETTER TOO.
YOU'RE GOING TO BE THE NEW
KID FLASH
KRA KOOOOOM

cover to FINAL CRISIS: ROGUES' REVENGE #2

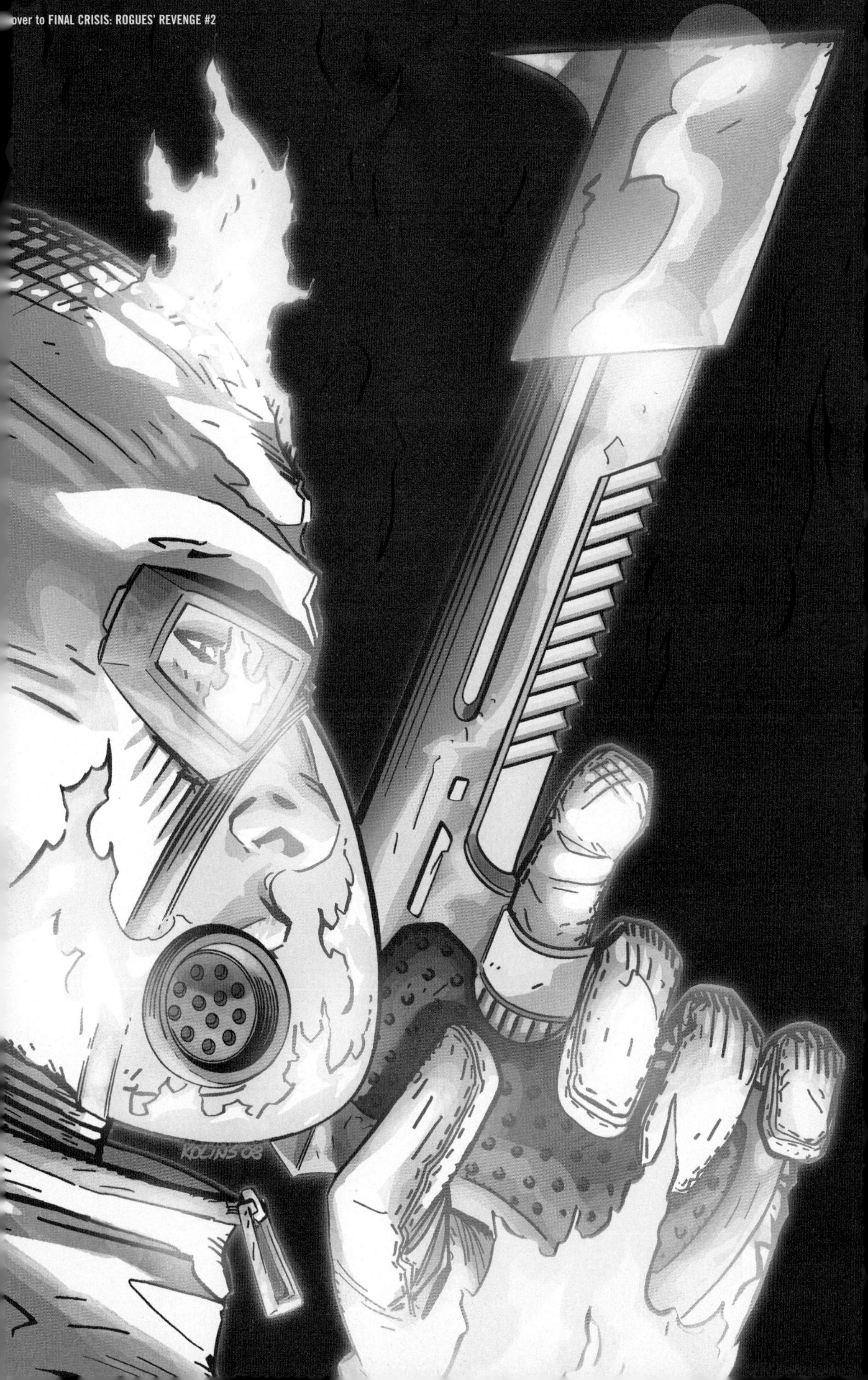
KOLINS '08

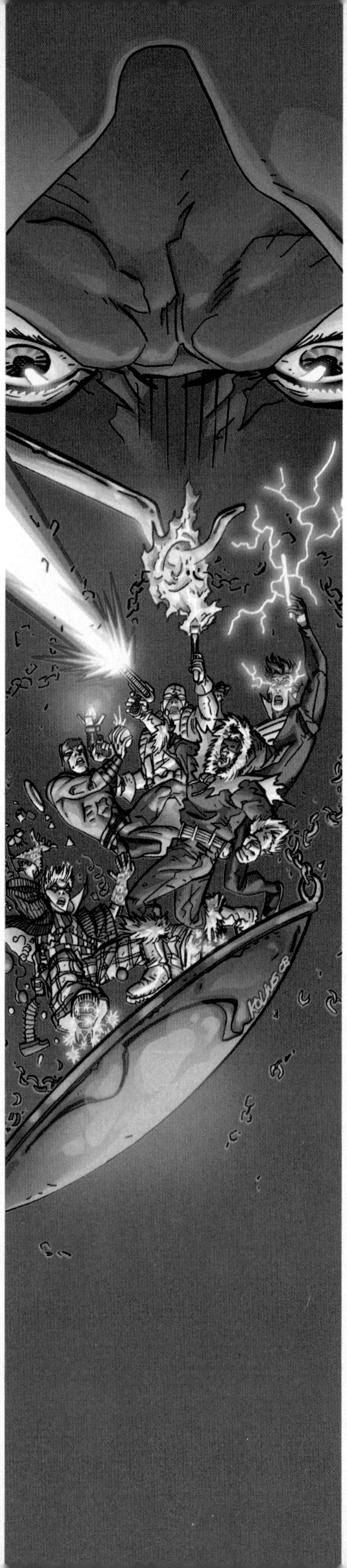

Sliver cover to FINAL CRISIS: ROGUES' REVENGE #2

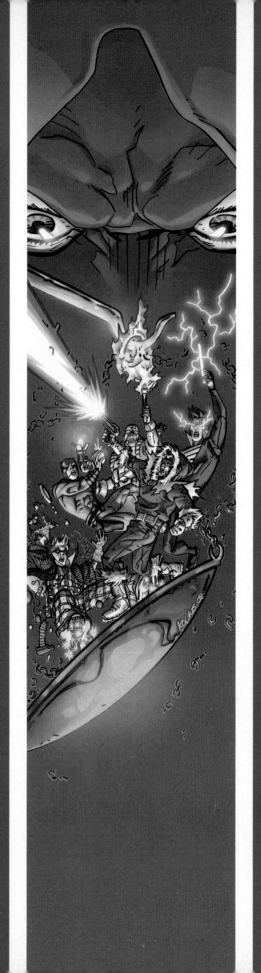

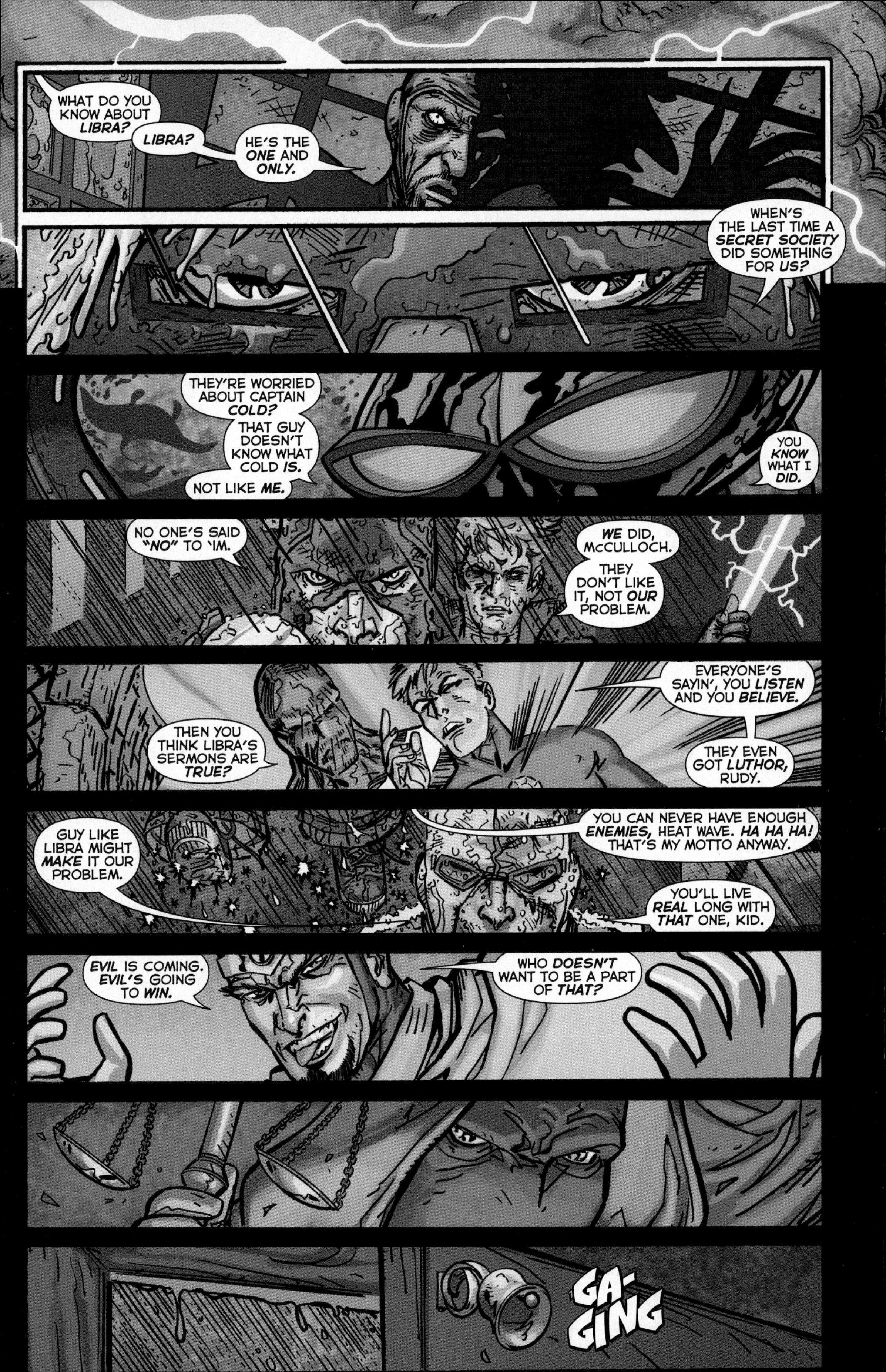

WHAT DO YOU KNOW ABOUT LIBRA?
LIBRA?
HE'S THE ONE AND ONLY.
WHEN'S THE LAST TIME A SECRET SOCIETY DID SOMETHING FOR US?
THEY'RE WORRIED ABOUT CAPTAIN COLD?
THAT GUY DOESN'T KNOW WHAT COLD IS.
NOT LIKE ME.
YOU KNOW WHAT I DID.
NO ONE'S SAID "NO" TO 'IM.
WE DID, McCULLOCH.
THEY DON'T LIKE IT, NOT OUR PROBLEM.
EVERYONE'S SAYIN', YOU LISTEN AND YOU BELIEVE.
THEN YOU THINK LIBRA'S SERMONS ARE TRUE?
THEY EVEN GOT LUTHOR, RUDY.
GUY LIKE LIBRA MIGHT MAKE IT OUR PROBLEM.
YOU CAN NEVER HAVE ENOUGH ENEMIES, HEAT WAVE. HA HA HA! THAT'S MY MOTTO ANYWAY.
YOU'LL LIVE REAL LONG WITH THAT ONE, KID.
EVIL IS COMING. EVIL'S GOING TO WIN.
WHO DOESN'T WANT TO BE A PART OF THAT?
GA-GING

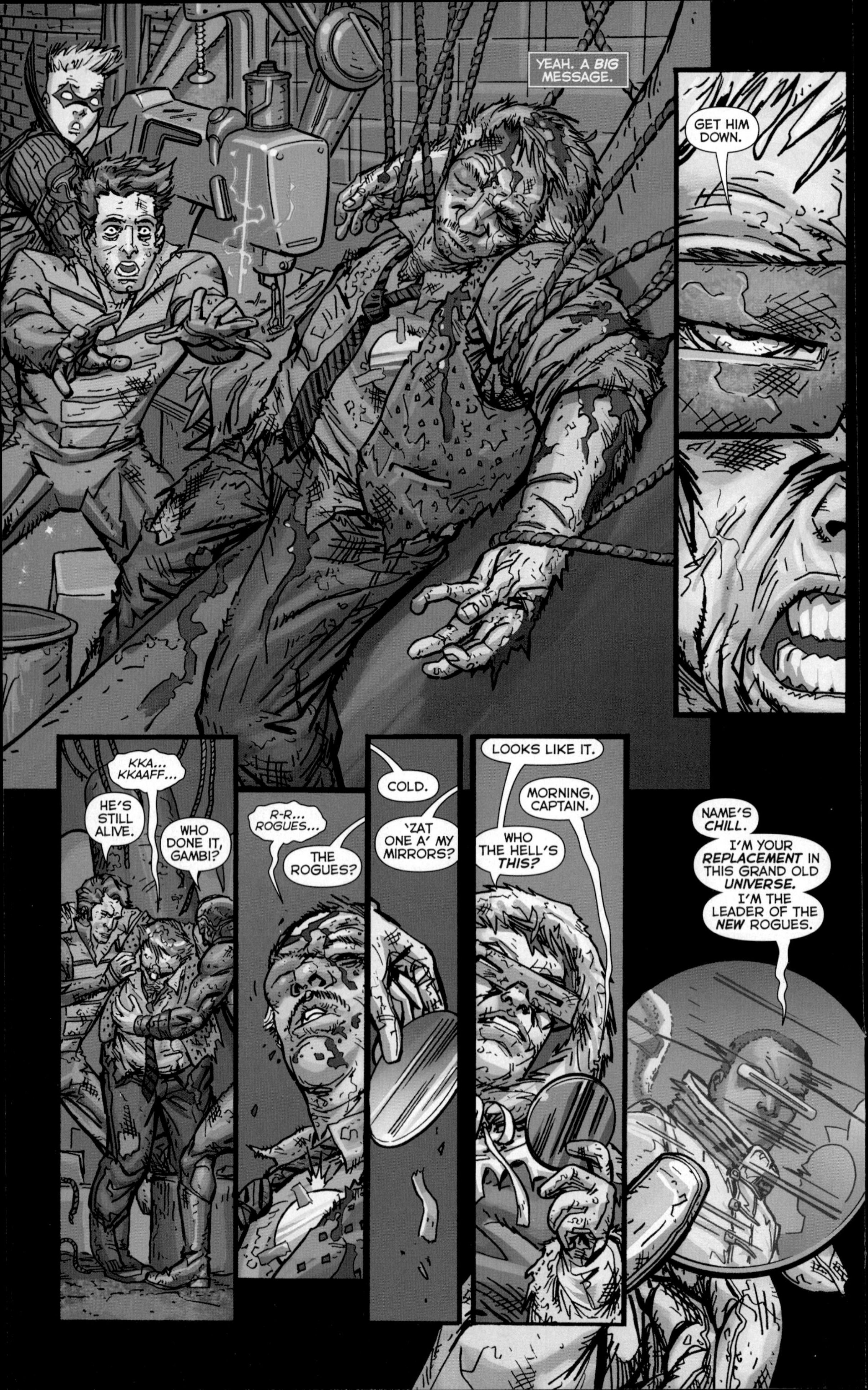
YEAH. A *BIG* MESSAGE.
GET HIM DOWN.
KKA... KKAAFF...
HE'S STILL ALIVE.
WHO DONE IT, GAMBI?
R-R... ROGUES...
THE ROGUES?
COLD.
'ZAT ONE A' MY MIRRORS?
LOOKS LIKE IT.
MORNING, CAPTAIN.
WHO THE HELL'S *THIS?*
NAME'S *CHILL*.
I'M YOUR *REPLACEMENT* IN THIS GRAND OLD *UNIVERSE.*
I'M THE LEADER OF THE *NEW* ROGUES.

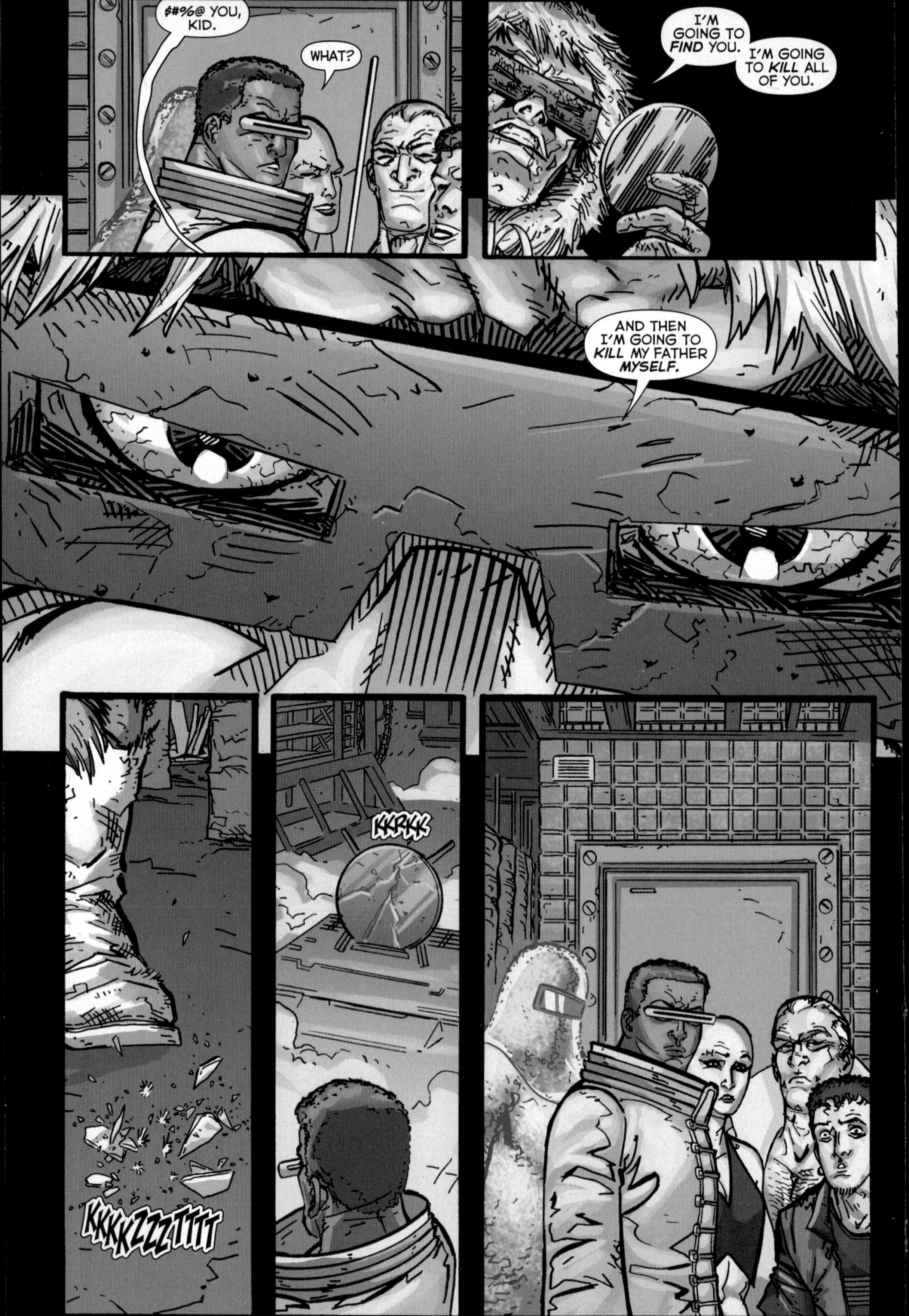
$#%@ YOU, KID.
WHAT?
I'M GOING TO FIND YOU.
I'M GOING TO KILL ALL OF YOU.
AND THEN I'M GOING TO KILL MY FATHER MYSELF.
KKKKZZZTTTT
KKRKK

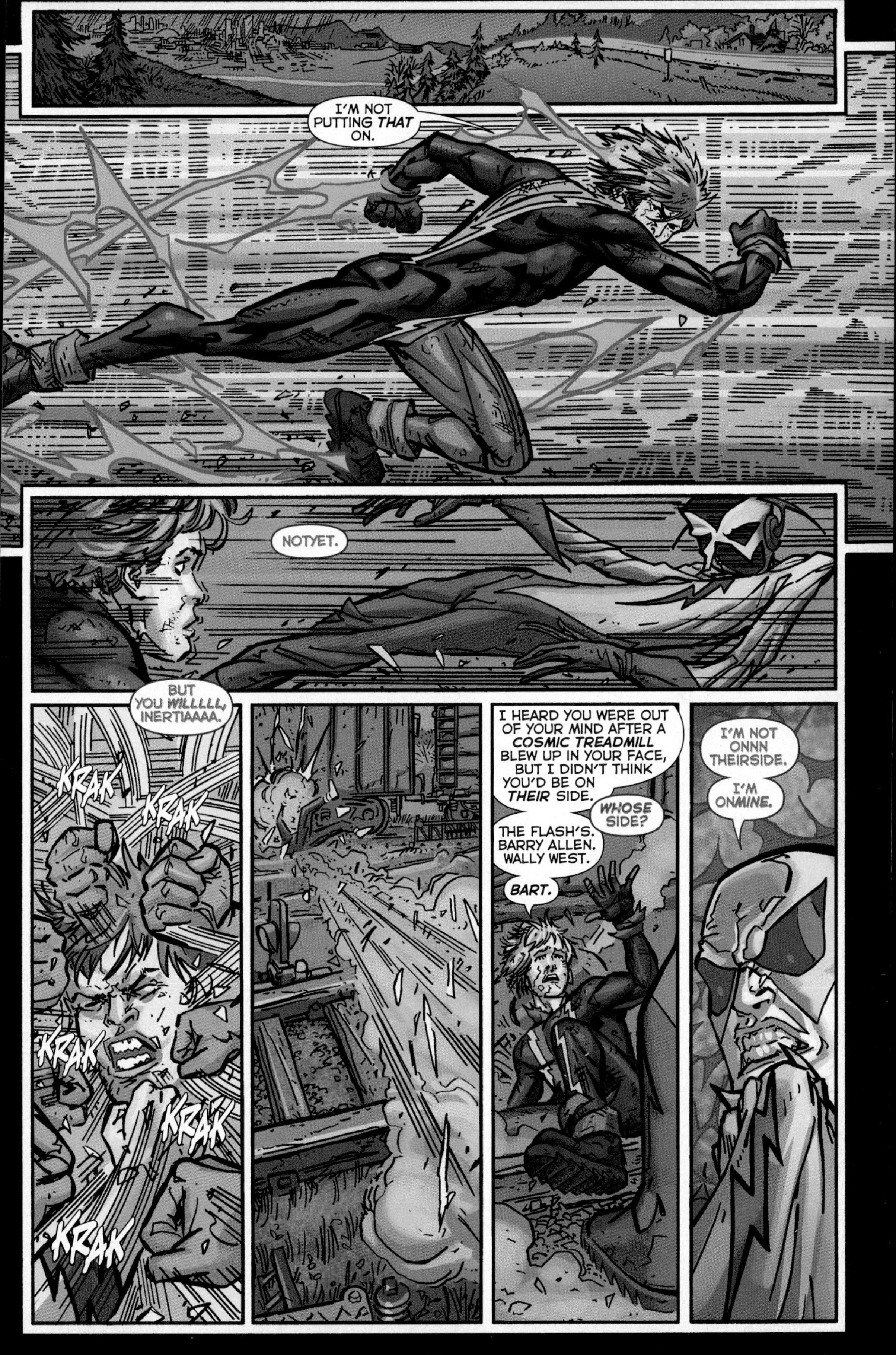
I'M NOT PUTTING THAT ON.
NOTYET.
BUT YOU WILLLLL, INERTIAAAA.
KRAK
KRAK
KRAK
KRAK
KRAK
I HEARD YOU WERE OUT OF YOUR MIND AFTER A COSMIC TREADMILL BLEW UP IN YOUR FACE, BUT I DIDN'T THINK YOU'D BE ON THEIR SIDE.
WHOSE SIDE?
THE FLASH'S. BARRY ALLEN. WALLY WEST.
BART.
I'M NOT ONNN THEIRSIDE.
I'M ONMINE.

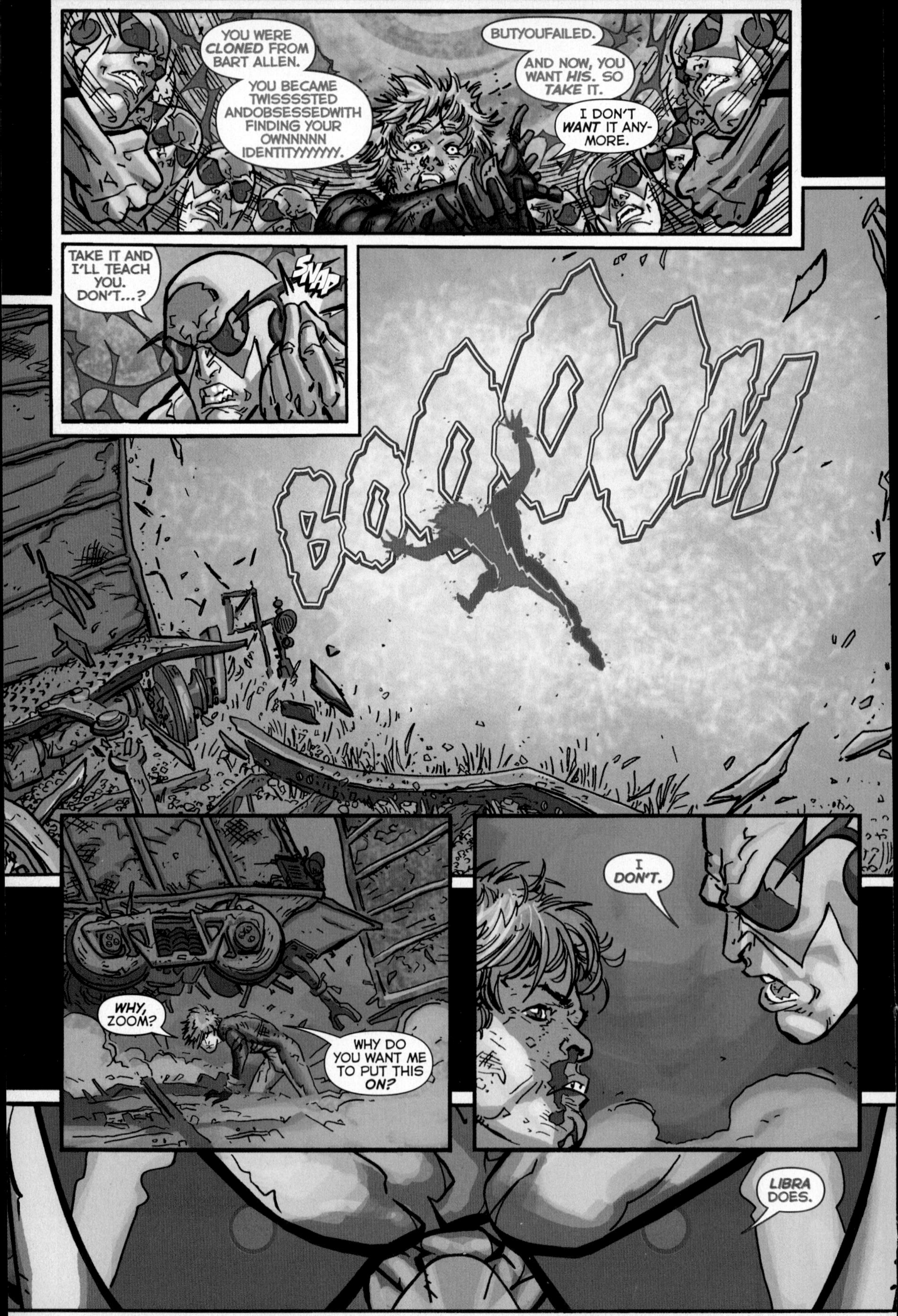

YOU WERE CLONED FROM BART ALLEN.
YOU BECAME TWISSSSTED ANDOBSESSEDWITH FINDING YOUR OWNNNNN IDENTITYYYYYYY.
BUTYOUFAILED.
AND NOW, YOU WANT HIS. SO TAKE IT.
I DON'T WANT IT ANY-MORE.
TAKE IT AND I'LL TEACH YOU. DON'T...?
SNAP
BOOOOOOM
WHY, ZOOM?
WHY DO YOU WANT ME TO PUT THIS ON?
I DON'T.
LIBRA DOES.

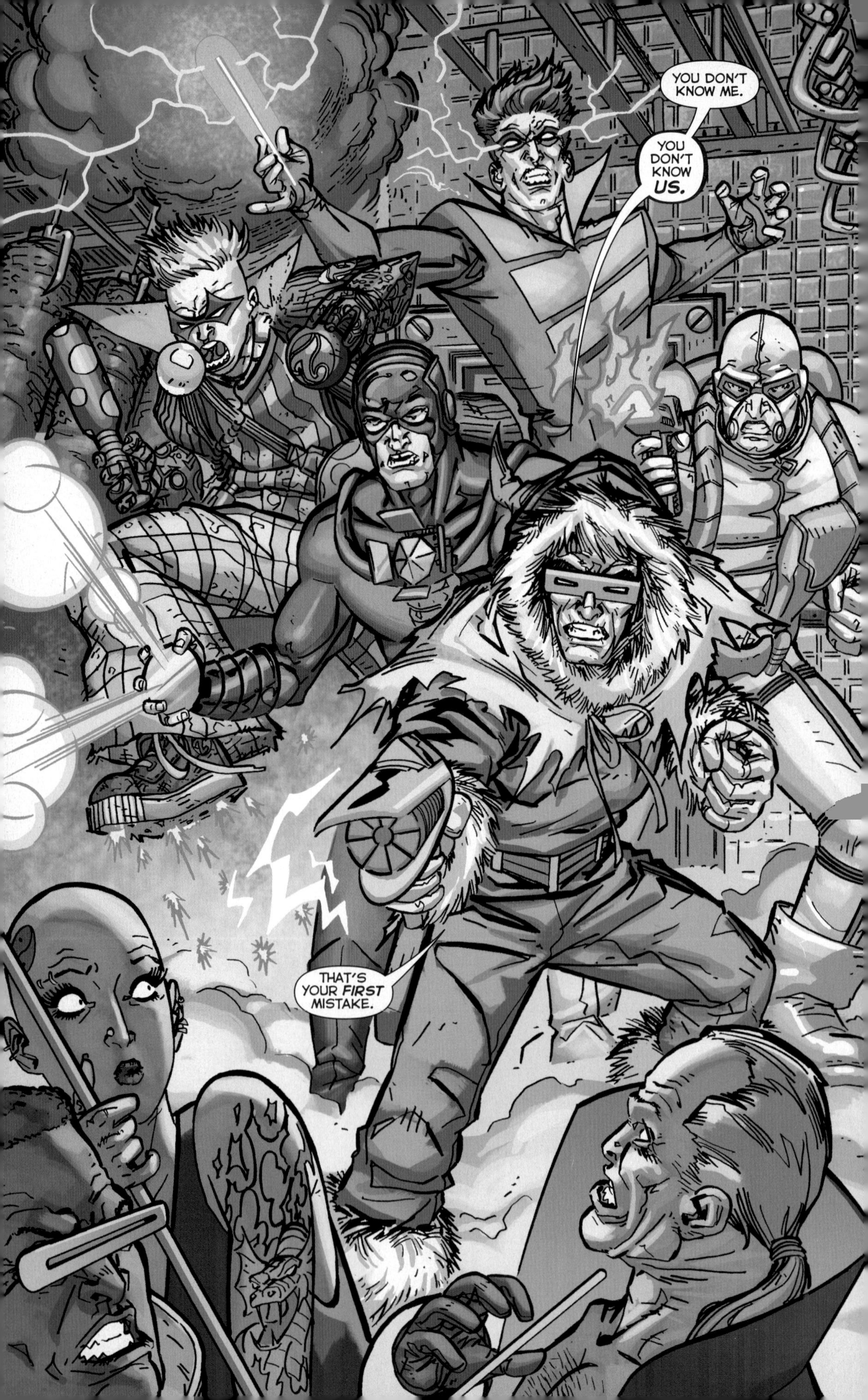
YOU DON'T KNOW ME.
YOU DON'T KNOW US.
THAT'S YOUR FIRST MISTAKE.

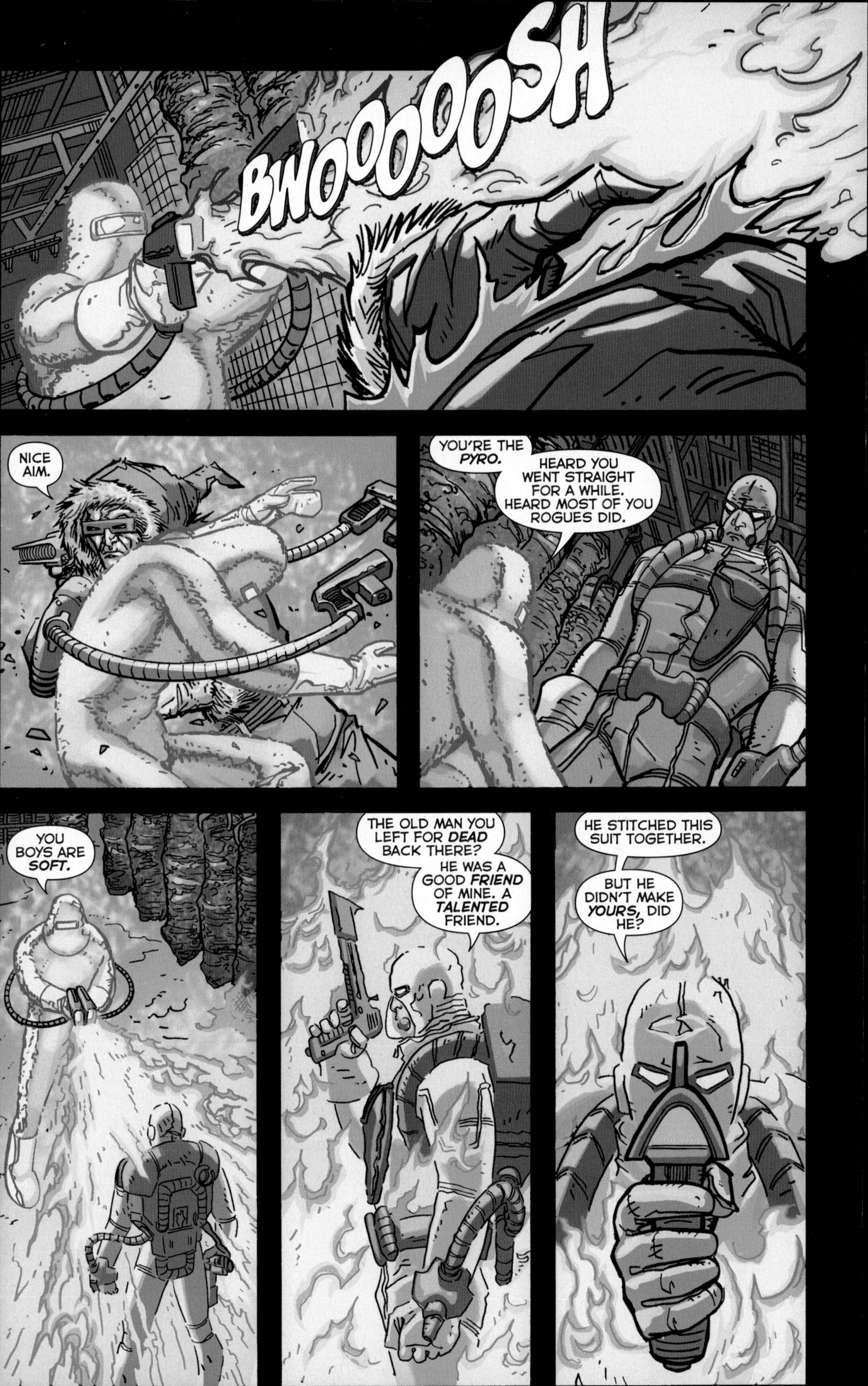
BWOOOOOOSH
NICE AIM.
YOU'RE THE PYRO.
HEARD YOU WENT STRAIGHT FOR A WHILE. HEARD MOST OF YOU ROGUES DID.
YOU BOYS ARE SOFT.
THE OLD MAN YOU LEFT FOR DEAD BACK THERE?
HE WAS A GOOD FRIEND OF MINE. A TALENTED FRIEND.
HE STITCHED THIS SUIT TOGETHER.
BUT HE DIDN'T MAKE YOURS, DID HE?

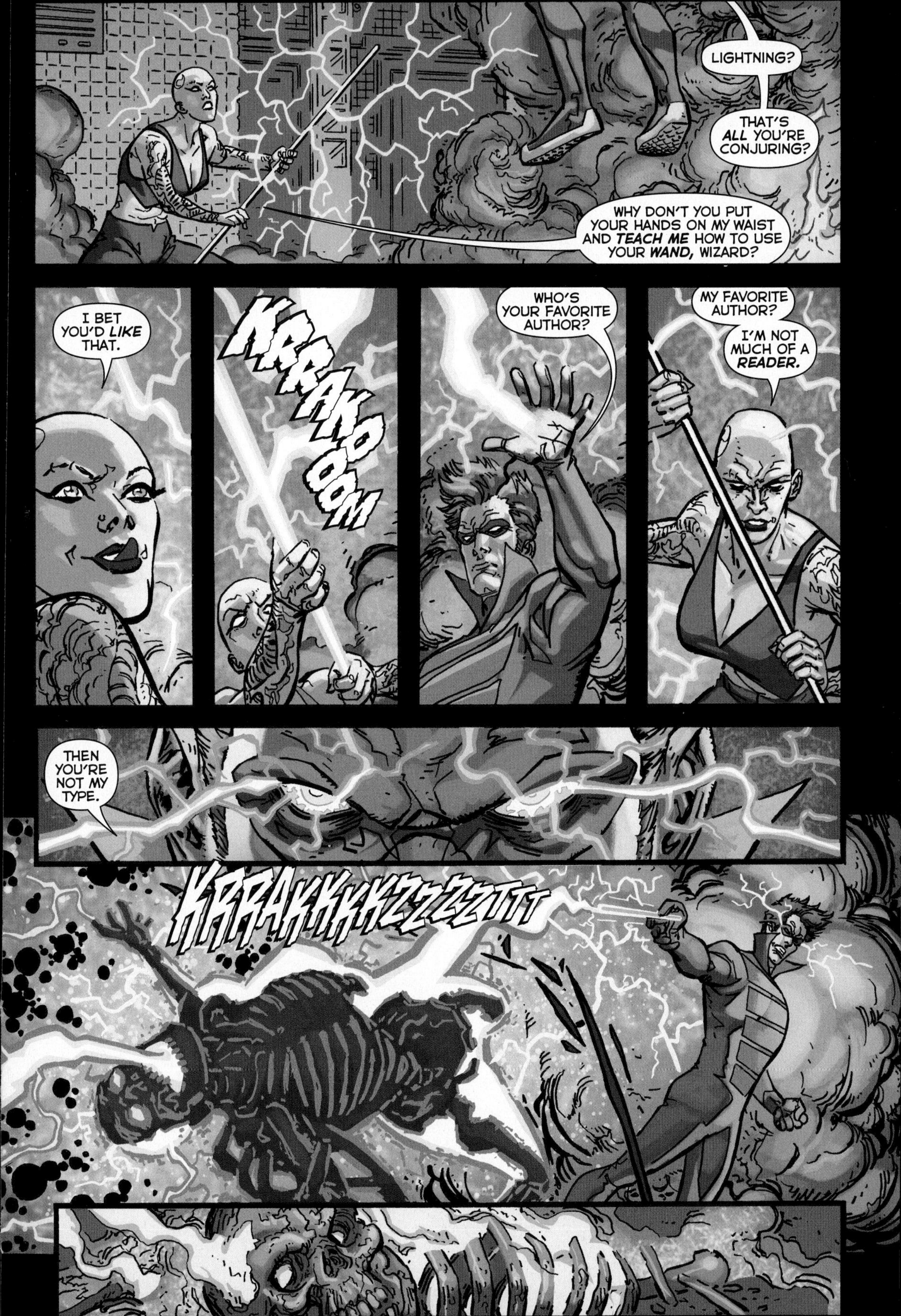

LIGHTNING?
THAT'S ALL YOU'RE CONJURING?
WHY DON'T YOU PUT YOUR HANDS ON MY WAIST AND TEACH ME HOW TO USE YOUR WAND, WIZARD?
I BET YOU'D LIKE THAT.
KRRAKOOOM
WHO'S YOUR FAVORITE AUTHOR?
MY FAVORITE AUTHOR?
I'M NOT MUCH OF A READER.
THEN YOU'RE NOT MY TYPE.
KRRAKKKKKZZZZZTTTT

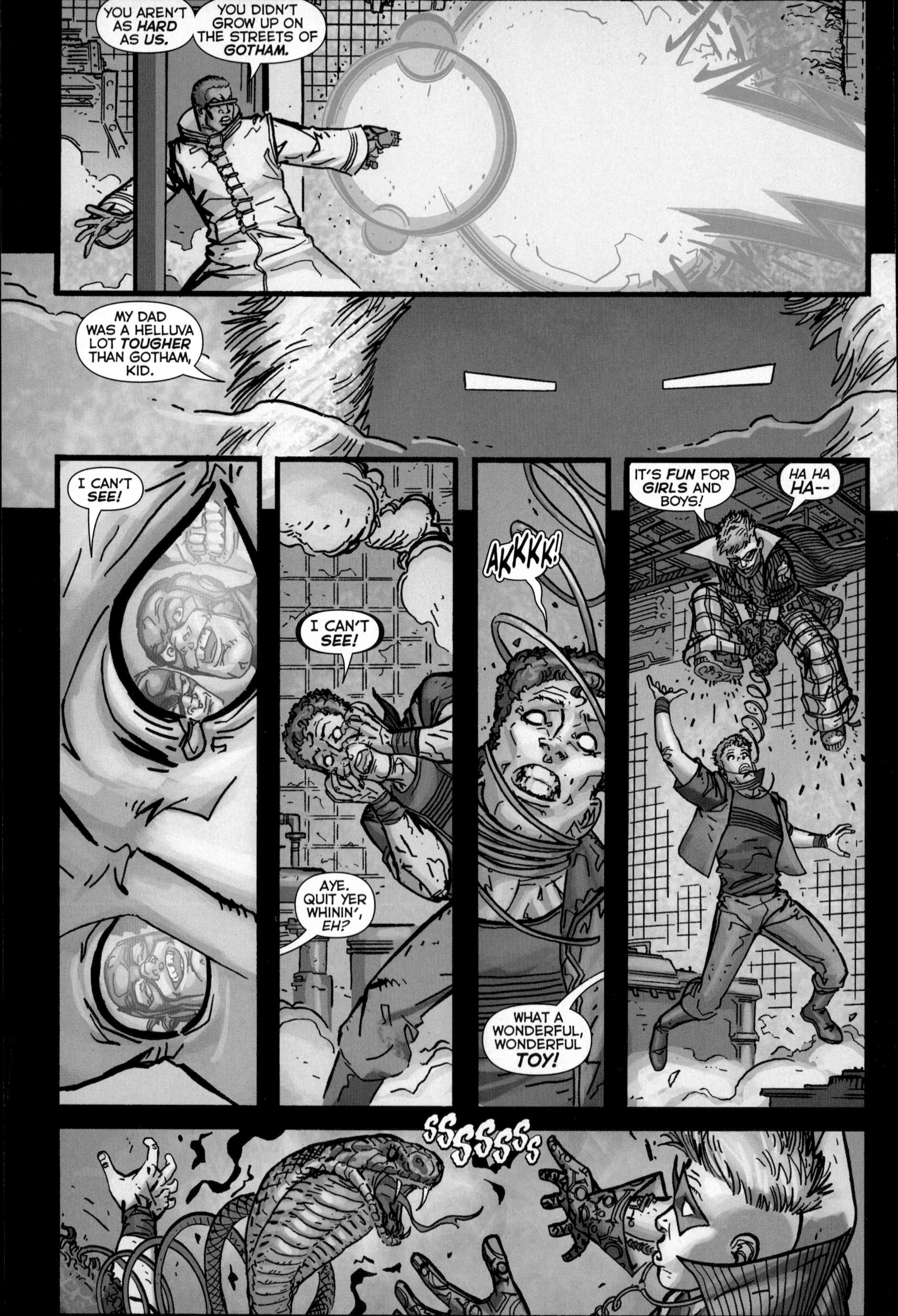

YOU AREN'T AS HARD AS US.
YOU DIDN'T GROW UP ON THE STREETS OF GOTHAM.
MY DAD WAS A HELLUVA LOT TOUGHER THAN GOTHAM, KID.
I CAN'T SEE!
I CAN'T SEE!
AYE. QUIT YER WHININ', EH?
AKKKK!
WHAT A WONDERFUL, WONDERFUL TOY!
IT'S FUN FOR GIRLS AND BOYS!
HA HA HA--
SSSSSSS

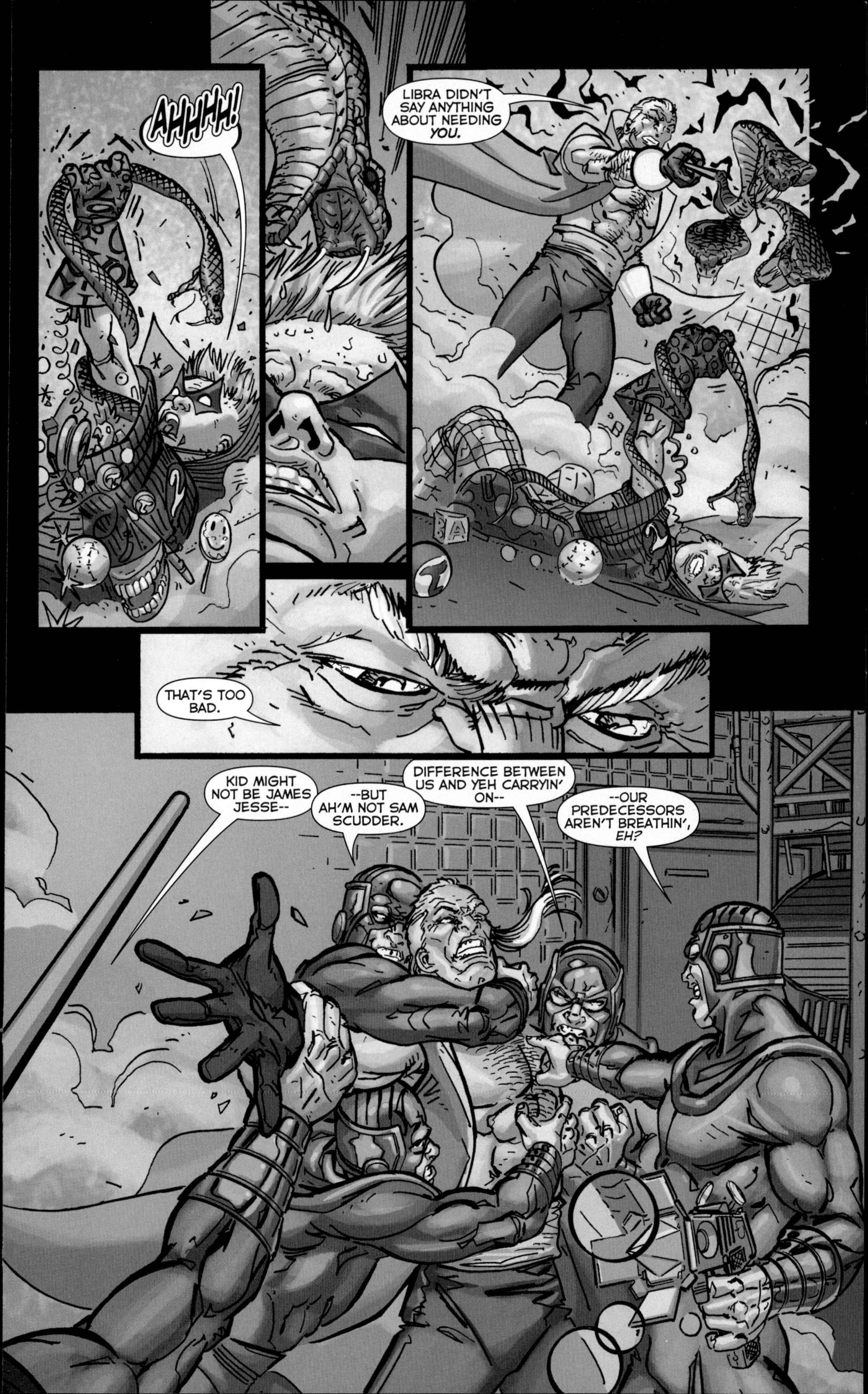
AHHHH!
LIBRA DIDN'T SAY ANYTHING ABOUT NEEDING *YOU.*
THAT'S TOO BAD.
KID MIGHT NOT BE JAMES JESSE--
--BUT AH'M NOT SAM SCUDDER.
DIFFERENCE BETWEEN US AND YEH CARRYIN' ON--
--OUR PREDECESSORS AREN'T BREATHIN', *EH?*

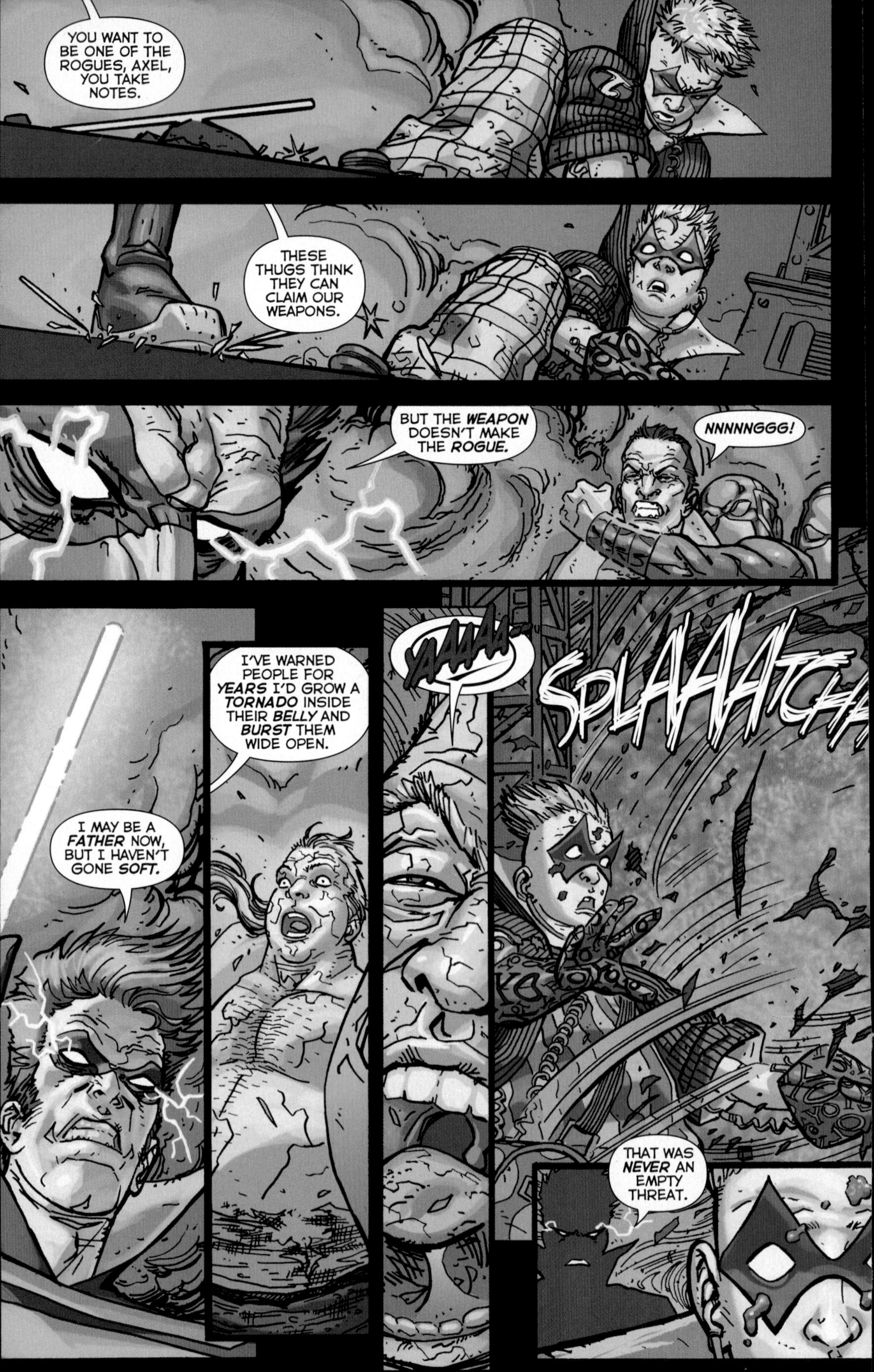
YOU WANT TO BE ONE OF THE ROGUES, AXEL, YOU TAKE NOTES.
THESE THUGS THINK THEY CAN CLAIM OUR WEAPONS.
BUT THE WEAPON DOESN'T MAKE THE ROGUE.
NNNNNGGG!
I MAY BE A FATHER NOW, BUT I HAVEN'T GONE SOFT.
I'VE WARNED PEOPLE FOR YEARS I'D GROW A TORNADO INSIDE THEIR BELLY AND BURST THEM WIDE OPEN.
YAAAAA--
SPLAAATCHA
THAT WAS NEVER AN EMPTY THREAT.

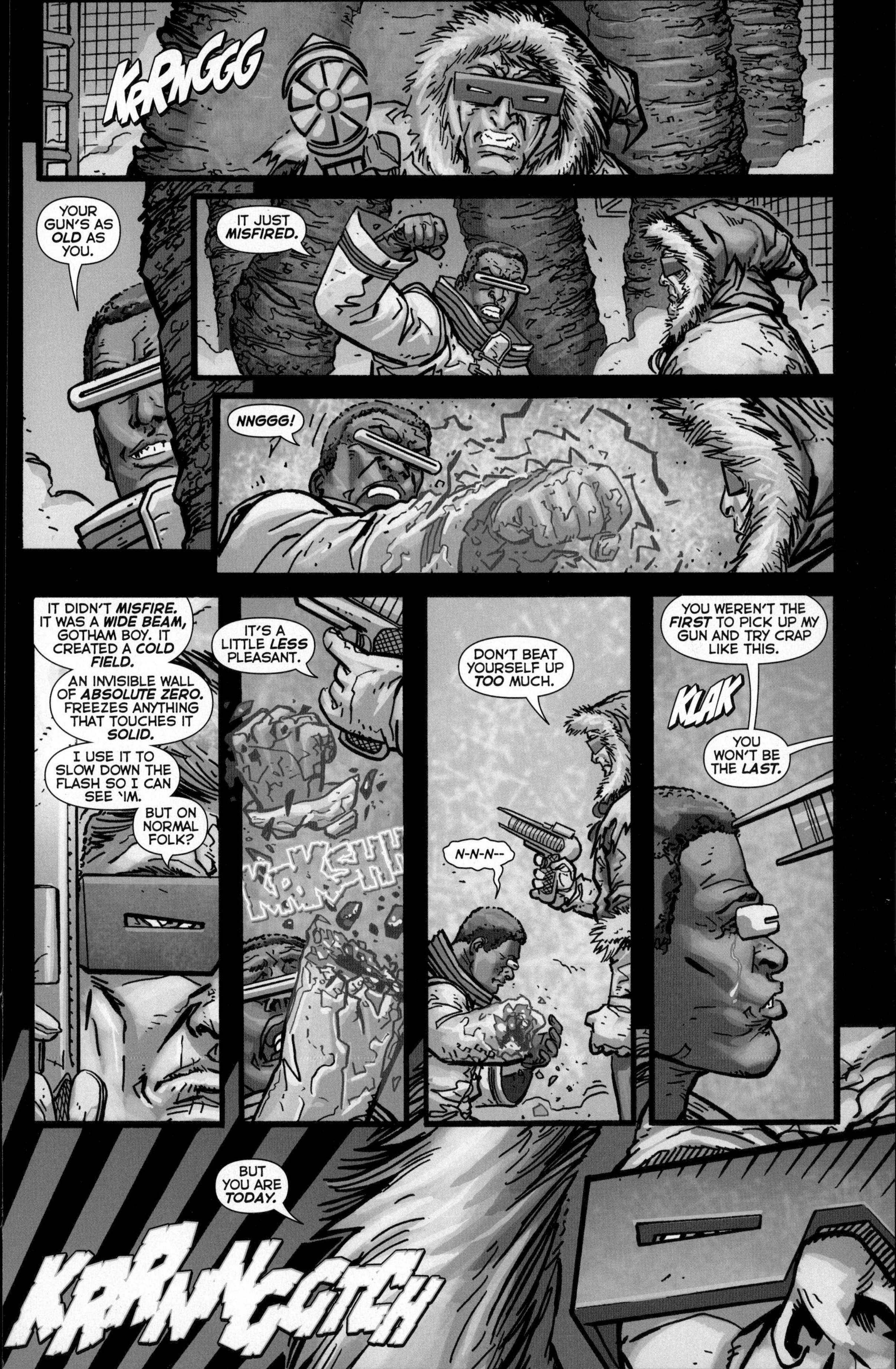
KRRNGGG
YOUR GUN'S AS OLD AS YOU.
IT JUST MISFIRED.
NNGGG!
IT DIDN'T MISFIRE. IT WAS A WIDE BEAM, GOTHAM BOY. IT CREATED A COLD FIELD.
AN INVISIBLE WALL OF ABSOLUTE ZERO. FREEZES ANYTHING THAT TOUCHES IT SOLID.
I USE IT TO SLOW DOWN THE FLASH SO I CAN SEE 'IM.
BUT ON NORMAL FOLK?
IT'S A LITTLE LESS PLEASANT.
KRKSHH
DON'T BEAT YOURSELF UP TOO MUCH.
N-N-N--
YOU WEREN'T THE FIRST TO PICK UP MY GUN AND TRY CRAP LIKE THIS.
KLAK
YOU WON'T BE THE LAST.
BUT YOU ARE TODAY.
KRRNGGTCH

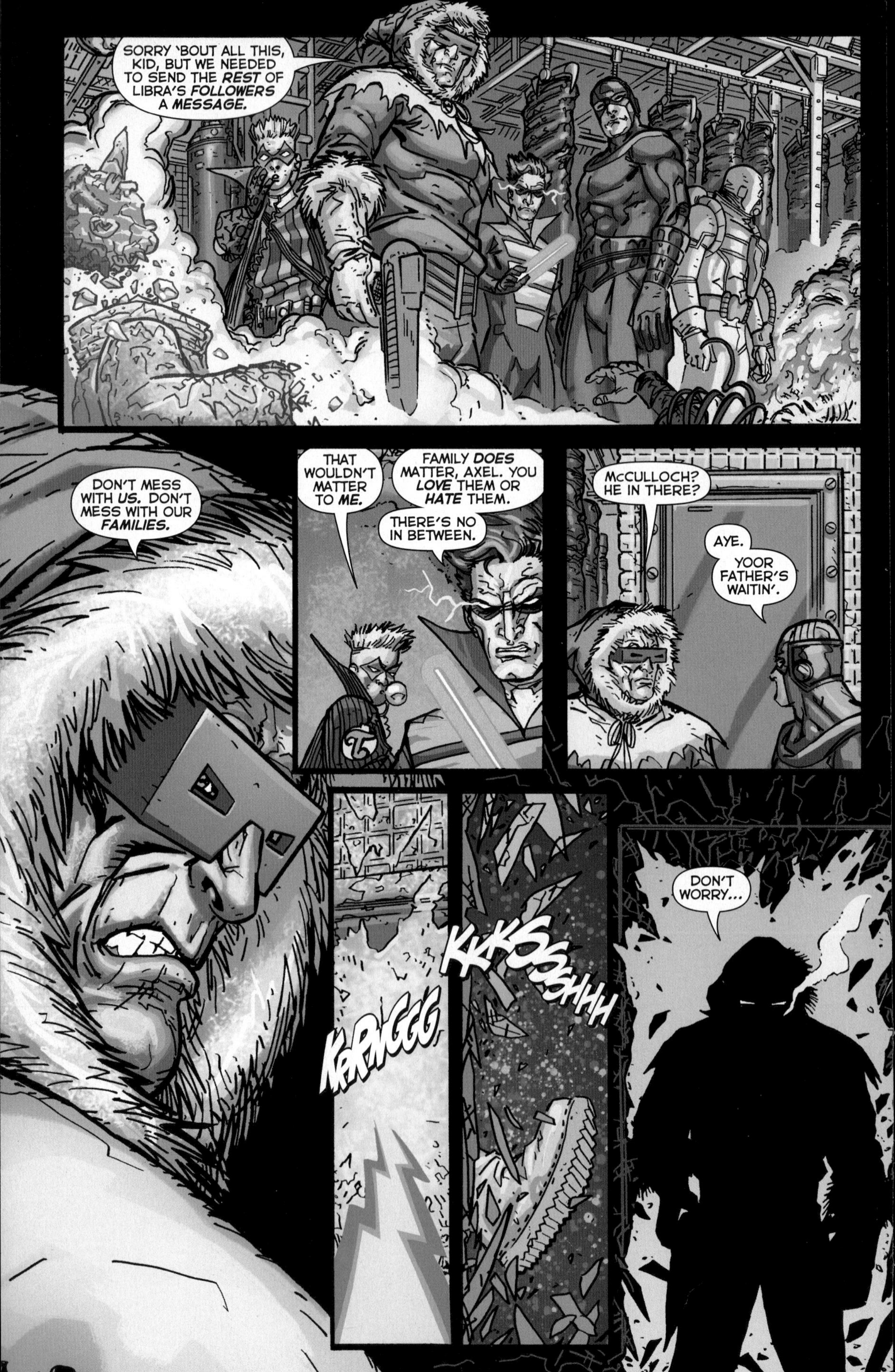
SORRY 'BOUT ALL THIS, KID, BUT WE NEEDED TO SEND THE REST OF LIBRA'S FOLLOWERS A MESSAGE.
DON'T MESS WITH US. DON'T MESS WITH OUR FAMILIES.
THAT WOULDN'T MATTER TO ME.
FAMILY DOES MATTER, AXEL. YOU LOVE THEM OR HATE THEM.
THERE'S NO IN BETWEEN.
McCULLOCH? HE IN THERE?
AYE.
YOOR FATHER'S WAITIN'.
KRRNGGG
KKKSSSSHHHH
DON'T WORRY...

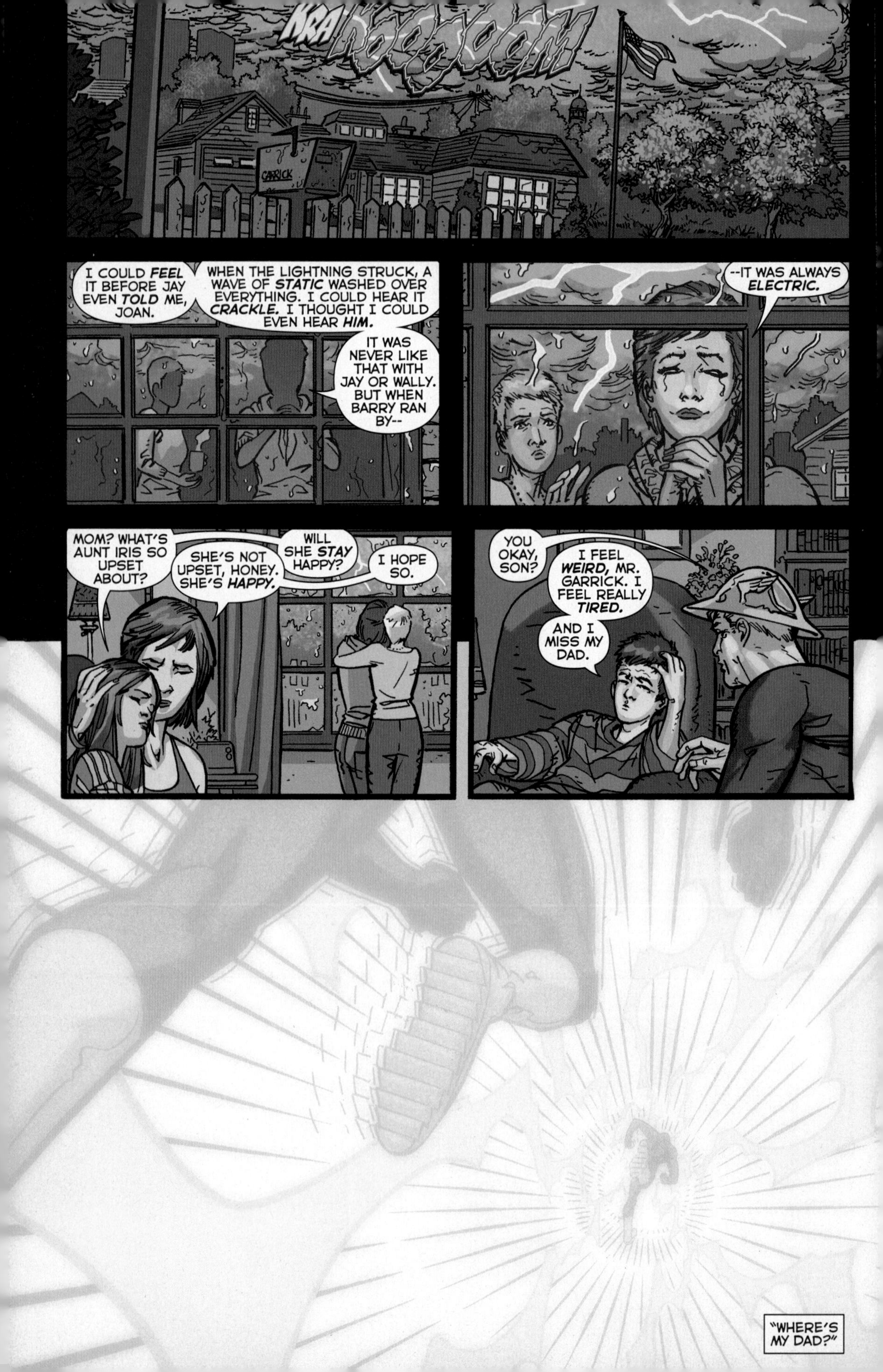
KRA-KOOOOOOOM
GARRICK
I COULD FEEL IT BEFORE JAY EVEN TOLD ME, JOAN.
WHEN THE LIGHTNING STRUCK, A WAVE OF STATIC WASHED OVER EVERYTHING. I COULD HEAR IT CRACKLE. I THOUGHT I COULD EVEN HEAR HIM.
IT WAS NEVER LIKE THAT WITH JAY OR WALLY. BUT WHEN BARRY RAN BY--
--IT WAS ALWAYS ELECTRIC.
MOM? WHAT'S AUNT IRIS SO UPSET ABOUT?
SHE'S NOT UPSET, HONEY. SHE'S HAPPY.
WILL SHE STAY HAPPY?
I HOPE SO.
YOU OKAY, SON?
I FEEL WEIRD, MR. GARRICK. I FEEL REALLY TIRED.
AND I MISS MY DAD.
"WHERE'S MY DAD?"

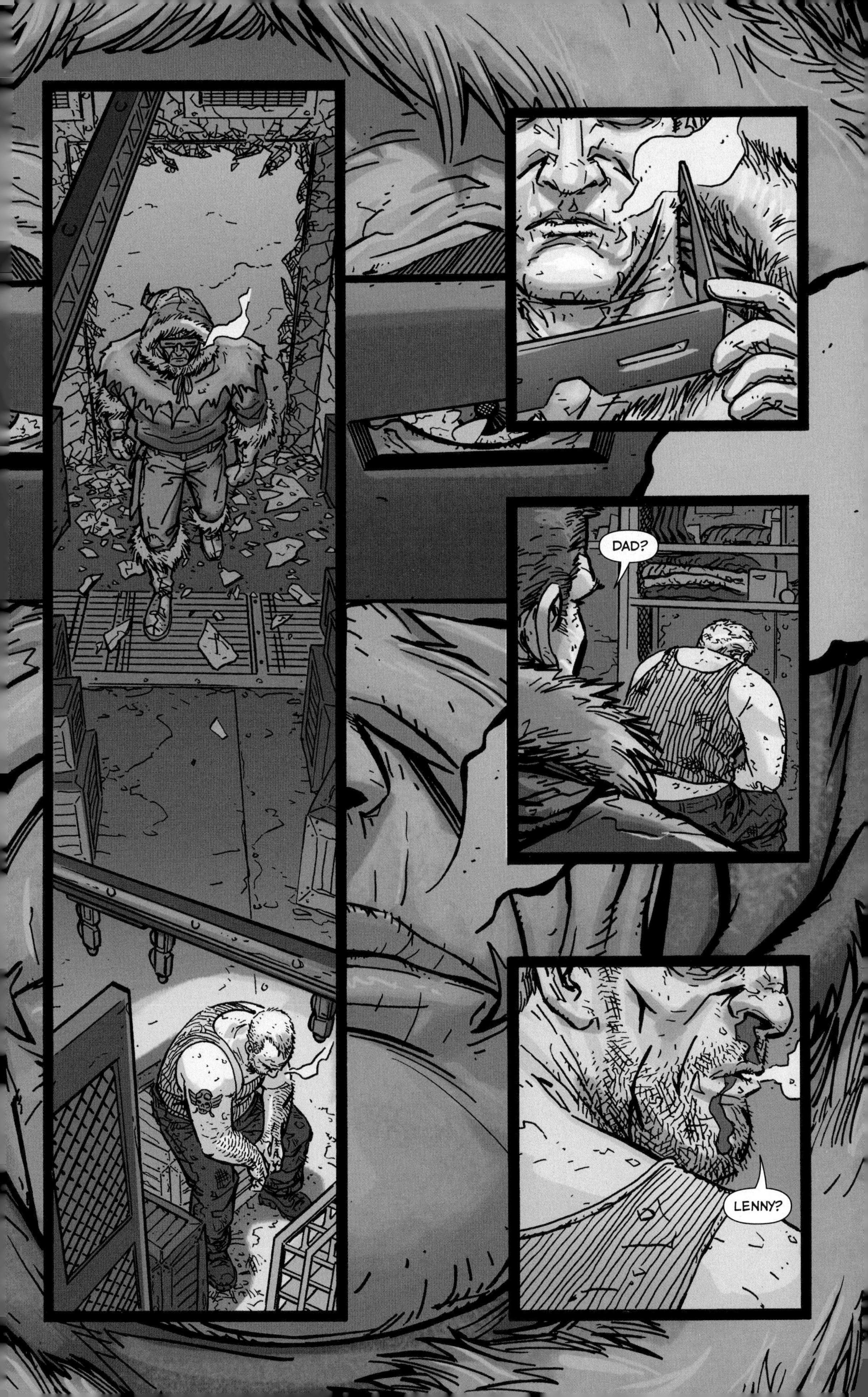
DAD?
LENNY?

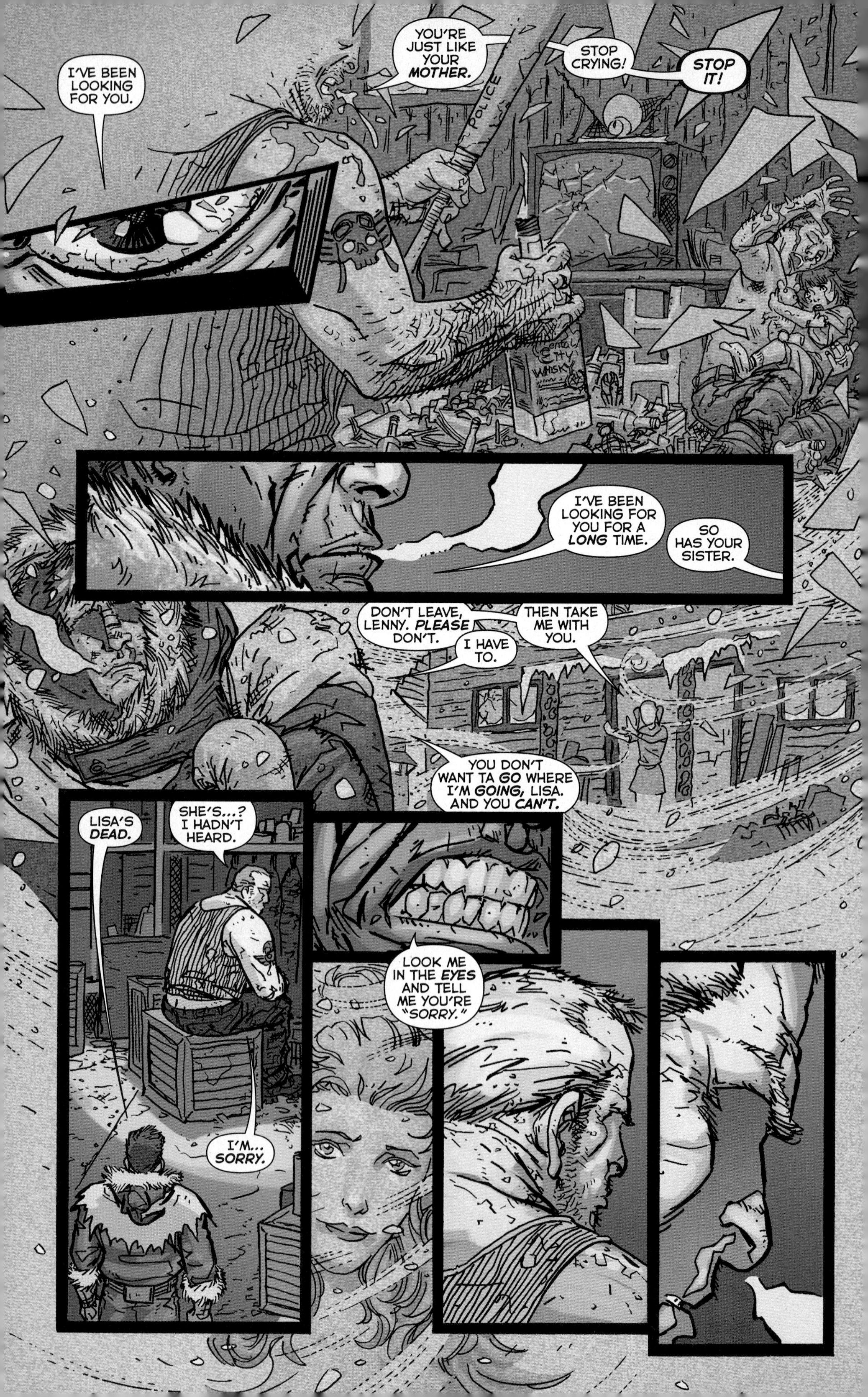

I'VE BEEN LOOKING FOR YOU.
YOU'RE JUST LIKE YOUR MOTHER.
STOP CRYING!
STOP IT!
POLICE
I'VE BEEN LOOKING FOR YOU FOR A LONG TIME.
SO HAS YOUR SISTER.
DON'T LEAVE, LENNY. PLEASE DON'T.
I HAVE TO.
THEN TAKE ME WITH YOU.
YOU DON'T WANT TA GO WHERE I'M GOING, LISA. AND YOU CAN'T.
LISA'S DEAD.
SHE'S...? I HADN'T HEARD.
I'M... SORRY.
LOOK ME IN THE EYES AND TELL ME YOU'RE "SORRY."

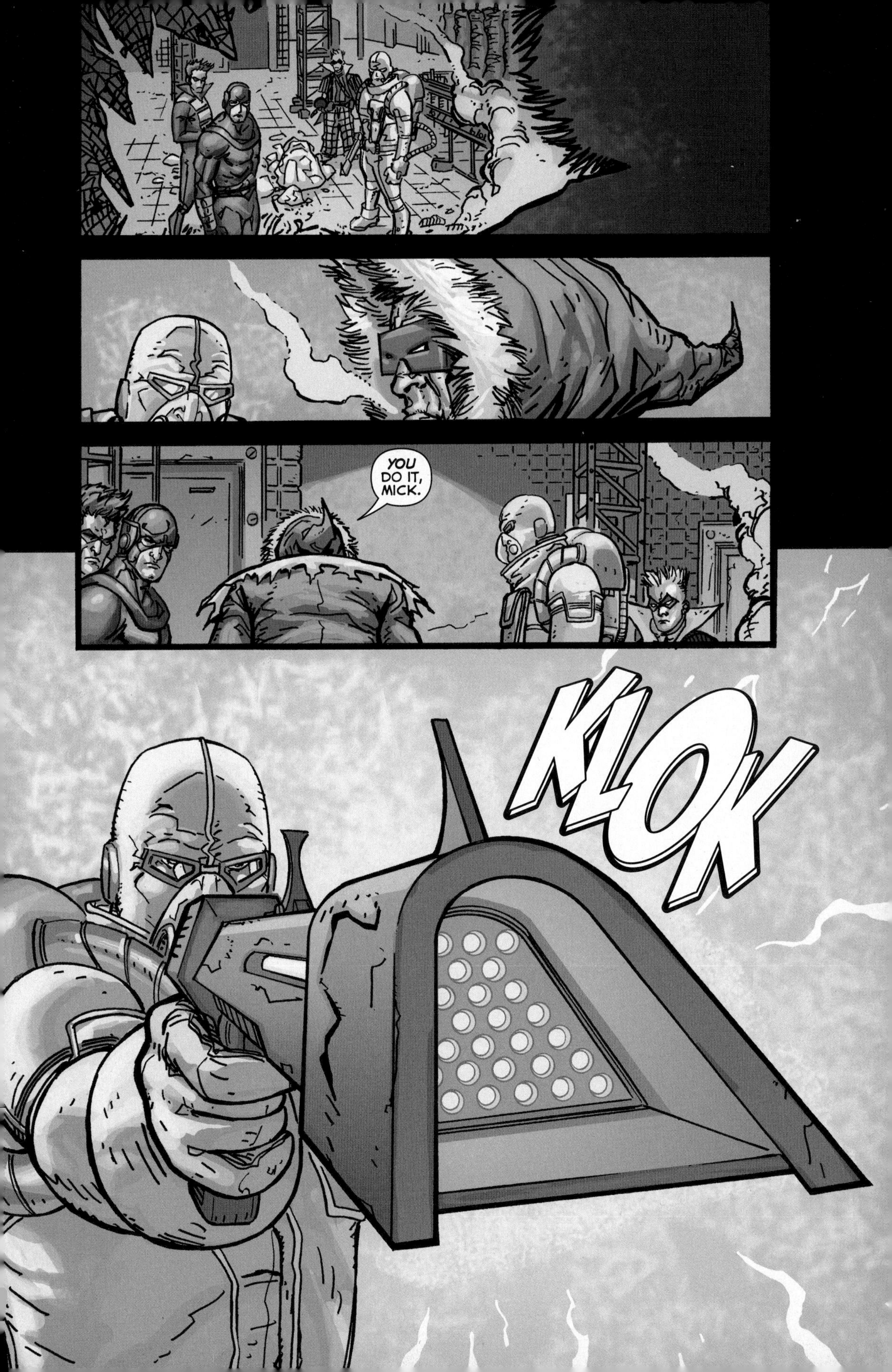
YOU DO IT, MICK.
KLOK

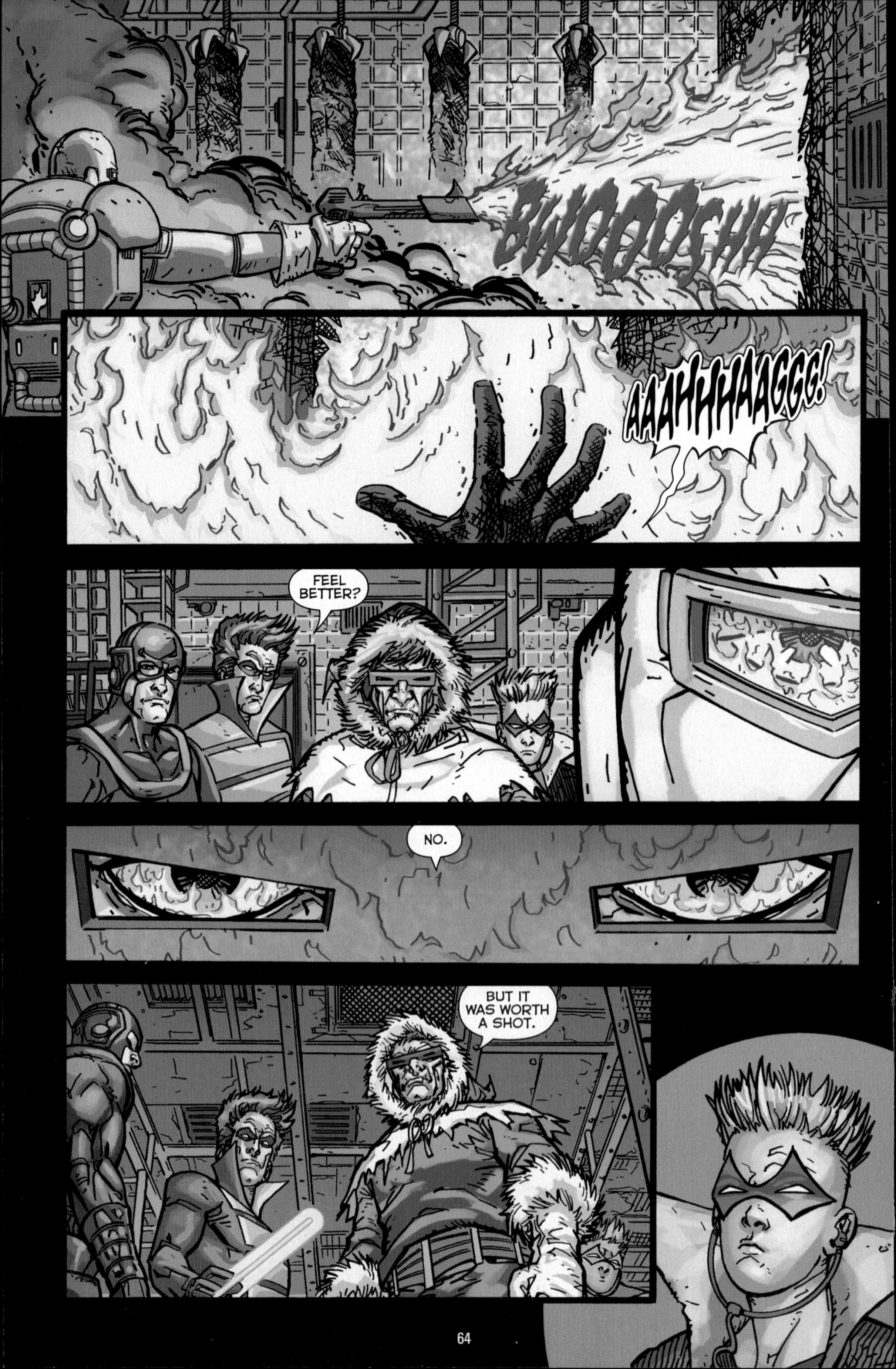

BWOOOSHH
AAAHHHAAGGG!
FEEL BETTER?
NO.
BUT IT WAS WORTH A SHOT.

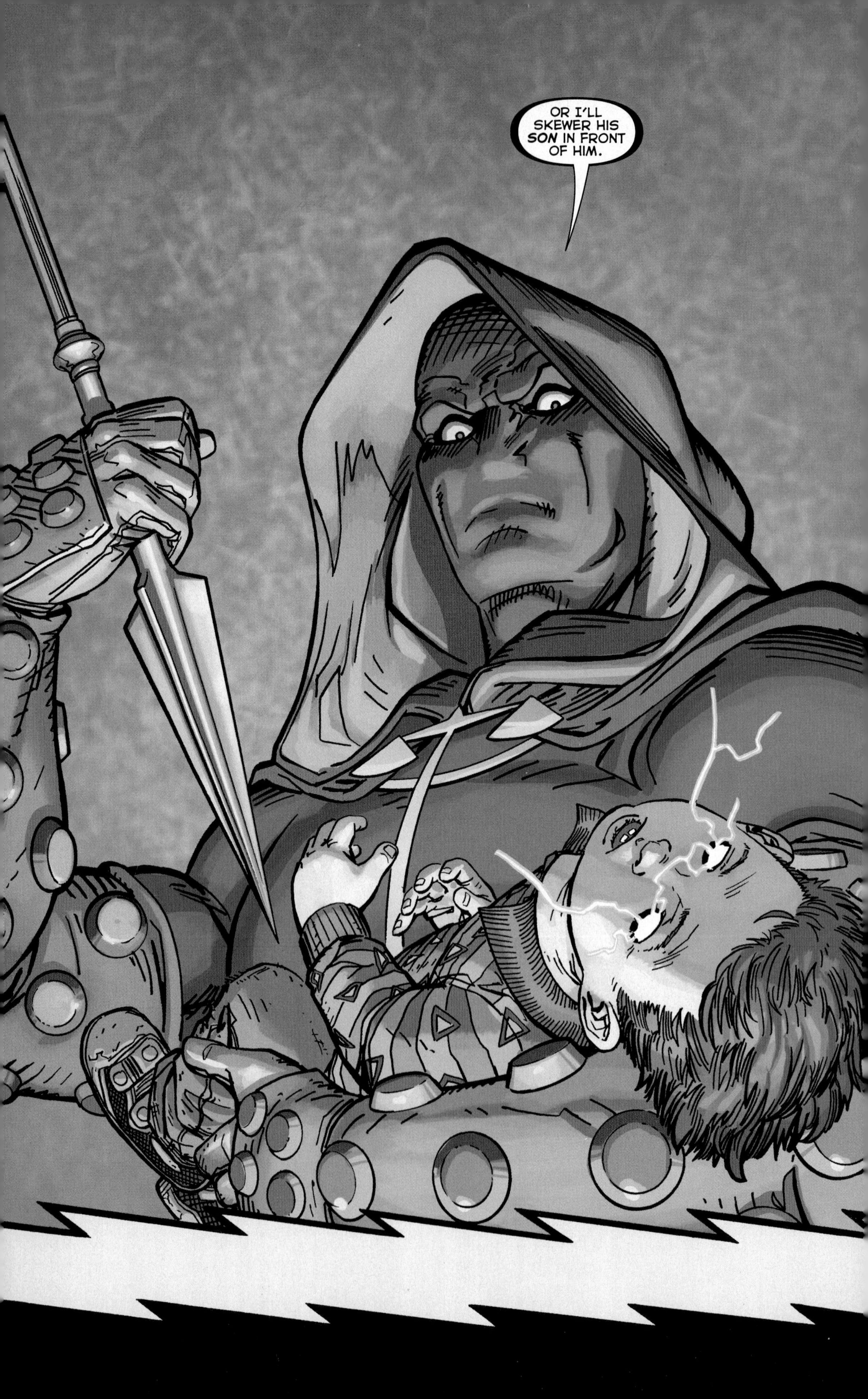
OR I'LL SKEWER HIS SON IN FRONT OF HIM.

Cover to FINAL CRISIS: ROGUES' REVENGE #3

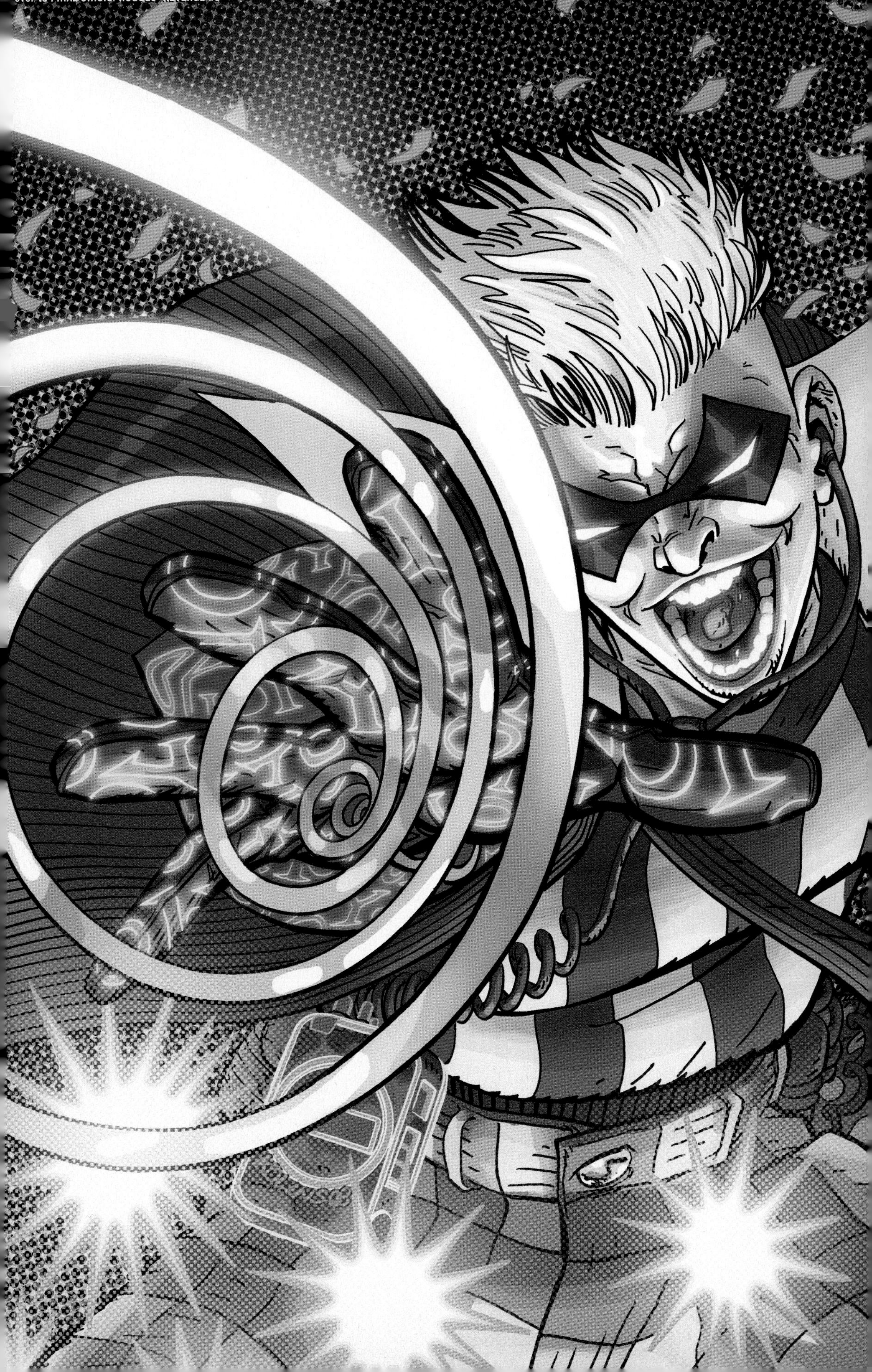

Sliver cover to FINAL CRISIS: ROGUES' REVENGE #3

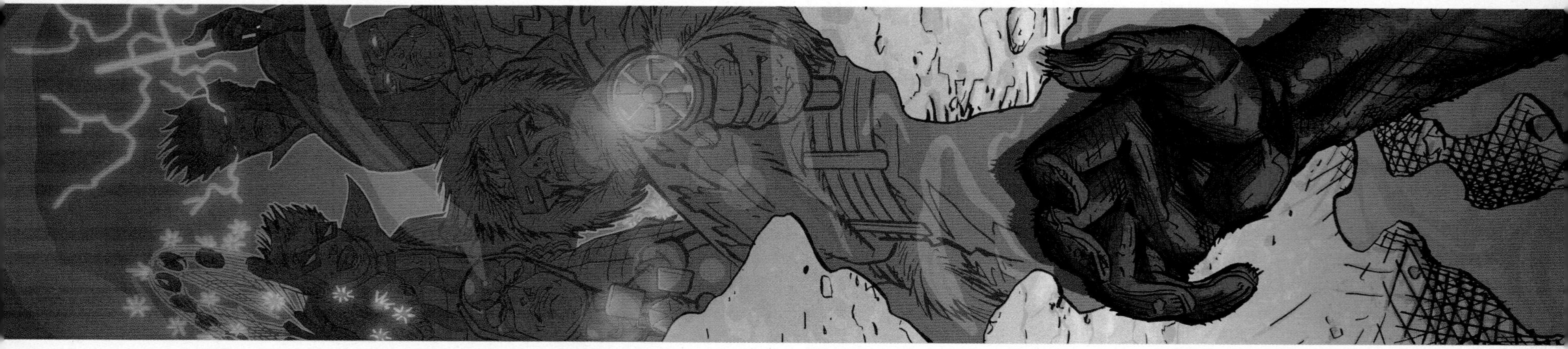

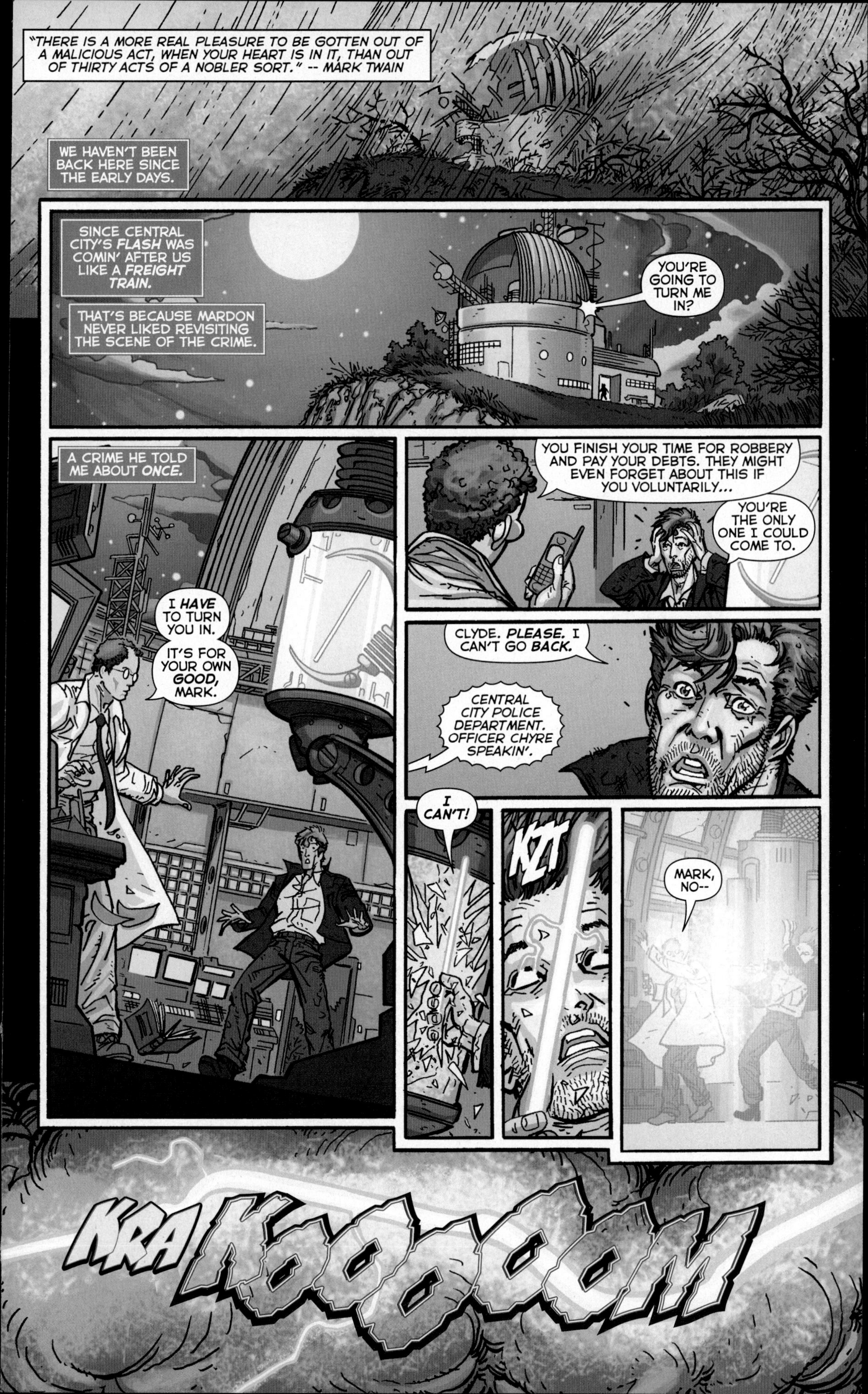
"THERE IS A MORE REAL PLEASURE TO BE GOTTEN OUT OF A MALICIOUS ACT, WHEN YOUR HEART IS IN IT, THAN OUT OF THIRTY ACTS OF A NOBLER SORT." -- MARK TWAIN
WE HAVEN'T BEEN BACK HERE SINCE THE EARLY DAYS.
SINCE CENTRAL CITY'S FLASH WAS COMIN' AFTER US LIKE A FREIGHT TRAIN.
THAT'S BECAUSE MARDON NEVER LIKED REVISITING THE SCENE OF THE CRIME.
YOU'RE GOING TO TURN ME IN?
A CRIME HE TOLD ME ABOUT ONCE.
I HAVE TO TURN YOU IN.
IT'S FOR YOUR OWN GOOD, MARK.
YOU FINISH YOUR TIME FOR ROBBERY AND PAY YOUR DEBTS. THEY MIGHT EVEN FORGET ABOUT THIS IF YOU VOLUNTARILY...
YOU'RE THE ONLY ONE I COULD COME TO.
CLYDE. PLEASE. I CAN'T GO BACK.
CENTRAL CITY POLICE DEPARTMENT. OFFICER CHYRE SPEAKIN'.
I CAN'T!
KZT
MARK, NO--
KRAKOOOOOM

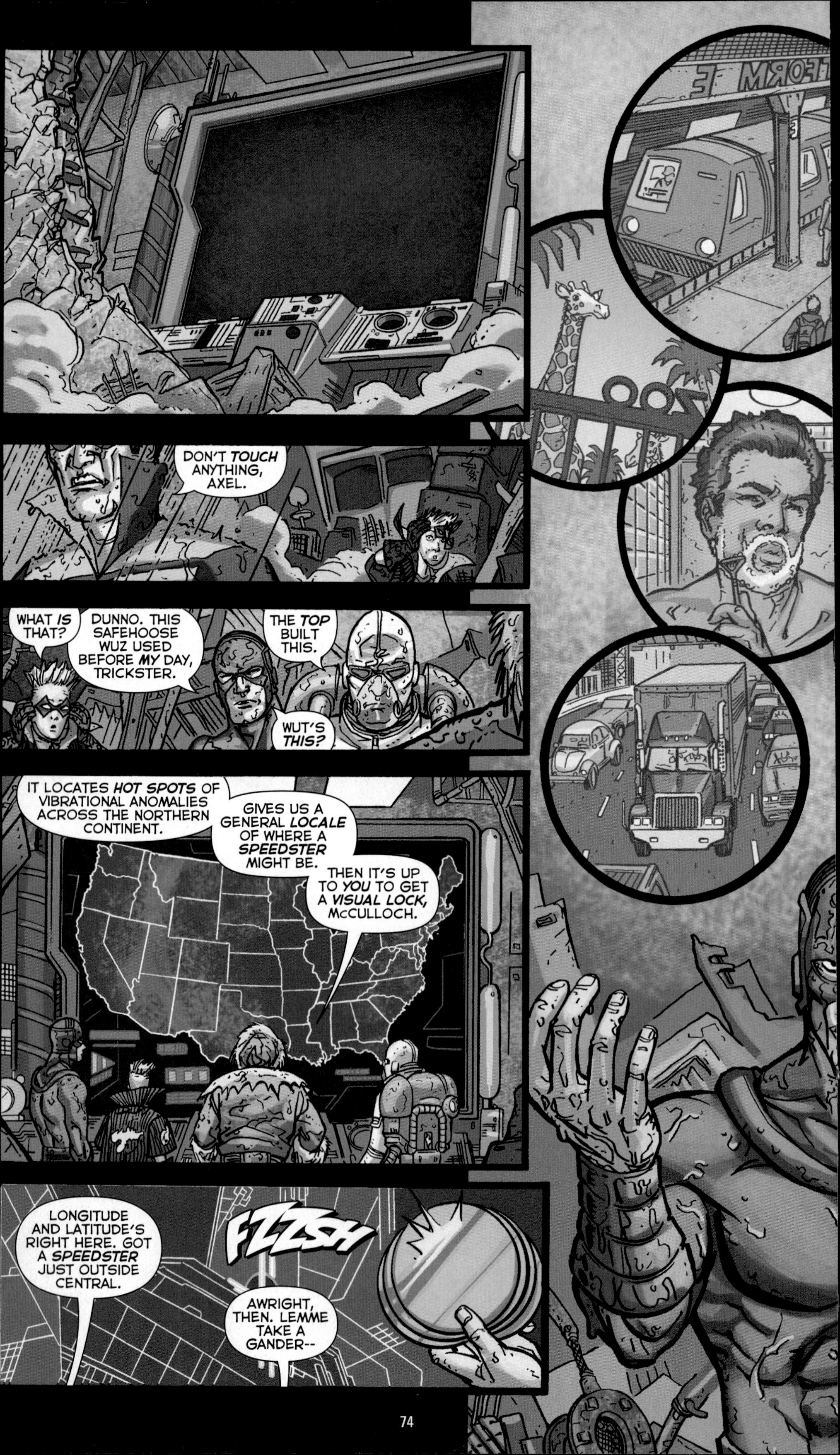
DON'T TOUCH ANYTHING, AXEL.
WHAT IS THAT?
DUNNO. THIS SAFEHOOSE WUZ USED BEFORE MY DAY, TRICKSTER.
THE TOP BUILT THIS.
WUT'S THIS?
IT LOCATES HOT SPOTS OF VIBRATIONAL ANOMALIES ACROSS THE NORTHERN CONTINENT.
GIVES US A GENERAL LOCALE OF WHERE A SPEEDSTER MIGHT BE.
THEN IT'S UP TO YOU TO GET A VISUAL LOCK, McCULLOCH.
LONGITUDE AND LATITUDE'S RIGHT HERE. GOT A SPEEDSTER JUST OUTSIDE CENTRAL.
FZZSH
AWRIGHT, THEN. LEMME TAKE A GANDER--

STOP.

WHAT? WHAT NOW? I PUT ON THE COSTUME (BECAUSE YOU TORE UP MY OLD ONE). I'VE RUN AROUND. WHAT NOW?

FEEL THE PRESENTTTTT PASS US BYYYY, THADDEUS?

LIKESTANDINGONA ROLLING BALL. YOU CAN CONTROL IT.

YOU CAN MOVE AS FAAAAAST ORASSLOW AS YOU WANT TO.

AND WHEN YOU RIDE TIME, EVEN THE SLIGHTEST OFMOVEMENTS CAN RESULT IN UNIMAGINABLE POWER.

I'LL TRY, I'LL TRY.

YOU BETTER BACK UP, THOUGH. THIS IS GONNA GO OFF!

SVP

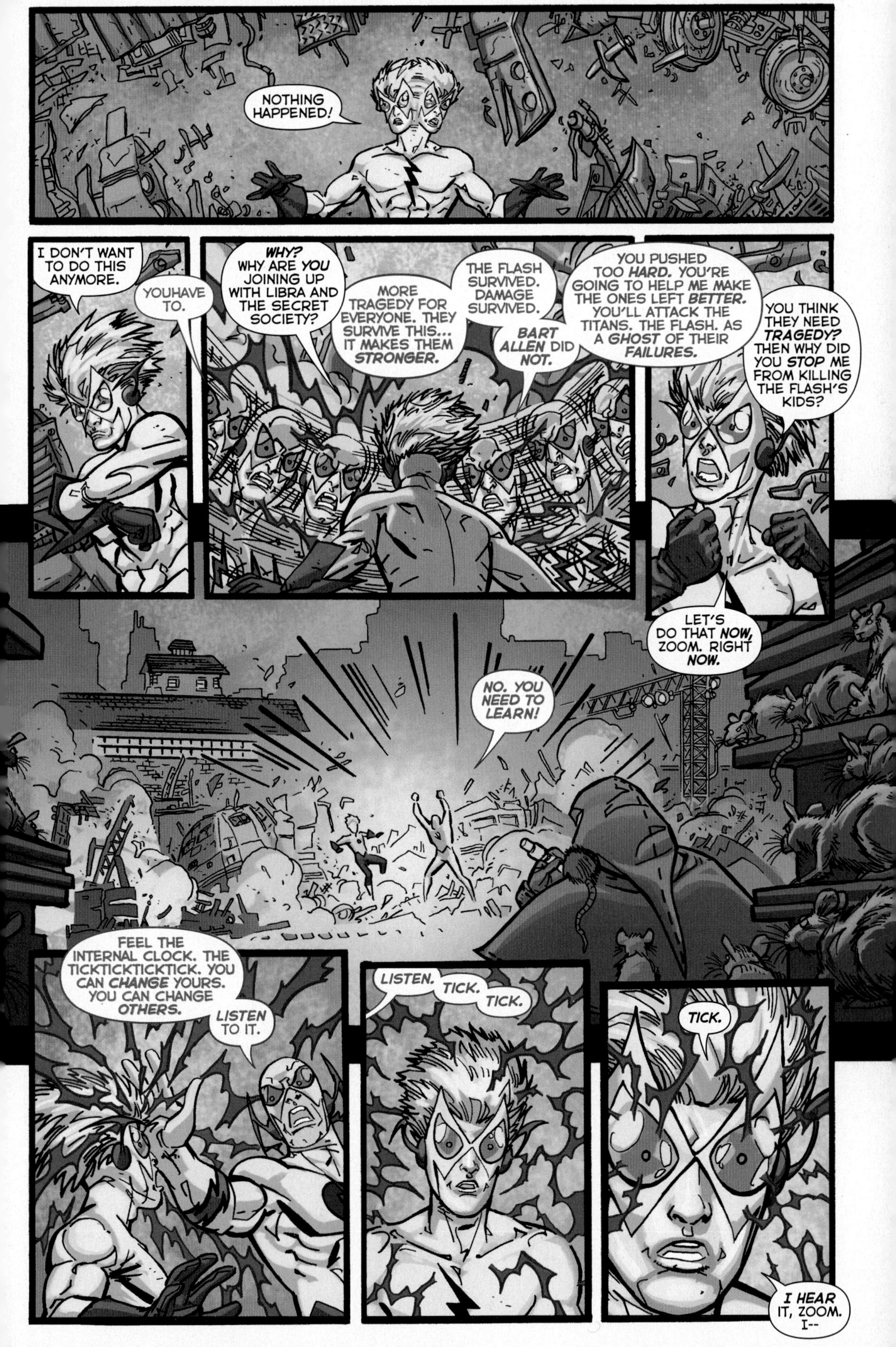

NOTHING HAPPENED!
I DON'T WANT TO DO THIS ANYMORE.
YOUHAVE TO.
WHY? WHY ARE YOU JOINING UP WITH LIBRA AND THE SECRET SOCIETY?
MORE TRAGEDY FOR EVERYONE. THEY SURVIVE THIS... IT MAKES THEM STRONGER.
THE FLASH SURVIVED. DAMAGE SURVIVED.
BART ALLEN DID NOT.
YOU PUSHED TOO HARD. YOU'RE GOING TO HELP ME MAKE THE ONES LEFT BETTER. YOU'LL ATTACK THE TITANS. THE FLASH. AS A GHOST OF THEIR FAILURES.
YOU THINK THEY NEED TRAGEDY? THEN WHY DID YOU STOP ME FROM KILLING THE FLASH'S KIDS?
LET'S DO THAT NOW, ZOOM. RIGHT NOW.
NO. YOU NEED TO LEARN!
FEEL THE INTERNAL CLOCK. THE TICKTICKTICKTICK. YOU CAN CHANGE YOURS. YOU CAN CHANGE OTHERS.
LISTEN TO IT.
LISTEN.
TICK.
TICK.
TICK.
I HEAR IT, ZOOM. I--

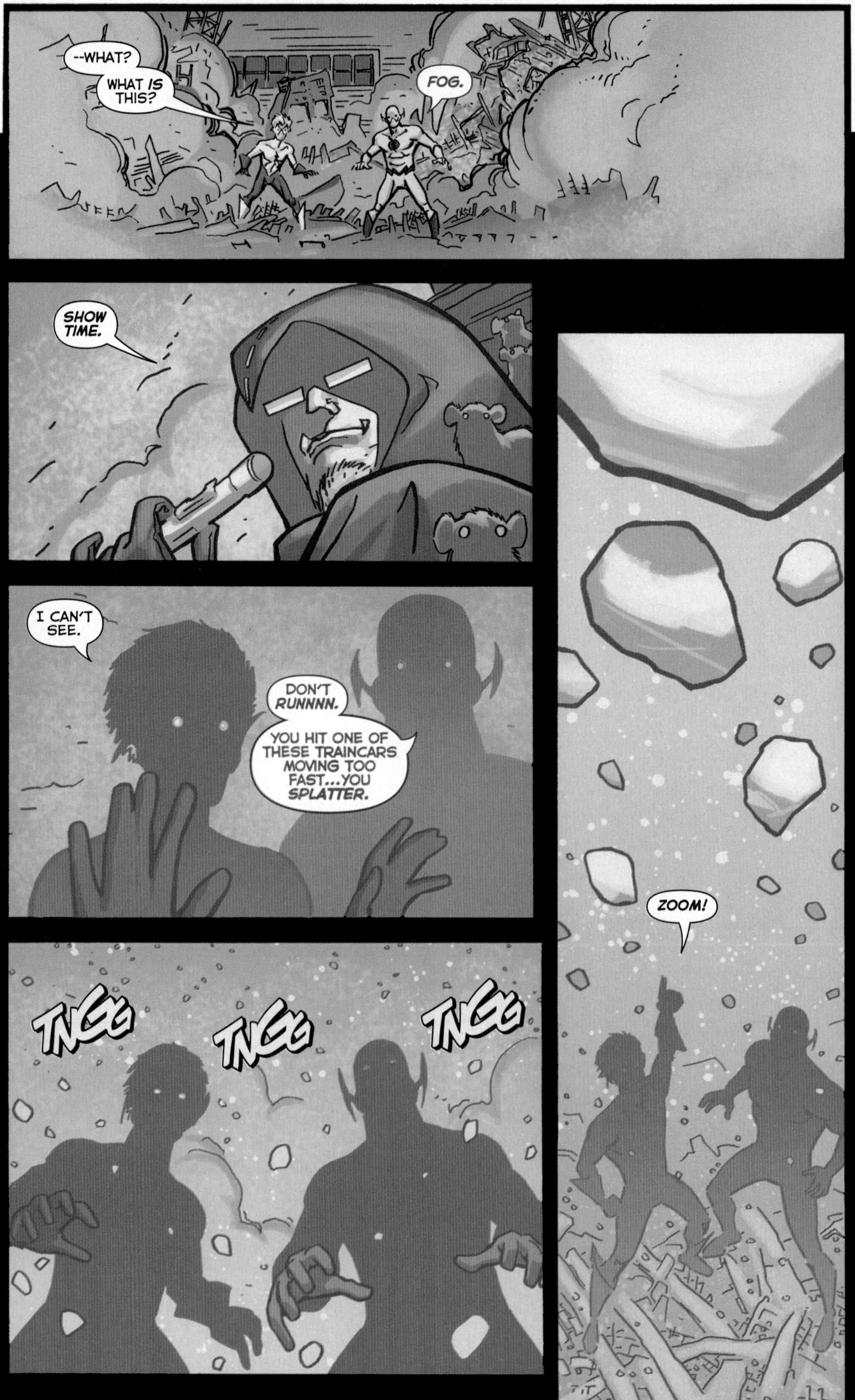
--WHAT?
WHAT IS THIS?
FOG.
SHOW TIME.
I CAN'T SEE.
DON'T RUNNNN.
YOU HIT ONE OF THESE TRAINCARS MOVING TOO FAST...YOU SPLATTER.
TNGG
TNGG
TNGG
ZOOM!

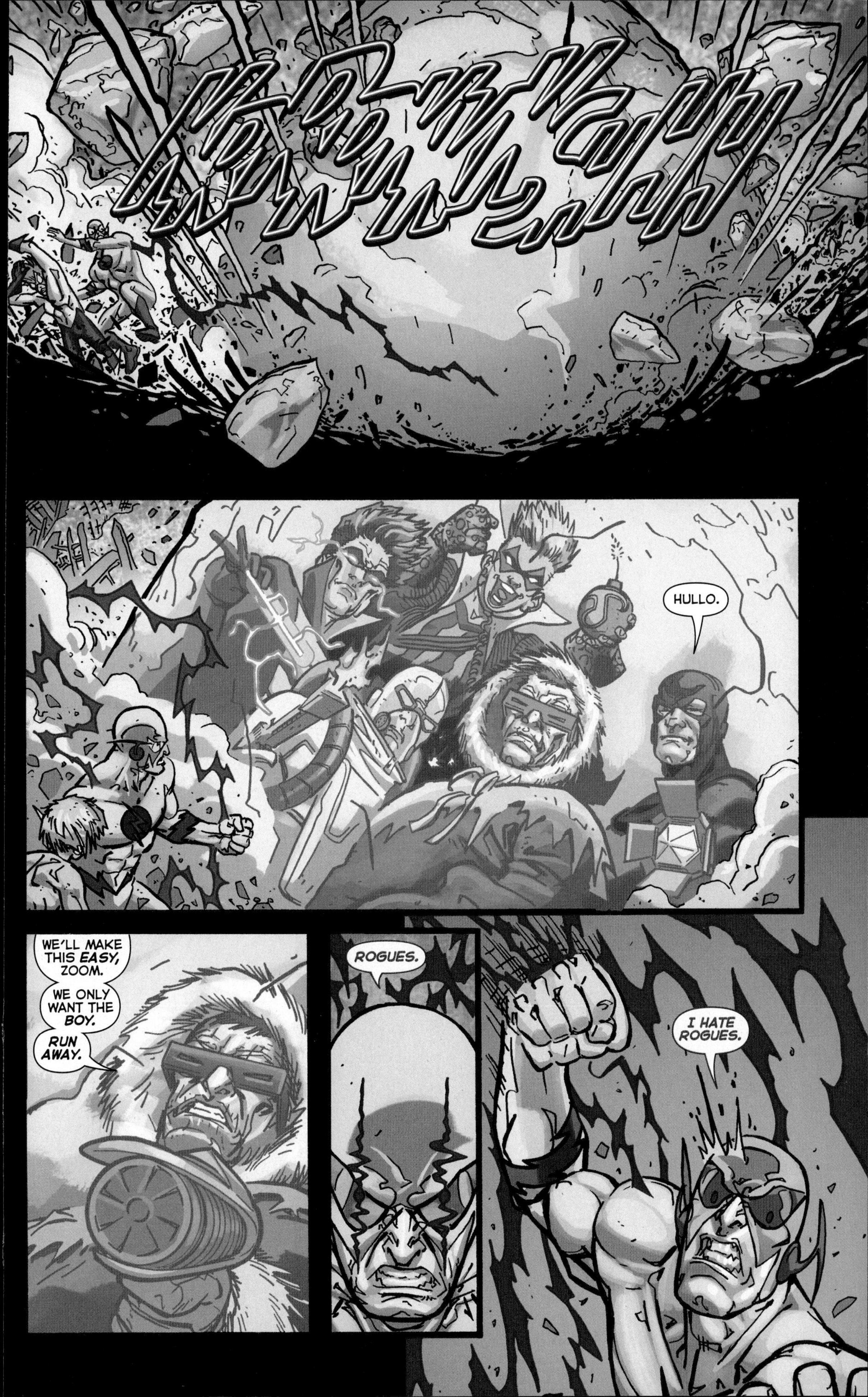

HULLO.
WE'LL MAKE THIS *EASY*, ZOOM.
WE ONLY WANT THE *BOY*.
RUN AWAY.
ROGUES.
I HATE ROGUES.

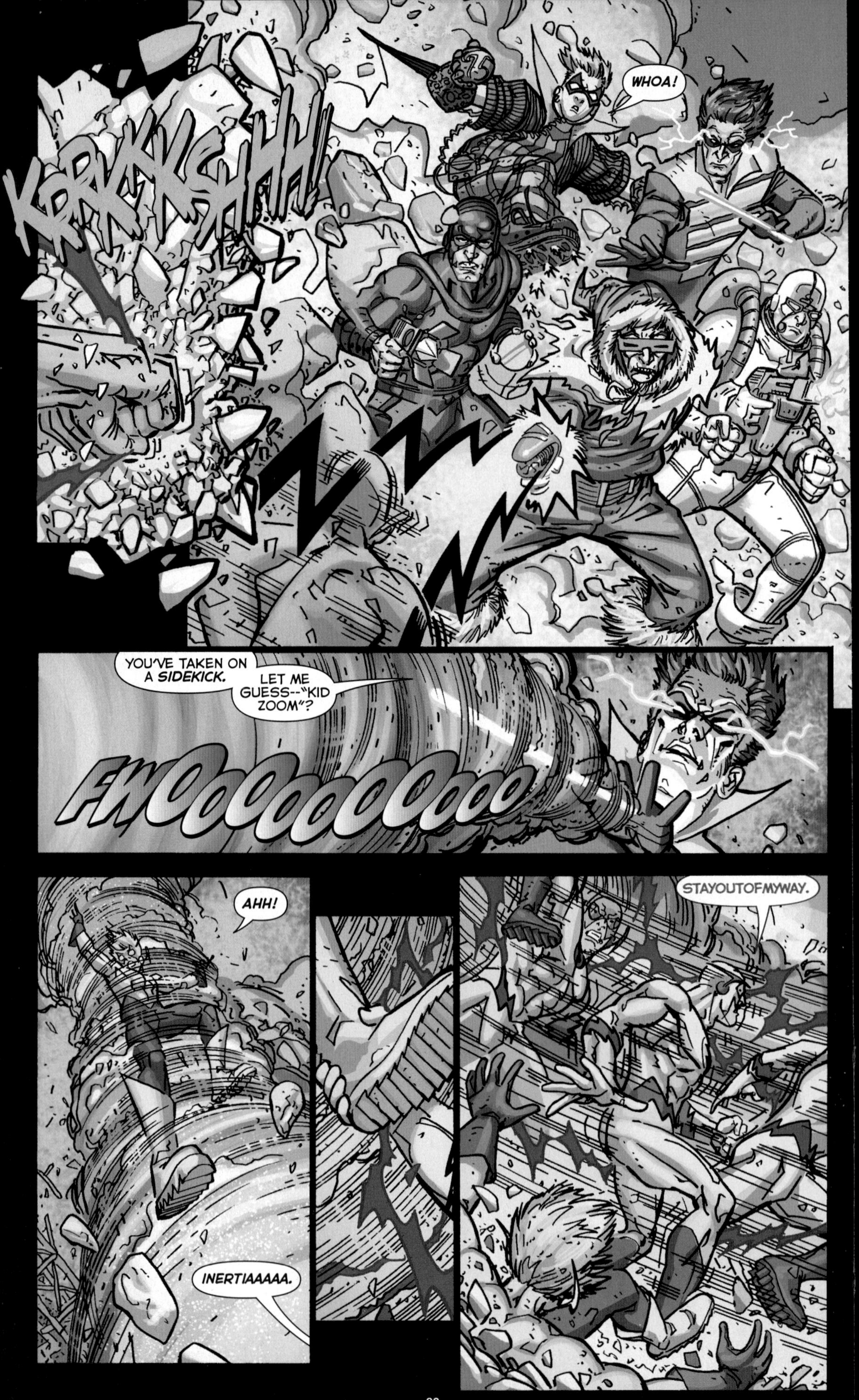
KRAKASHH!
WHOA!
YOU'VE TAKEN ON A SIDEKICK.
LET ME GUESS--"KID ZOOM"?
FWOOOOOOOOOOO
AHH!
INERTIAAAAA.
STAYOUTOFMYWAY.

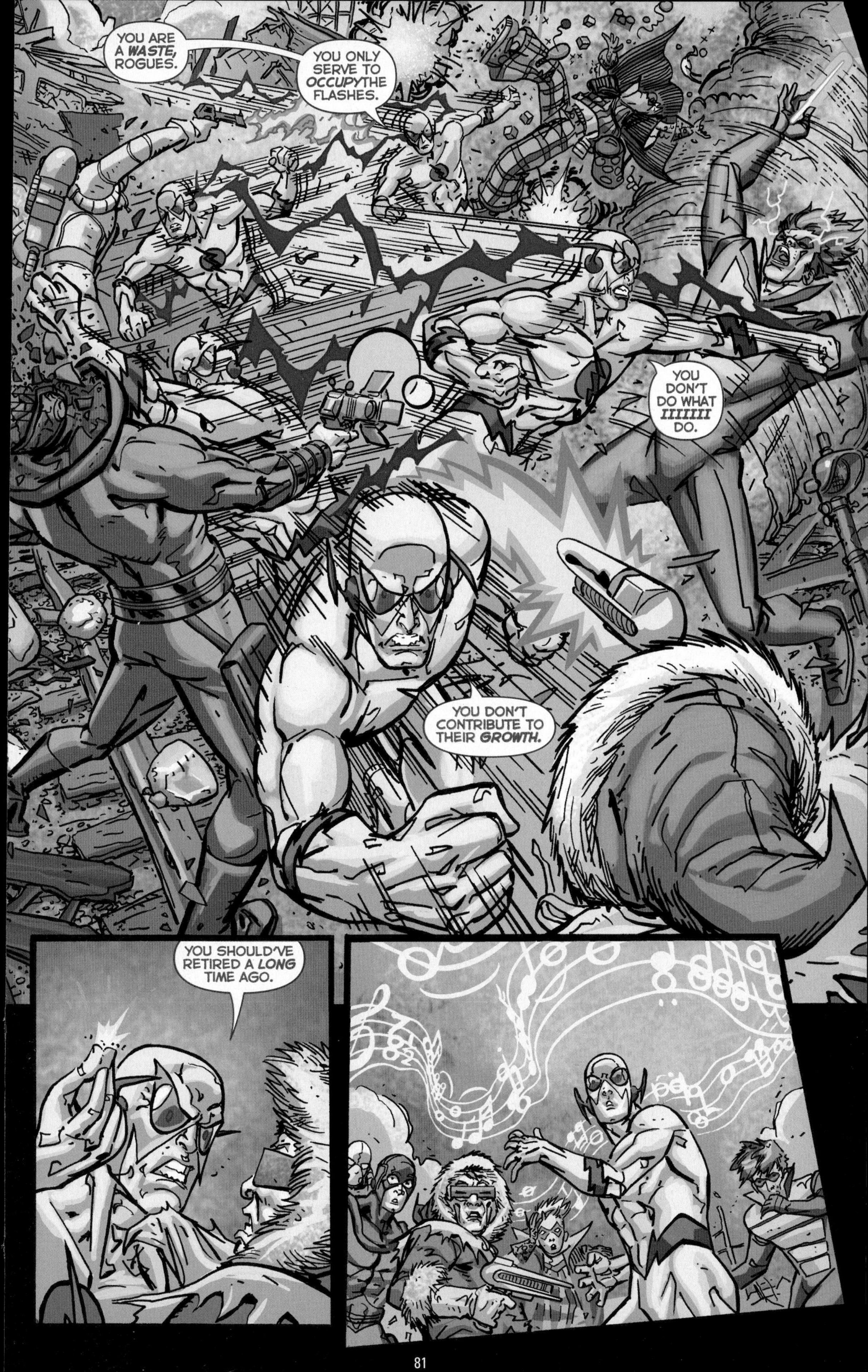
YOU ARE A WASTE, ROGUES.
YOU ONLY SERVE TO OCCUPY THE FLASHES.
YOU DON'T DO WHAT IIIIIII DO.
YOU DON'T CONTRIBUTE TO THEIR GROWTH.
YOU SHOULD'VE RETIRED A LONG TIME AGO.

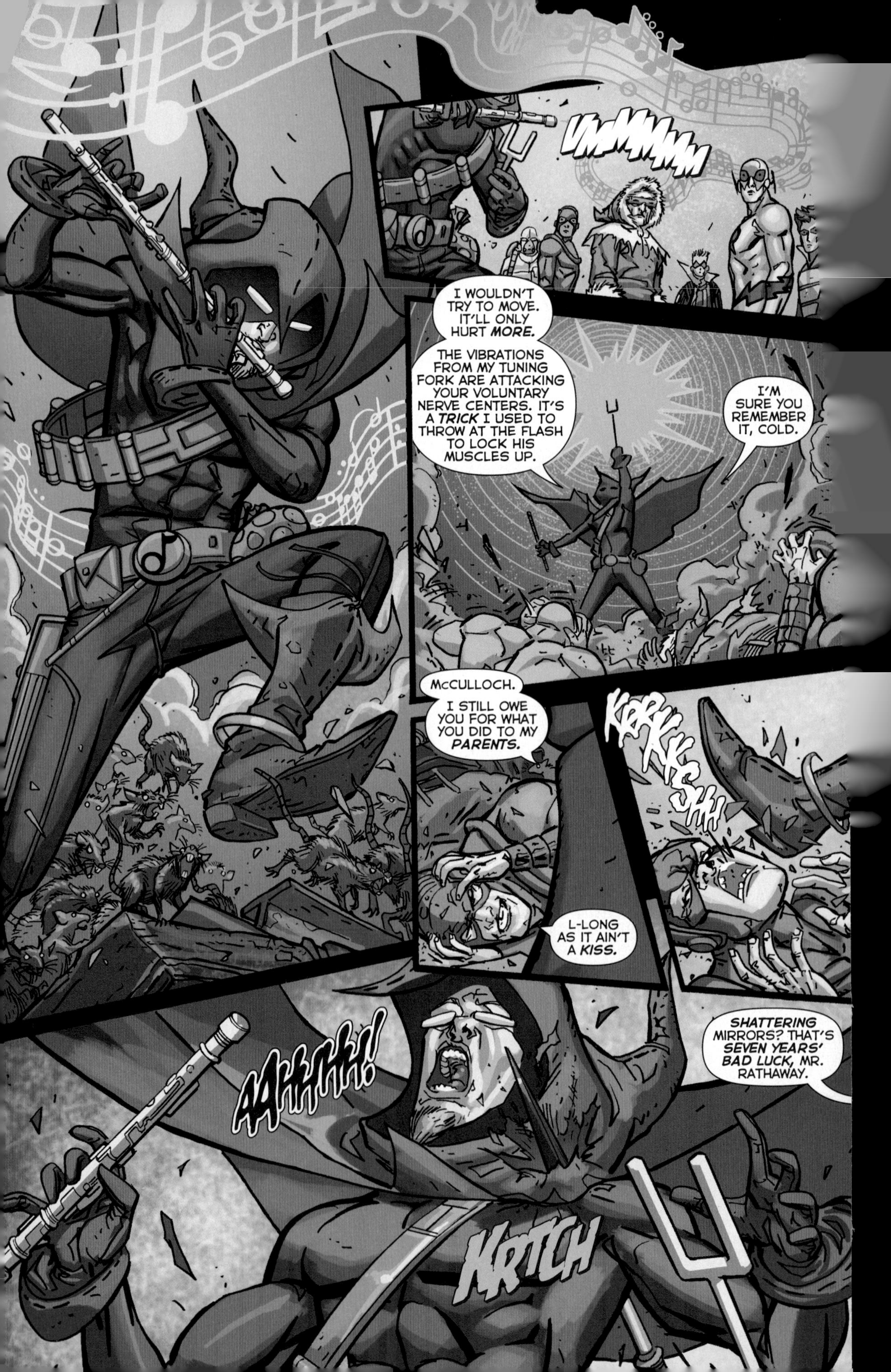
UMMMMMM
I WOULDN'T TRY TO MOVE. IT'LL ONLY HURT MORE.
THE VIBRATIONS FROM MY TUNING FORK ARE ATTACKING YOUR VOLUNTARY NERVE CENTERS. IT'S A TRICK I USED TO THROW AT THE FLASH TO LOCK HIS MUSCLES UP.
I'M SURE YOU REMEMBER IT, COLD.
McCULLOCH.
I STILL OWE YOU FOR WHAT YOU DID TO MY PARENTS.
L-LONG AS IT AIN'T A KISS.
KRRKSHH
AAHHHH!
SHATTERING MIRRORS? THAT'S SEVEN YEARS' BAD LUCK, MR. RATHAWAY.
KRTCH

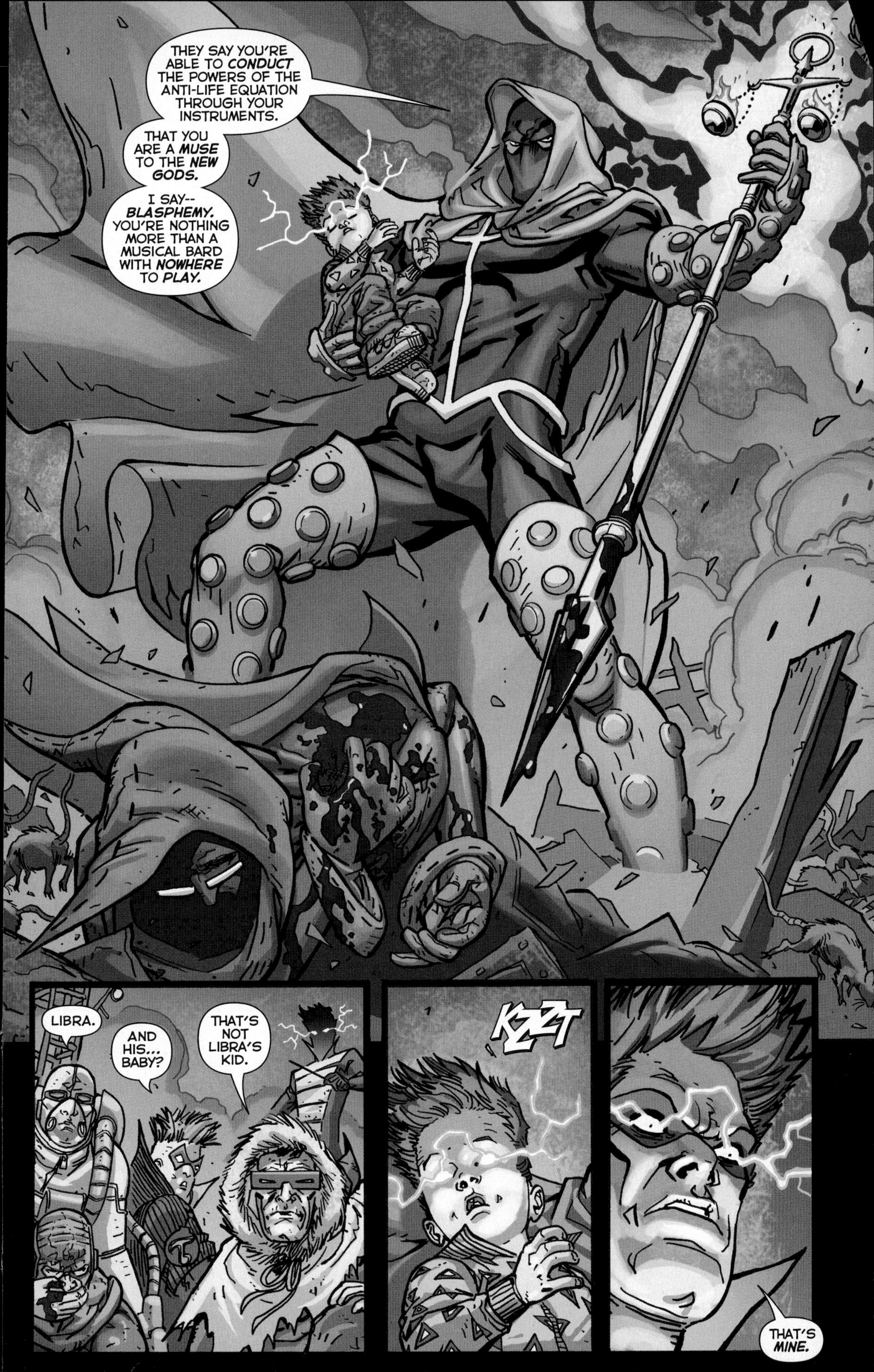
THEY SAY YOU'RE ABLE TO CONDUCT THE POWERS OF THE ANTI-LIFE EQUATION THROUGH YOUR INSTRUMENTS.
THAT YOU ARE A MUSE TO THE NEW GODS.
I SAY-- BLASPHEMY. YOU'RE NOTHING MORE THAN A MUSICAL BARD WITH NOWHERE TO PLAY.
LIBRA.
AND HIS... BABY?
THAT'S NOT LIBRA'S KID.
KZZT
THAT'S MINE.

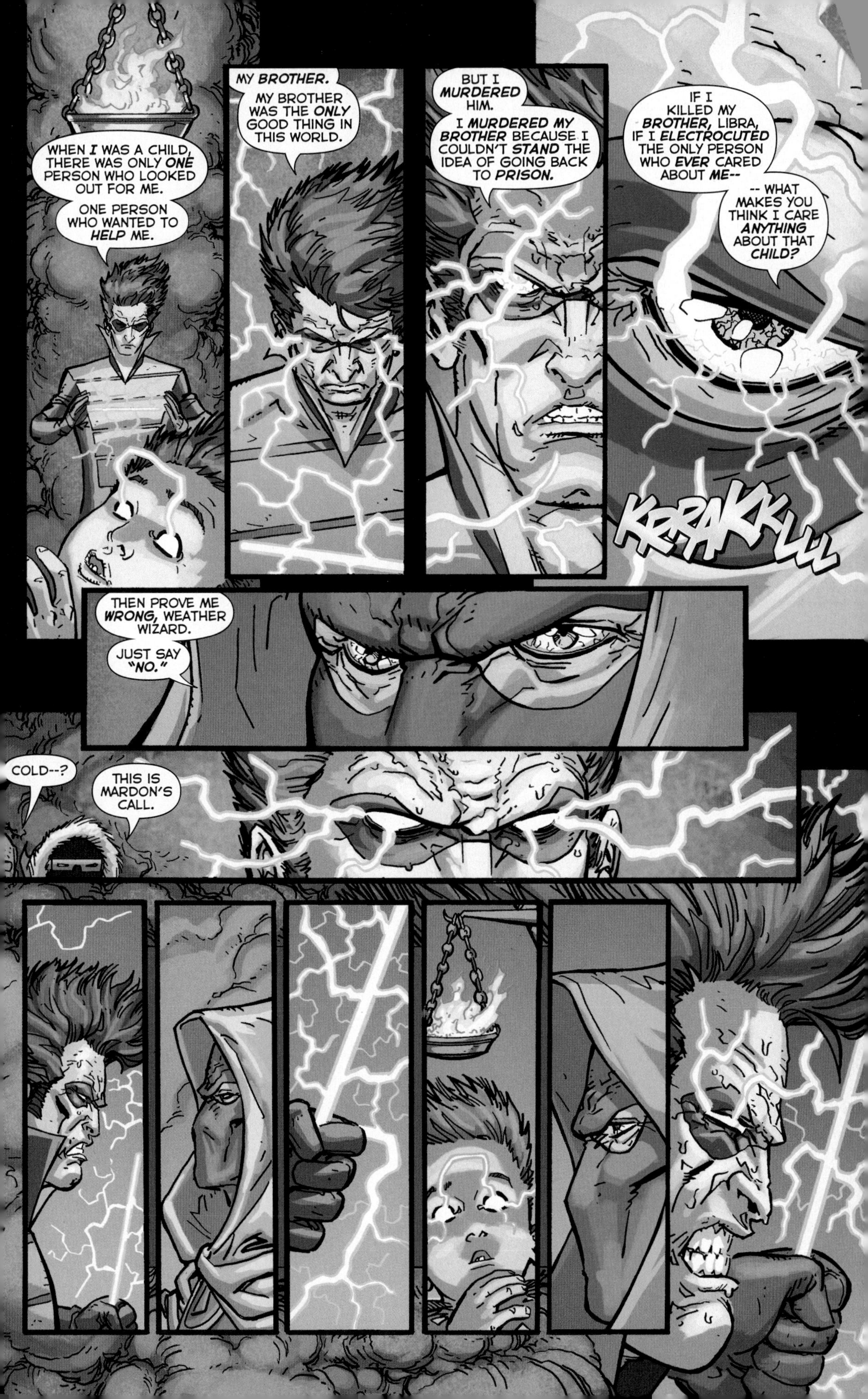
WHEN I WAS A CHILD, THERE WAS ONLY ONE PERSON WHO LOOKED OUT FOR ME.
ONE PERSON WHO WANTED TO HELP ME.
MY BROTHER.
MY BROTHER WAS THE ONLY GOOD THING IN THIS WORLD.
BUT I MURDERED HIM.
I MURDERED MY BROTHER BECAUSE I COULDN'T STAND THE IDEA OF GOING BACK TO PRISON.
IF I KILLED MY BROTHER, LIBRA, IF I ELECTROCUTED THE ONLY PERSON WHO EVER CARED ABOUT ME--
-- WHAT MAKES YOU THINK I CARE ANYTHING ABOUT THAT CHILD?
KRRAKKLLL
THEN PROVE ME WRONG, WEATHER WIZARD.
JUST SAY "NO."
COLD--?
THIS IS MARDON'S CALL.

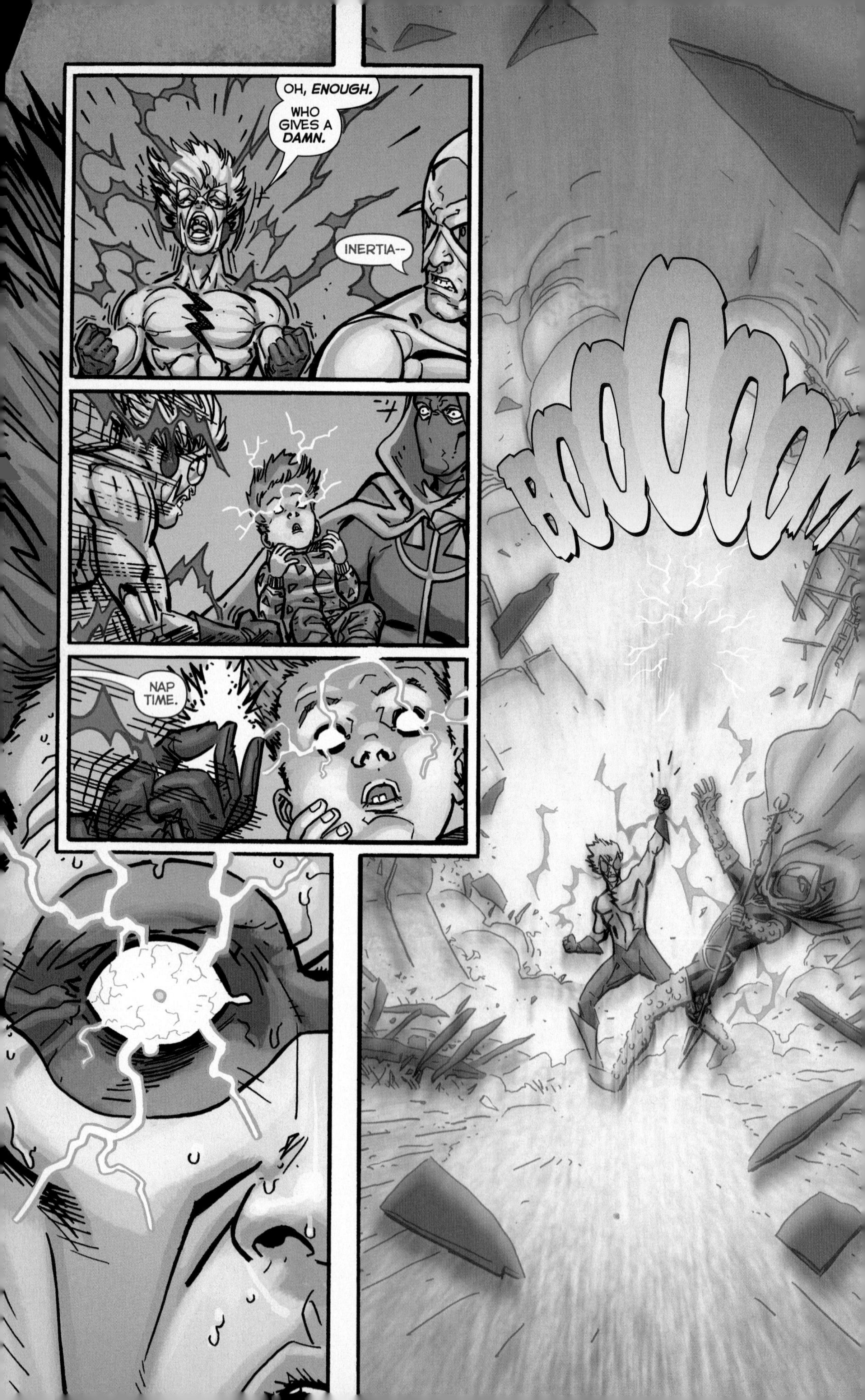
OH, ENOUGH.
WHO GIVES A DAMN.
INERTIA--
NAP TIME.
BOOOOOM

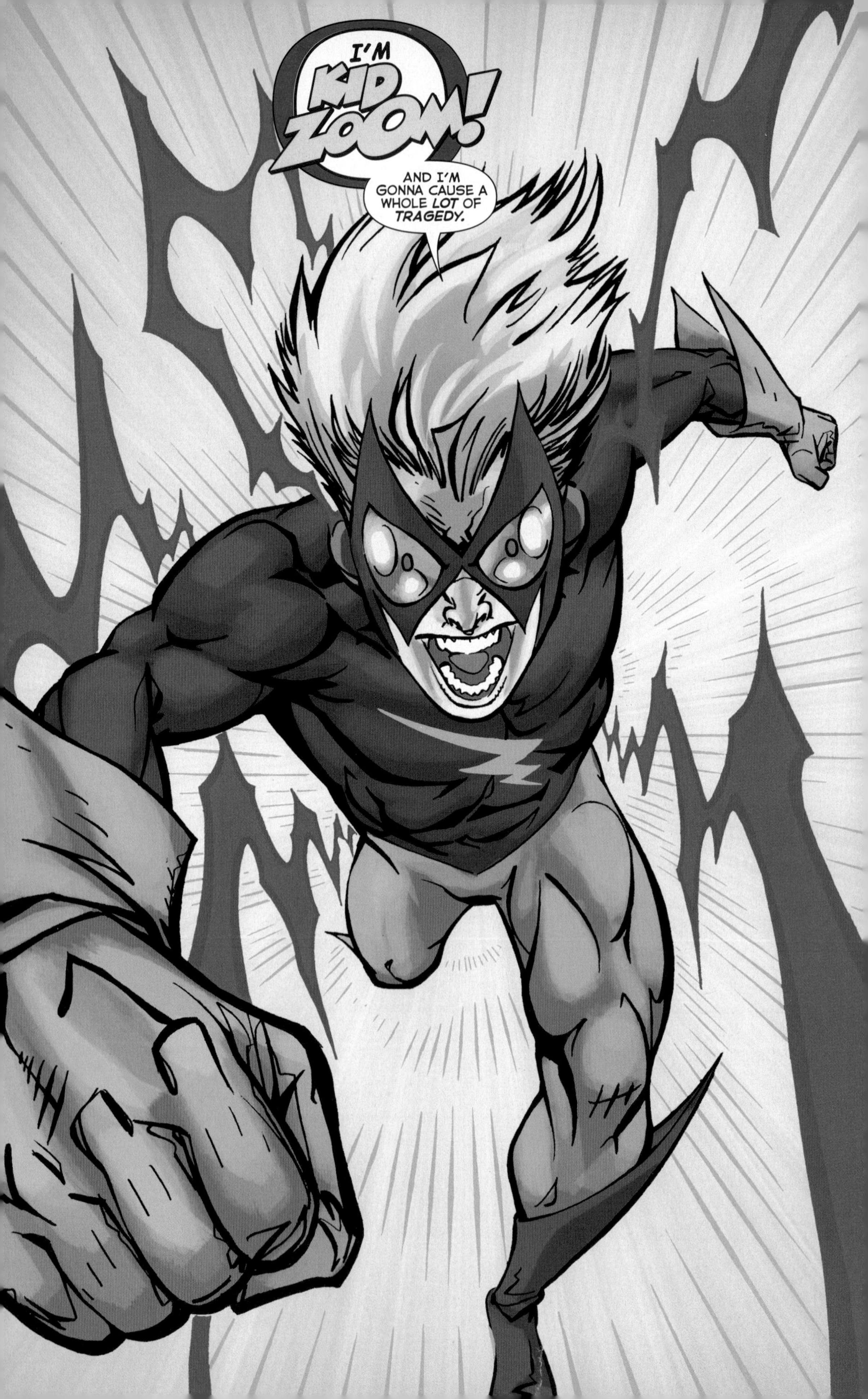
I'M KID ZOOM!
AND I'M GONNA CAUSE A WHOLE LOT OF TRAGEDY.

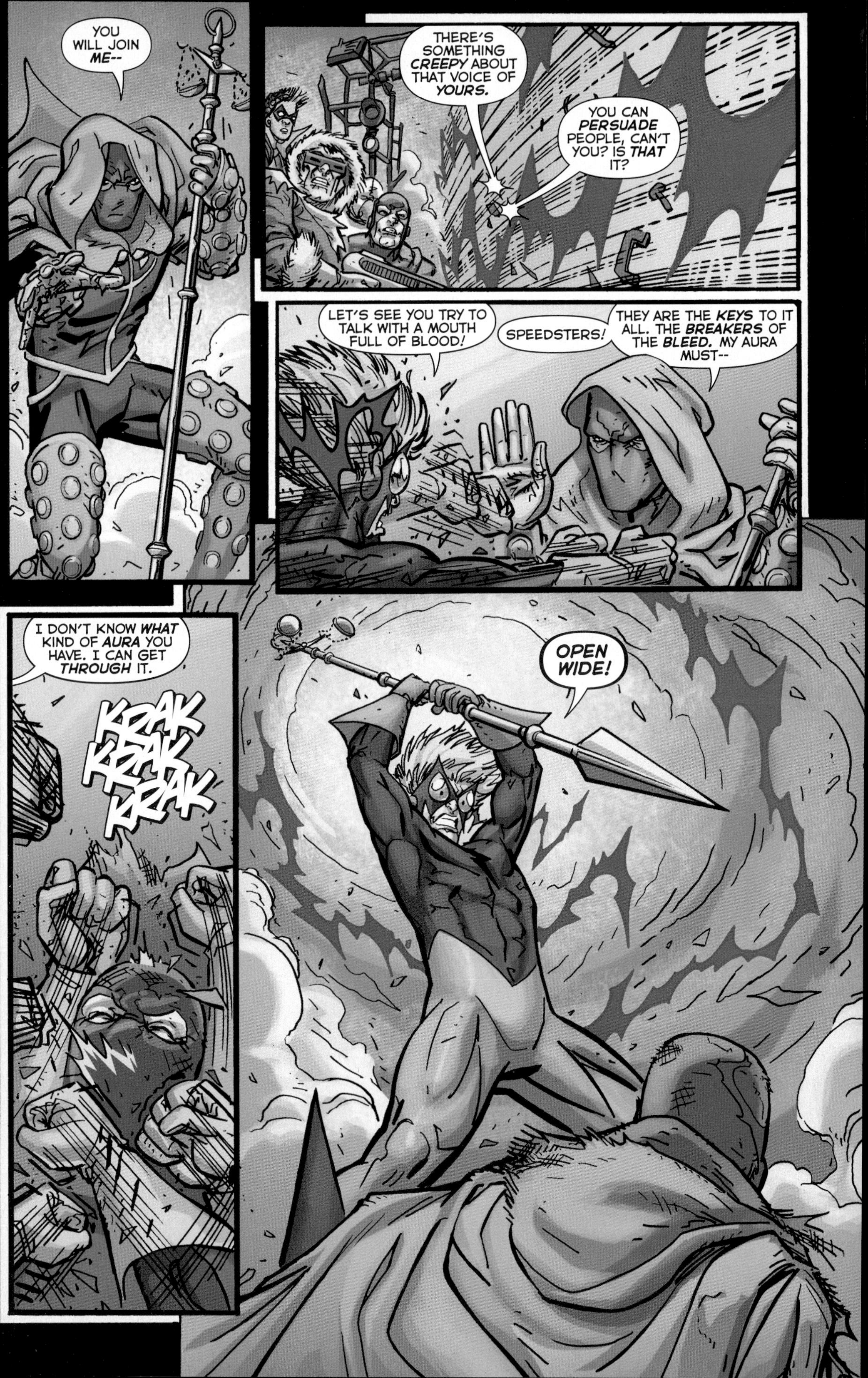
YOU WILL JOIN *ME*--
THERE'S SOMETHING *CREEPY* ABOUT THAT VOICE OF *YOURS.*
YOU CAN *PERSUADE* PEOPLE, CAN'T YOU? IS *THAT* IT?
LET'S SEE YOU TRY TO TALK WITH A MOUTH FULL OF BLOOD!
SPEEDSTERS!
THEY ARE THE *KEYS* TO IT ALL. THE *BREAKERS* OF THE *BLEED.* MY AURA MUST--
I DON'T KNOW *WHAT* KIND OF *AURA* YOU HAVE. I CAN GET *THROUGH* IT.
KRAK KRAK KRAK
OPEN WIDE!

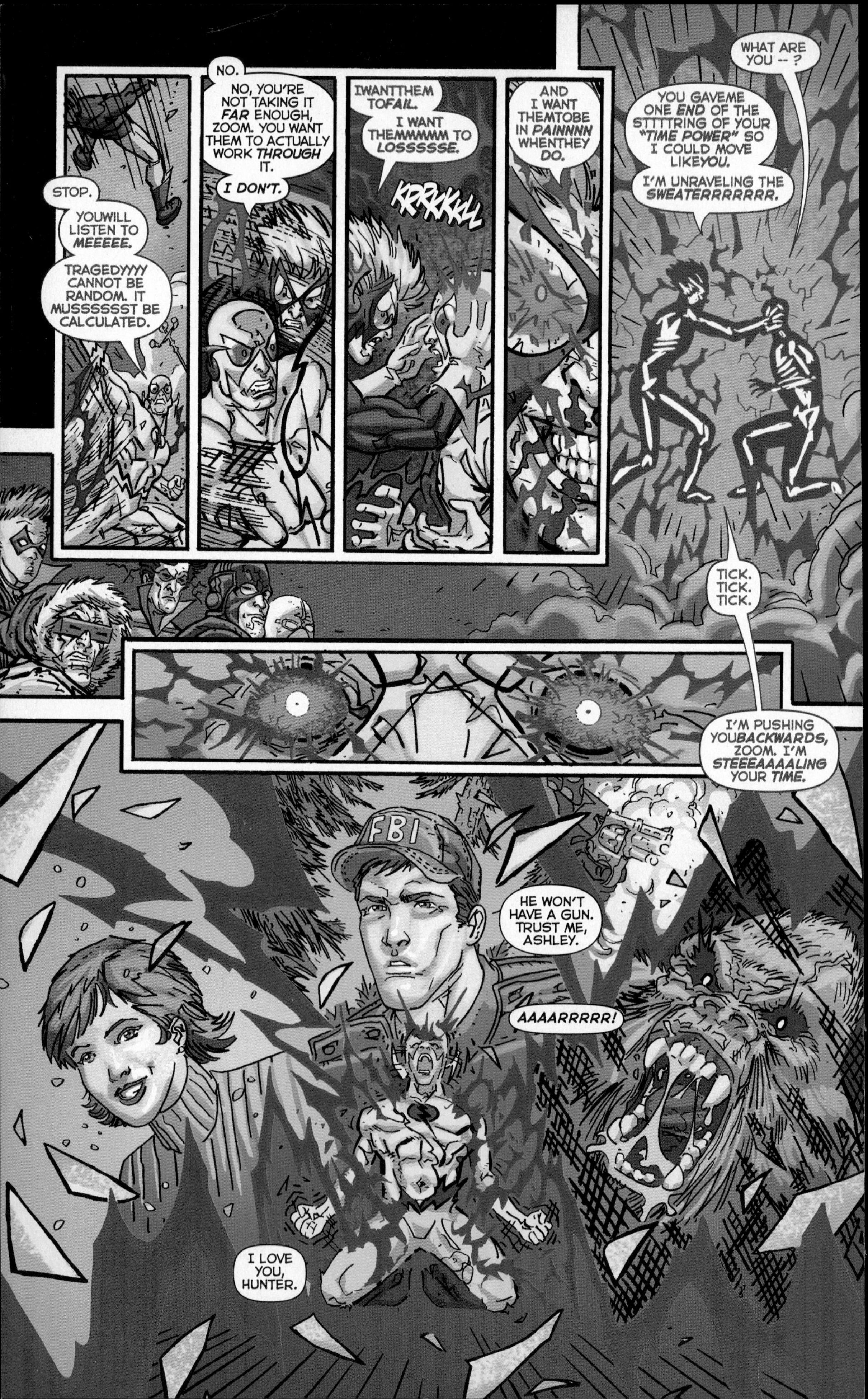
STOP.
YOUWILL LISTEN TO MEEEEE.
TRAGEDYYYY CANNOT BE RANDOM. IT MUSSSSSST BE CALCULATED.
NO.
NO, YOU'RE NOT TAKING IT FAR ENOUGH, ZOOM. YOU WANT THEM TO ACTUALLY WORK THROUGH IT.
I DON'T.
IWANTTHEM TOFAIL.
I WANT THEMMMMM TO LOSSSSSE.
KRRKKKLL
AND I WANT THEMTOBE IN PAINNNN WHENTHEY DO.
WHAT ARE YOU -- ?
YOU GAVEME ONE END OF THE STTTTRING OF YOUR "TIME POWER" SO I COULD MOVE LIKEYOU.
I'M UNRAVELING THE SWEATERRRRRRR.
TICK. TICK. TICK.
I'M PUSHING YOUBACKWARDS, ZOOM. I'M STEEEAAAALING YOUR TIME.
FBI
HE WON'T HAVE A GUN. TRUST ME, ASHLEY.
AAAARRRRR!
I LOVE YOU, HUNTER.

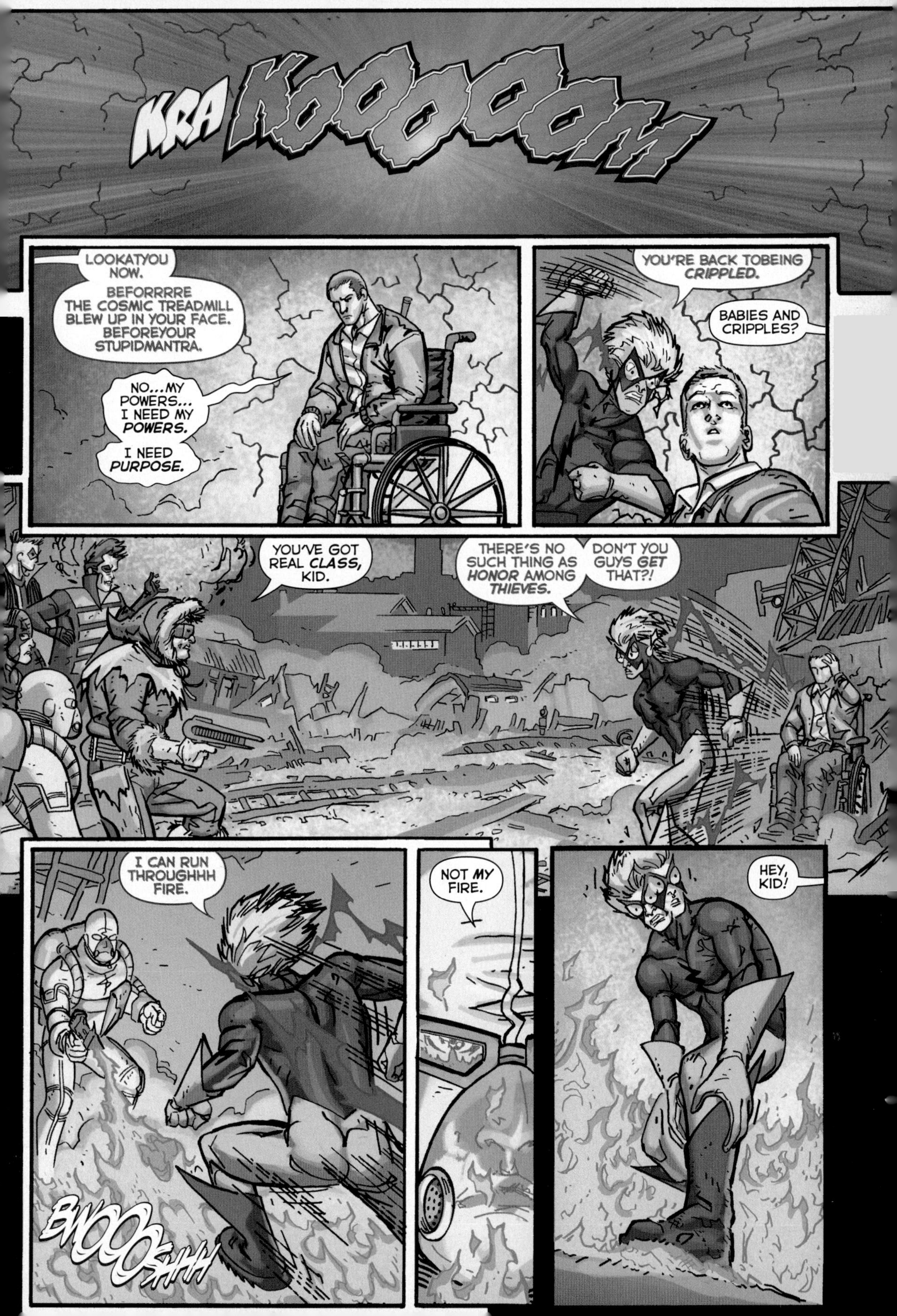
KRA KOOOOOOM
LOOKATYOU NOW.
BEFORRRRE THE COSMIC TREADMILL BLEW UP IN YOUR FACE. BEFOREYOUR STUPIDMANTRA.
NO...MY POWERS... I NEED MY POWERS.
I NEED PURPOSE.
YOU'RE BACK TOBEING CRIPPLED.
BABIES AND CRIPPLES?
YOU'VE GOT REAL CLASS, KID.
THERE'S NO SUCH THING AS HONOR AMONG THIEVES.
DON'T YOU GUYS GET THAT?!
I CAN RUN THROUGHHH FIRE.
BWOOOSHHH
NOT MY FIRE.
HEY, KID!

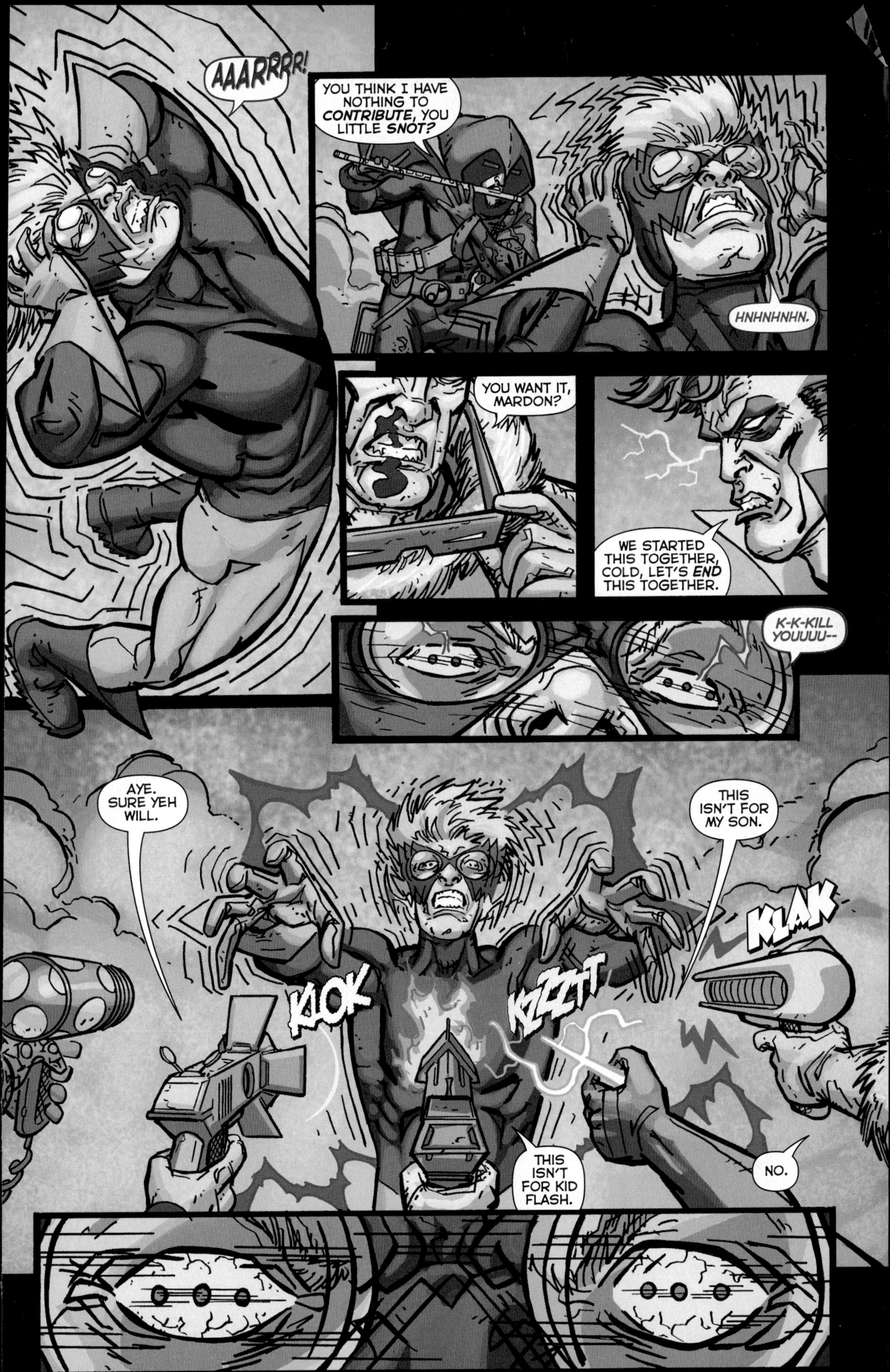
AAARRRR!
YOU THINK I HAVE NOTHING TO CONTRIBUTE, YOU LITTLE SNOT?
HNHNHNHN.
YOU WANT IT, MARDON?
WE STARTED THIS TOGETHER, COLD, LET'S END THIS TOGETHER.
K-K-KILL YOUUUU--
AYE. SURE YEH WILL.
THIS ISN'T FOR MY SON.
KLAK
KLOK
KZZZTT
THIS ISN'T FOR KID FLASH.
NO.

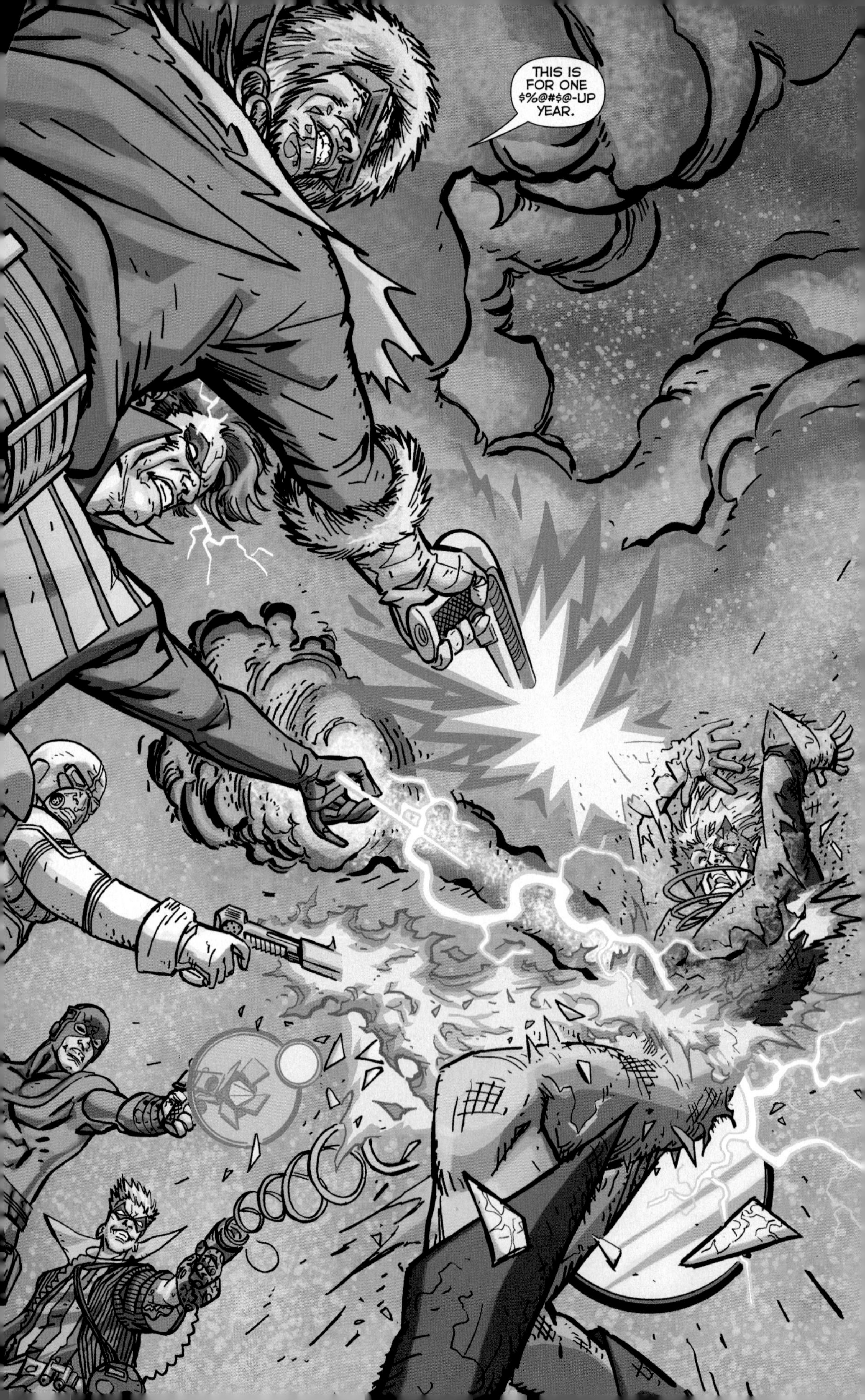
THIS IS FOR ONE $%@#$@-UP YEAR.

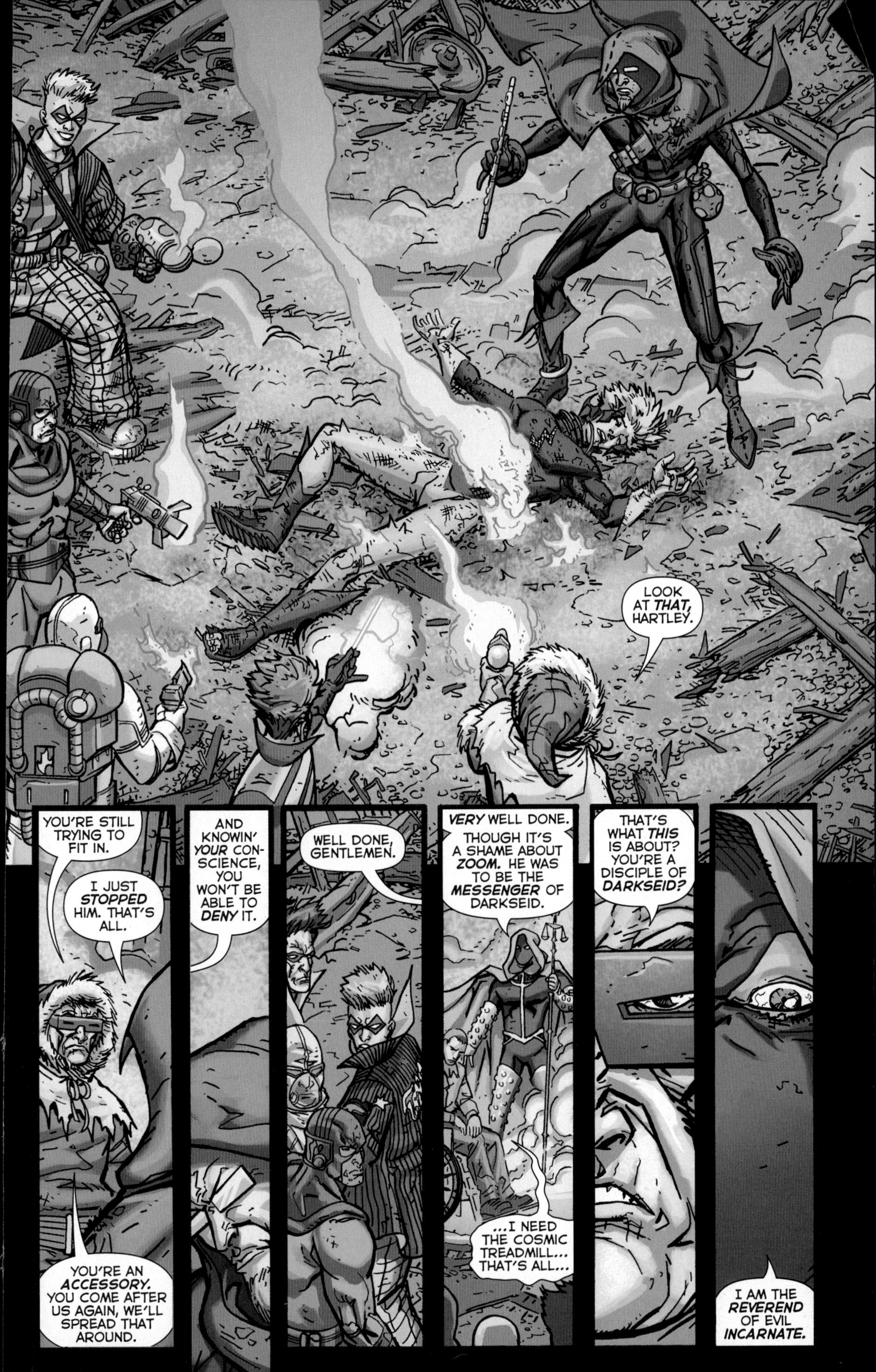
LOOK AT *THAT,* HARTLEY.
YOU'RE STILL TRYING TO FIT IN.
I JUST *STOPPED* HIM. THAT'S ALL.
YOU'RE AN *ACCESSORY.* YOU COME AFTER US AGAIN, WE'LL SPREAD THAT AROUND.
AND KNOWIN' *YOUR* CONSCIENCE, YOU WON'T BE ABLE TO *DENY* IT.
WELL DONE, GENTLEMEN.
VERY WELL DONE.
THOUGH IT'S A SHAME ABOUT *ZOOM.* HE WAS TO BE THE *MESSENGER* OF DARKSEID.
...I NEED THE COSMIC TREADMILL... THAT'S ALL...
THAT'S WHAT *THIS* IS ABOUT? YOU'RE A DISCIPLE OF *DARKSEID?*
I AM THE *REVEREND* OF EVIL *INCARNATE.*

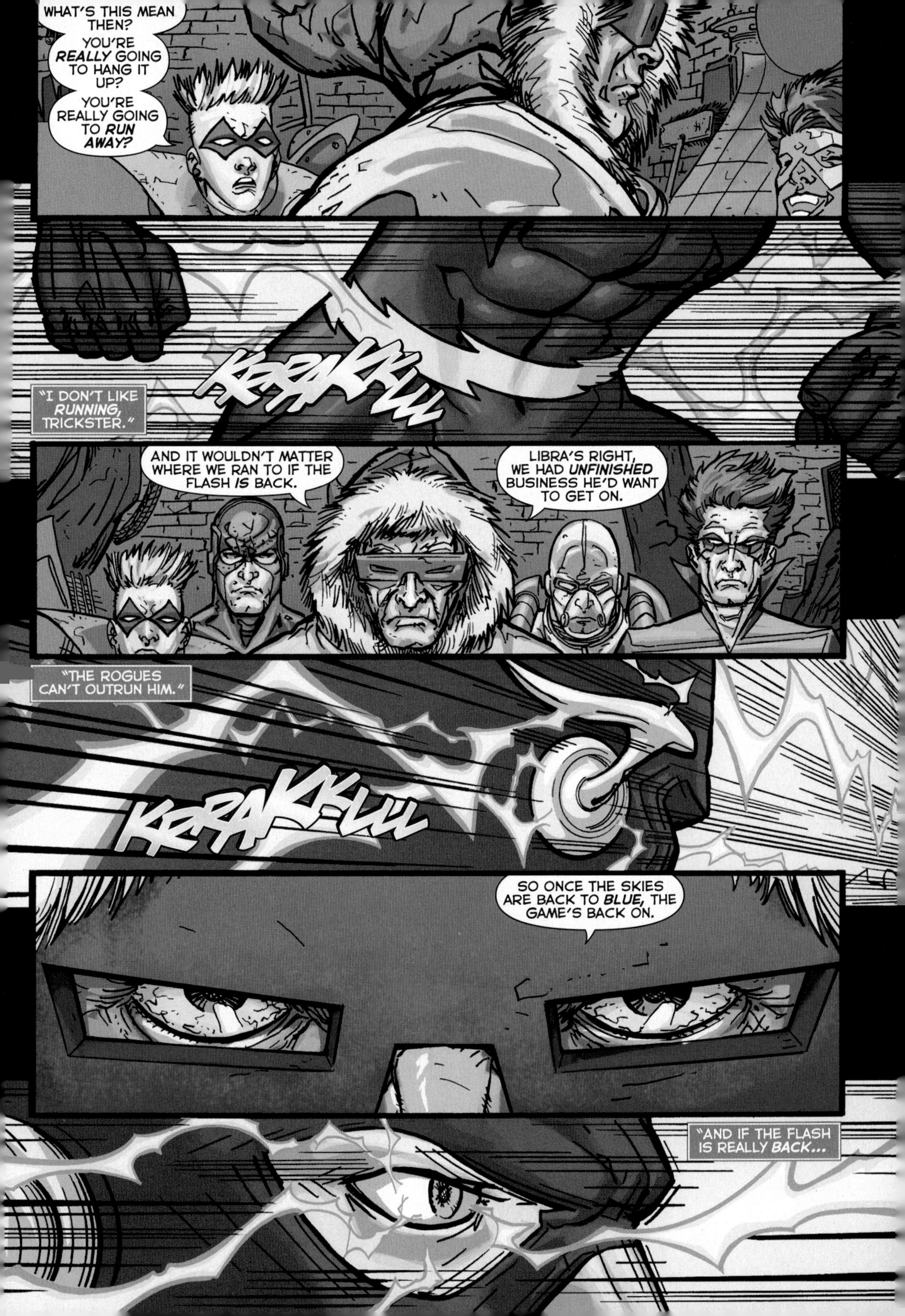
WHAT'S THIS MEAN THEN?
YOU'RE *REALLY* GOING TO HANG IT UP?
YOU'RE REALLY GOING TO *RUN AWAY?*
KRRAKKLUU
"I DON'T LIKE *RUNNING*, TRICKSTER."
AND IT WOULDN'T MATTER WHERE WE RAN TO IF THE FLASH *IS* BACK.
LIBRA'S RIGHT, WE HAD *UNFINISHED* BUSINESS HE'D WANT TO GET ON.
"THE ROGUES CAN'T OUTRUN HIM."
KRRAKKLUU
SO ONCE THE SKIES ARE BACK TO *BLUE*, THE GAME'S BACK ON.
"AND IF THE FLASH IS REALLY *BACK*...

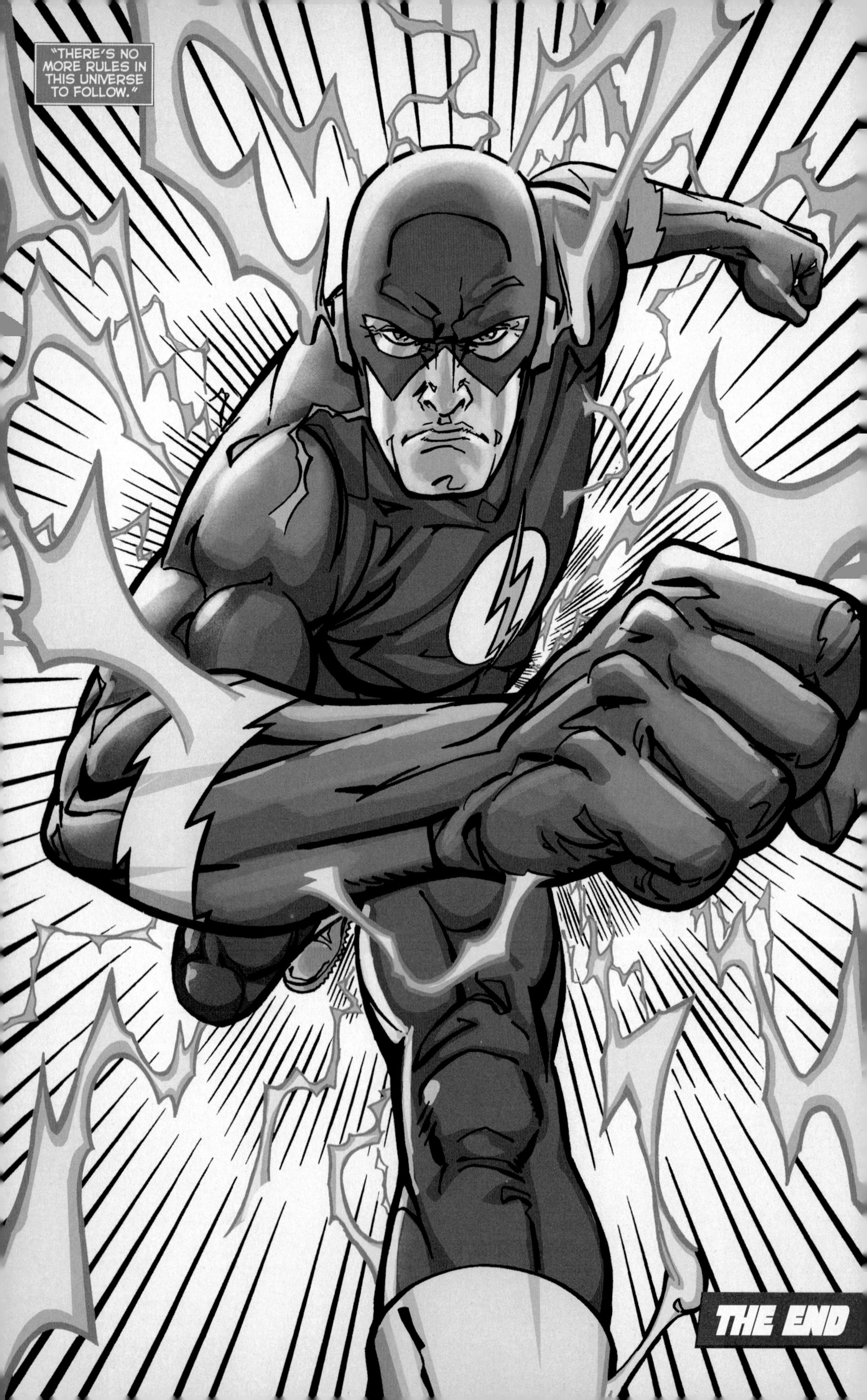
"THERE'S NO MORE RULES IN THIS UNIVERSE TO FOLLOW."
THE END

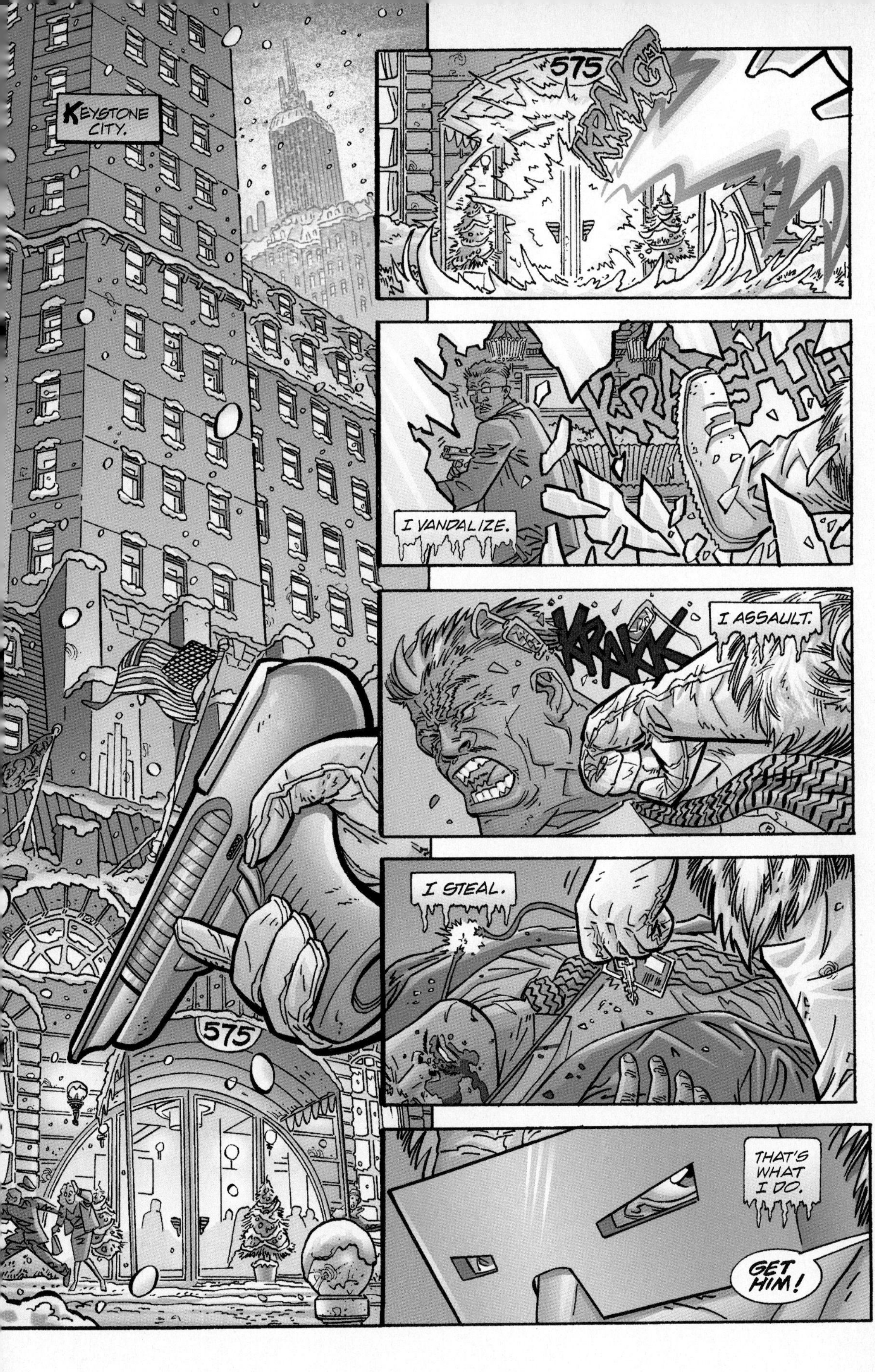
KEYSTONE CITY.
575
I VANDALIZE.
I ASSAULT.
KRAKK
I STEAL.
575
THAT'S WHAT I DO.
GET HIM!

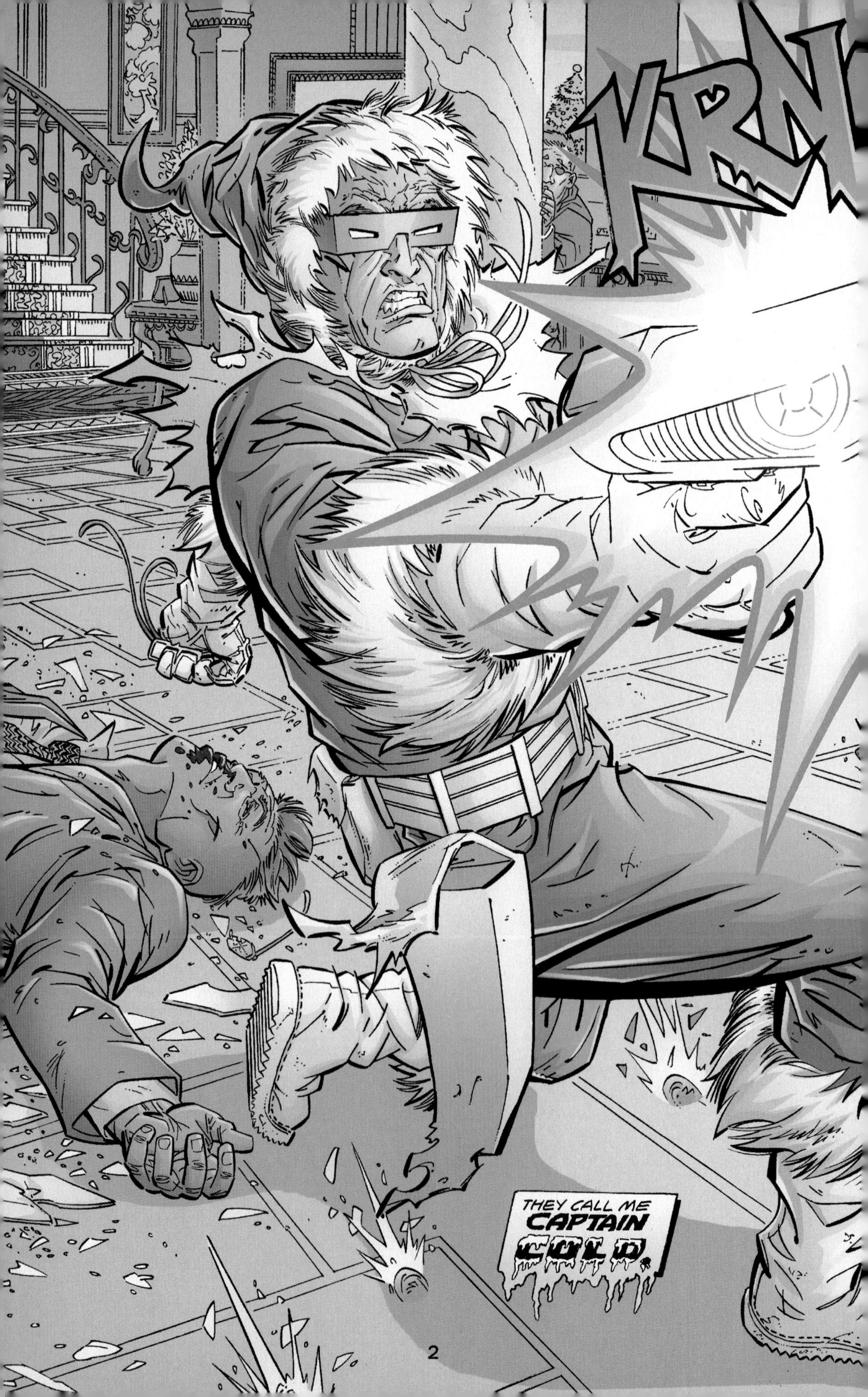
KRN
THEY CALL ME CAPTAIN COLD.

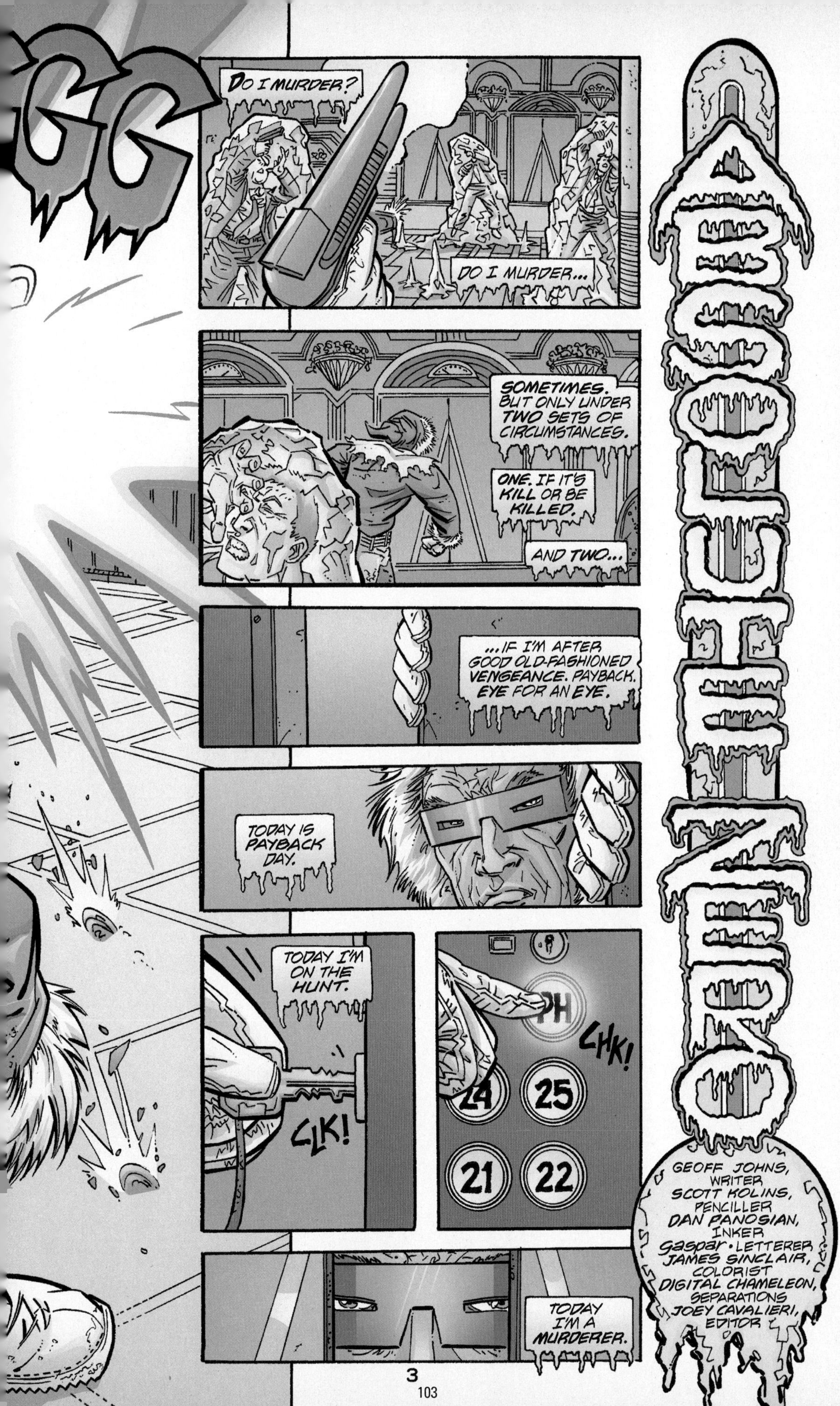
DO I MURDER?
DO I MURDER...
SOMETIMES. BUT ONLY UNDER TWO SETS OF CIRCUMSTANCES.
ONE. IF IT'S KILL OR BE KILLED.
AND TWO...
...IF I'M AFTER GOOD OLD-FASHIONED VENGEANCE. PAYBACK. EYE FOR AN EYE.
TODAY IS PAYBACK DAY.
TODAY I'M ON THE HUNT.
CLK!
PH
CHK!
24
25
21
22
TODAY I'M A MURDERER.
GEOFF JOHNS, WRITER
SCOTT KOLINS, PENCILLER
DAN PANOSIAN, INKER
Gaspar • LETTERER
JAMES SINCLAIR, COLORIST
DIGITAL CHAMELEON, SEPARATIONS
JOEY CAVALIERI, EDITOR

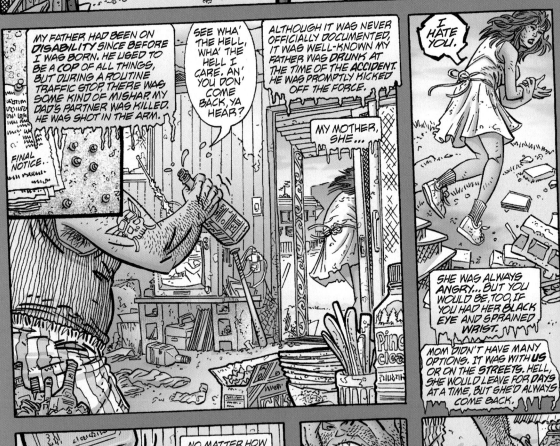

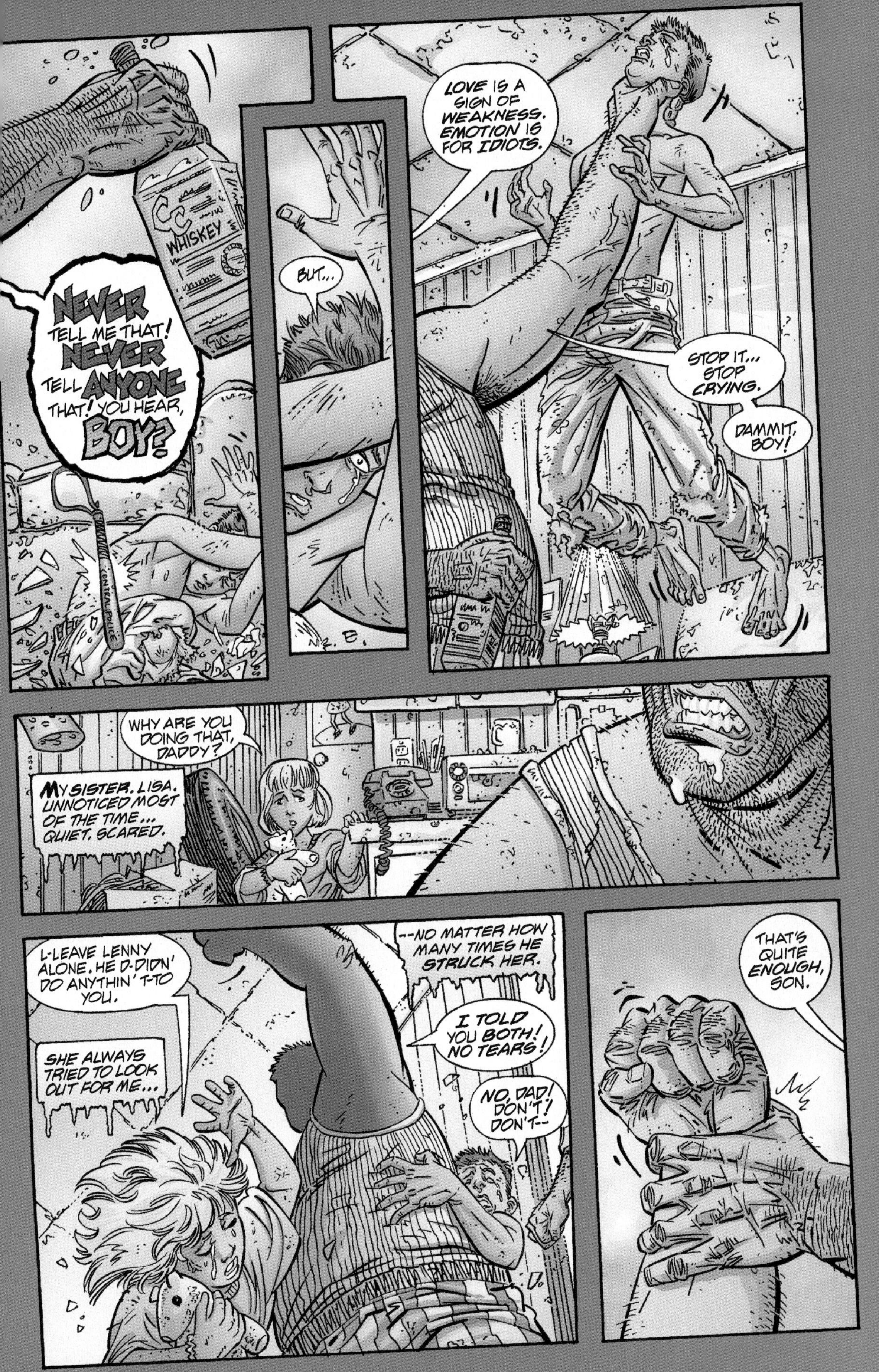
LOVE IS A SIGN OF WEAKNESS. EMOTION IS FOR IDIOTS.
BUT...
NEVER TELL ME THAT! NEVER TELL ANYONE THAT! YOU HEAR, BOY?
STOP IT... STOP CRYING.
DAMMIT, BOY!
WHISKEY
CENTRAL POLICE
WHY ARE YOU DOING THAT, DADDY?
MY SISTER. LISA. UNNOTICED MOST OF THE TIME... QUIET. SCARED.
L-LEAVE LENNY ALONE. HE D-DIDN' DO ANYTHIN' T-TO YOU.
SHE ALWAYS TRIED TO LOOK OUT FOR ME...
--NO MATTER HOW MANY TIMES HE STRUCK HER.
I TOLD YOU BOTH! NO TEARS!
NO, DAD! DON'T! DON'T--
THAT'S QUITE ENOUGH, SON.

KRKKK

MY GRANDFATHER WAS THE ONLY REAL ADULT IN MY YOUNG LIFE. HE WASN'T PROUD OF HIS SON, BUT WITH HIS AILING HEALTH I GUESS HE DIDN'T THINK THERE WAS MUCH HE COULD DO.

SLEEP IT OFF, AND STAY OFF THIS DAMN POISON.

WHERE'S YOUR WIFE?

GUG GUG GUG GUG

MOM LEFT AGAIN.

WELL, THEN, I'M TAKING YOU TWO FOR THE REST OF THE DAY.

MY GRANDFATHER DELIVERED ICE. TOOK IT TO RESTAURANTS, THE BALL PARK, FANCY PLACES MY SISTER AND I NEVER WENT TO.

WE THOUGHT HE HAD THE BEST JOB IN THE WORLD. HE GOT TO MEET ALL THESE NICE PEOPLE.

GOT ICE?

POLAR ICE

IT WAS ALWAYS A LITTLE COLD IN HIS TRUCK... BUT IT WAS ALWAYS SAFE, TOO.

I WISH I COULD REMEMBER HIM BETTER.

HE DIED BEFORE I TURNED TWELVE.

AND ALL OF THE GOOD THINGS IN OUR LIFE DIED WITH HIM.

BY THEN, MY SISTER AND I HAD LEARNED NOT TO SHED A SINGLE TEAR.

I NEVER CRIED AGAIN. NOT FOR ANYTHING.

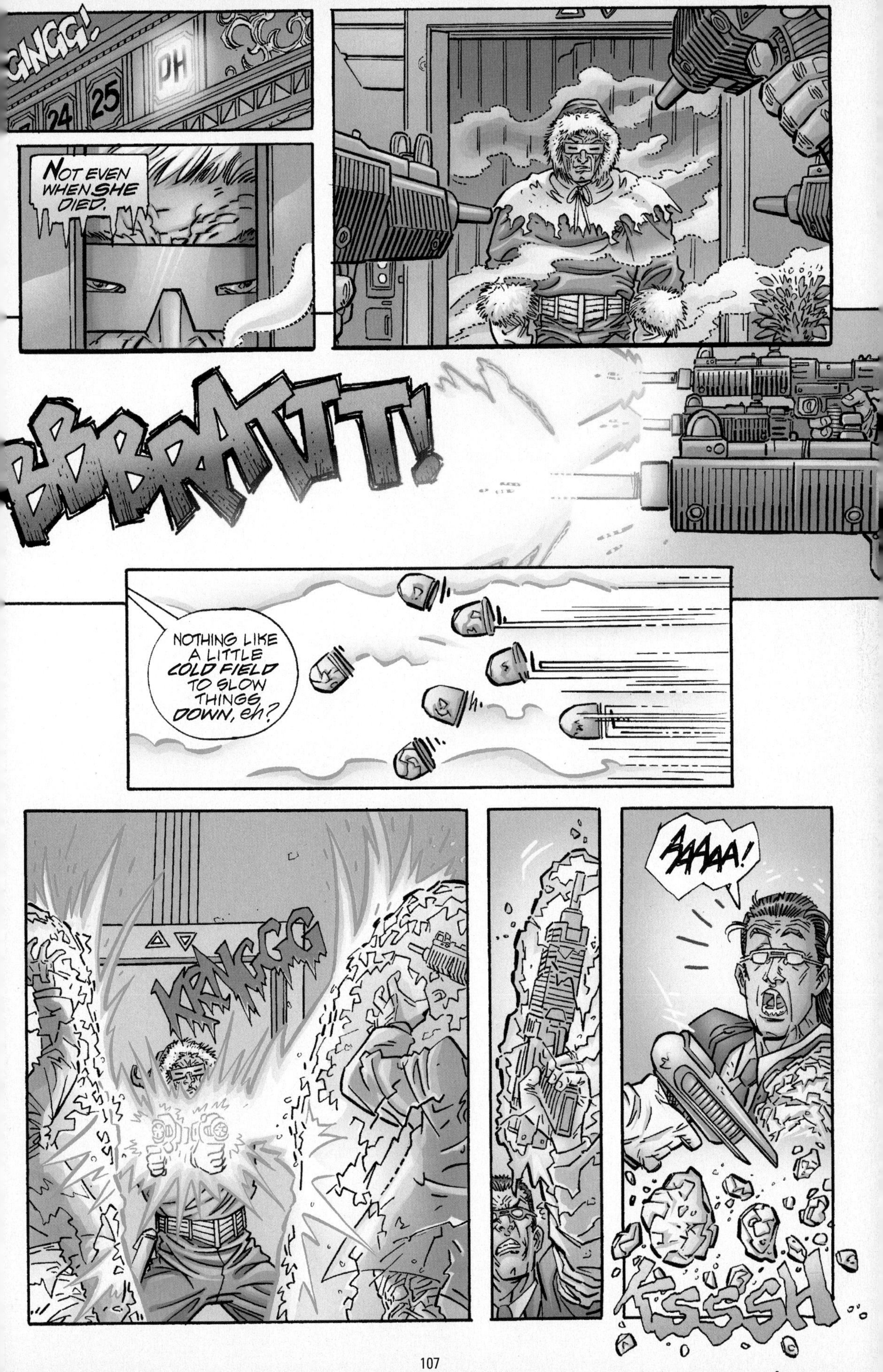
GNGG!
DH
24
25
NOT EVEN WHEN SHE DIED.
BBBRATTT!
NOTHING LIKE A LITTLE COLD FIELD TO SLOW THINGS DOWN, eh?
KRACGG
AAAAA!
KSSSH

QUIT YOUR **WHINING,** LOOK AT ME AND **LISTEN.** I DON'T WANT YOU GOING INTO **SHOCK.** THE PAIN WON'T HIT FOR AT LEAST **TWENTY** MINUTES.

BY THEN, ONE OF YOUR FELLOW GUN-TOTING MORONS WILL PROBABLY HAVE YOU IN A NICE **WARM** ROOM AT ST. JOHN'S. IF YOU'RE **LUCKY,** THEY'LL BE ABLE TO PIECE TOGETHER THAT ARM... AS LONG AS IT STAYS **FROZEN.**

IF YOU'RE NOT **LUCKY,** I'LL HELP SPREAD THE **FROSTBITE.**

UNDERSTAND?

DAMMIT...

WHERE'S **CHILLBLAINE?**

CHILLBLAINE? I DON'T KNOW WHO YOU'RE--

WRONG ANSWER.

KRNNNGG

AARRGH!

LET'S TRY **AGAIN,** CHILLBLAINE. **PLINK** WITH A **COLD-GUN** JUST LIKE **THIS.**

I DON'T KNOW, MAN. SOMEWHERE AROUND. HE'S WITH THE **CANDYMAN.**

YEAH, THE DRUG KING OF KEYSTONE. I HEARD HE WAS WORKING FOR YOUR **BOSS** NOW. HIS **BODYGUARD,** RIGHT?

W-WHAT'S YOUR P-PROBLEM WITH HIM ANYWAY?

CHILLBLAINE WANTED EVERYONE TO THINK HE WAS **DEAD.** THE FLASH, DR. POLARIS, THE COPS... AND **ESPECIALLY** ME.

I FOUND OUT HE OFFED SOME OTHER POOR **SAP,** DRESSED HIM UP IN HIS COSTUME. TRACED DOWN SOME LEADS FOR MONTHS. TO HERE... THE STRONGHOLD OF THE **CANDYMAN.**

CHILLBLAINE KILLED MY SISTER.

AND NOW WE GONNA KILL YOU!

KLAK!

CH-KAK! KAK!

ALWAYS GETTING IN OVER MY HEAD. BEGINNING BACK IN THE DAY...

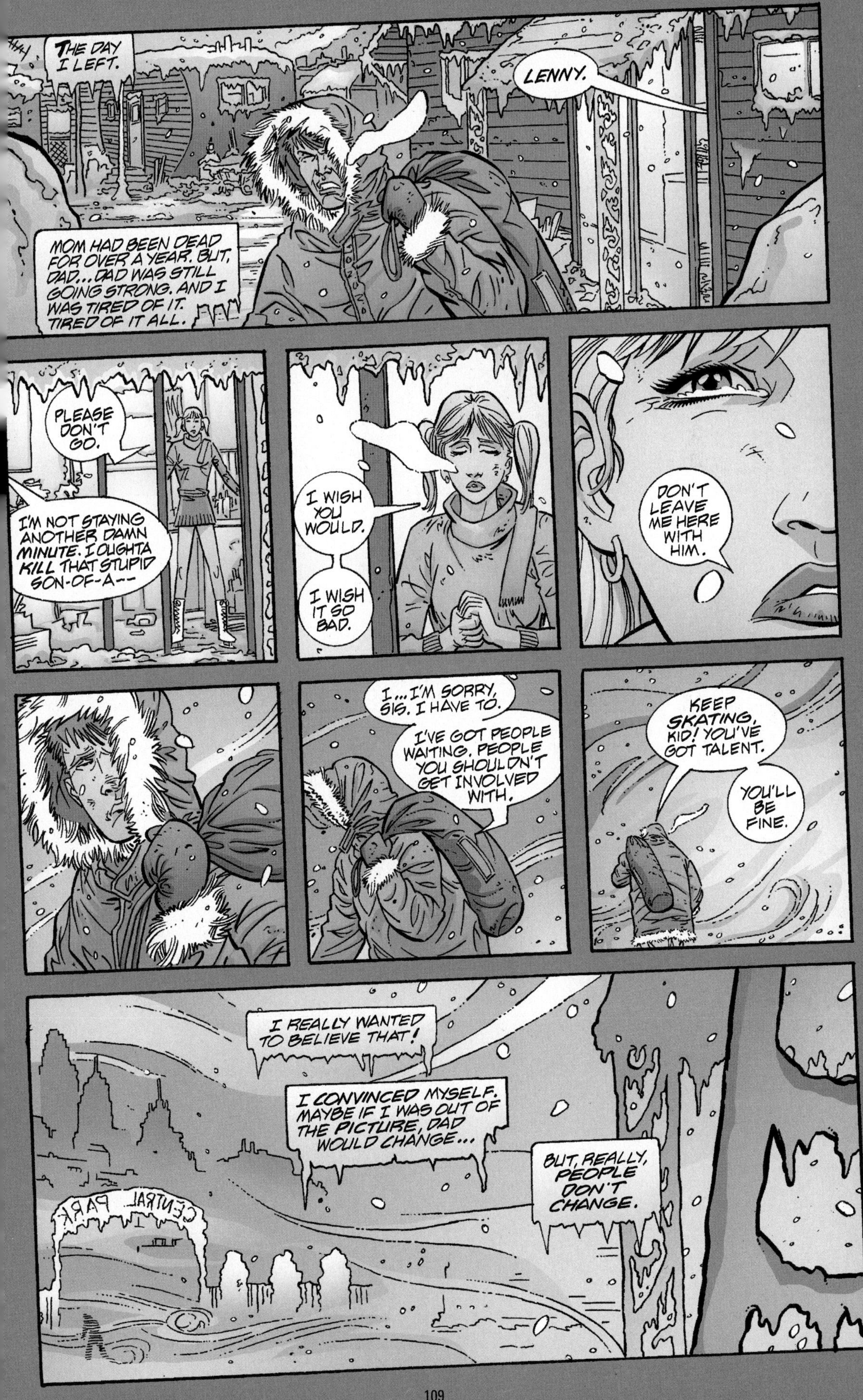
THE DAY I LEFT.
LENNY.
MOM HAD BEEN DEAD FOR OVER A YEAR. BUT, DAD... DAD WAS STILL GOING STRONG. AND I WAS TIRED OF IT. TIRED OF IT ALL.
PLEASE DON'T GO.
I'M NOT STAYING ANOTHER DAMN MINUTE. I OUGHTA KILL THAT STUPID SON-OF-A--
I WISH YOU WOULD.
I WISH IT SO BAD.
DON'T LEAVE ME HERE WITH HIM.
I... I'M SORRY, SIG. I HAVE TO.
I'VE GOT PEOPLE WAITING. PEOPLE YOU SHOULDN'T GET INVOLVED WITH.
KEEP SKATING, KID! YOU'VE GOT TALENT.
YOU'LL BE FINE.
I REALLY WANTED TO BELIEVE THAT!
I CONVINCED MYSELF. MAYBE IF I WAS OUT OF THE PICTURE, DAD WOULD CHANGE...
BUT, REALLY, PEOPLE DON'T CHANGE.
CENTRAL PARK

I NEVER DID.

SO, YOU IN, LENNY, OR WHAT?

COURSE. TOLD YOU I'M IN.

HERE.

WHAT THE HELL ARE THESE? 3-D GLASSES?

NO. THEY'LL PROTECT YOUR EYES FROM THE FLARE OF GUNFIRE.

AND THERE'S A POLICE BAND RECEIVER ON THE END HERE. WE CAN HEAR THE PIGS CHATTING, SEE IF WE TRIP A SILENT ALARM. MADE 'EM MYSELF, MAN.

COOL.

THE CORS HAD TO TELL US HOW WE ENDED UP IN CUSTODY. ONE MINUTE WE'RE INSIDE THE STORE, THE NEXT WE'RE HAND-CUFFED AND SITTING OUT FRONT.

FIVE MINUTES LATER I WAS ON MY WAY TO PRISON. WE HAD NEVER HEARD OF THE FLASH. IT WAS RIGHT WHEN HE STORMED ON TO THE SCENE. THE FLASH WAS BARRY ALLEN BACK THEN. FOUND OUT AFTER HIS DEATH, HE HAD A DAY JOB. WORKED ON THE POLICE FORCE AS A FORENSICS SCIENTIST.

IF I HAD KNOWN THE FLASH WAS REALLY A COP--

--I WOULD'VE HATED HIM EVEN MORE.

POLICE
TO PROTECT & SERVE
CENTRAL CITY
1956

110

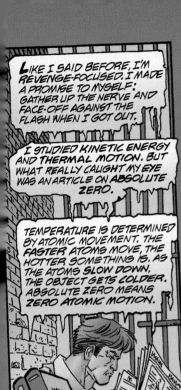

LIKE I SAID BEFORE, I'M REVENGE-FOCUSED. I MADE A PROMISE TO MYSELF: GATHER UP THE NERVE AND FACE-OFF AGAINST THE FLASH WHEN I GOT OUT.

I STUDIED KINETIC ENERGY AND THERMAL MOTION. BUT WHAT REALLY CAUGHT MY EYE WAS AN ARTICLE ON ABSOLUTE ZERO.

TEMPERATURE IS DETERMINED BY ATOMIC MOVEMENT. THE FASTER ATOMS MOVE, THE HOTTER SOMETHING IS. AS THE ATOMS SLOW DOWN, THE OBJECT GETS COLDER. ABSOLUTE ZERO MEANS ZERO ATOMIC MOTION.

WHEN I GOT OUT ON PAROLE, I BROKE INTO ONE OF THE LABS I'D READ ABOUT. I NEVER WAS TOO GREAT AT ALL THE SCIENCE SO I NEEDED SOME HELP. I STOLE SOME BLUE-PRINTS.

AND I MADE A WEAPON.

I JUST NEEDED TO POWER IT. I HAD READ SOMEWHERE A SIMPLE FORM OF CEN-TRALIZED RADIATION, LIKE THE MAGNETIC CIRCLES OF CYCLOTRON RADIATION, WOULD ACTIVATE THE ENGINE IN MY GUN INDEFINITELY.

ONCE ENERGIZED, IT WOULD NEGATE KINETIC ENERGY—

—AND SLOW ANYTHING, EVEN THE FLASH, DOWN TO A STANDSTILL.

I QUICKLY FOUND OUT MY "COLD-GUN" DID A WHOLE LOT MORE THAN SIMPLY SLOW THINGS DOWN.

IT ICED THINGS UP. BIG TIME.

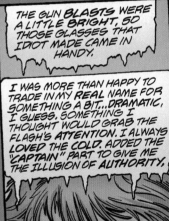

THE GUN BLASTS WERE A LITTLE BRIGHT, SO THOSE GLASSES THAT IDIOT MADE CAME IN HANDY.

I WAS MORE THAN HAPPY TO TRADE IN MY REAL NAME FOR SOMETHING A BIT...DRAMATIC, I GUESS. SOMETHING I THOUGHT WOULD GRAB THE FLASH'S ATTENTION. I ALWAYS LOVED THE COLD. ADDED THE "CAPTAIN" PART TO GIVE ME THE ILLUSION OF AUTHORITY.

GOOD-BYE, LENNY SNART—

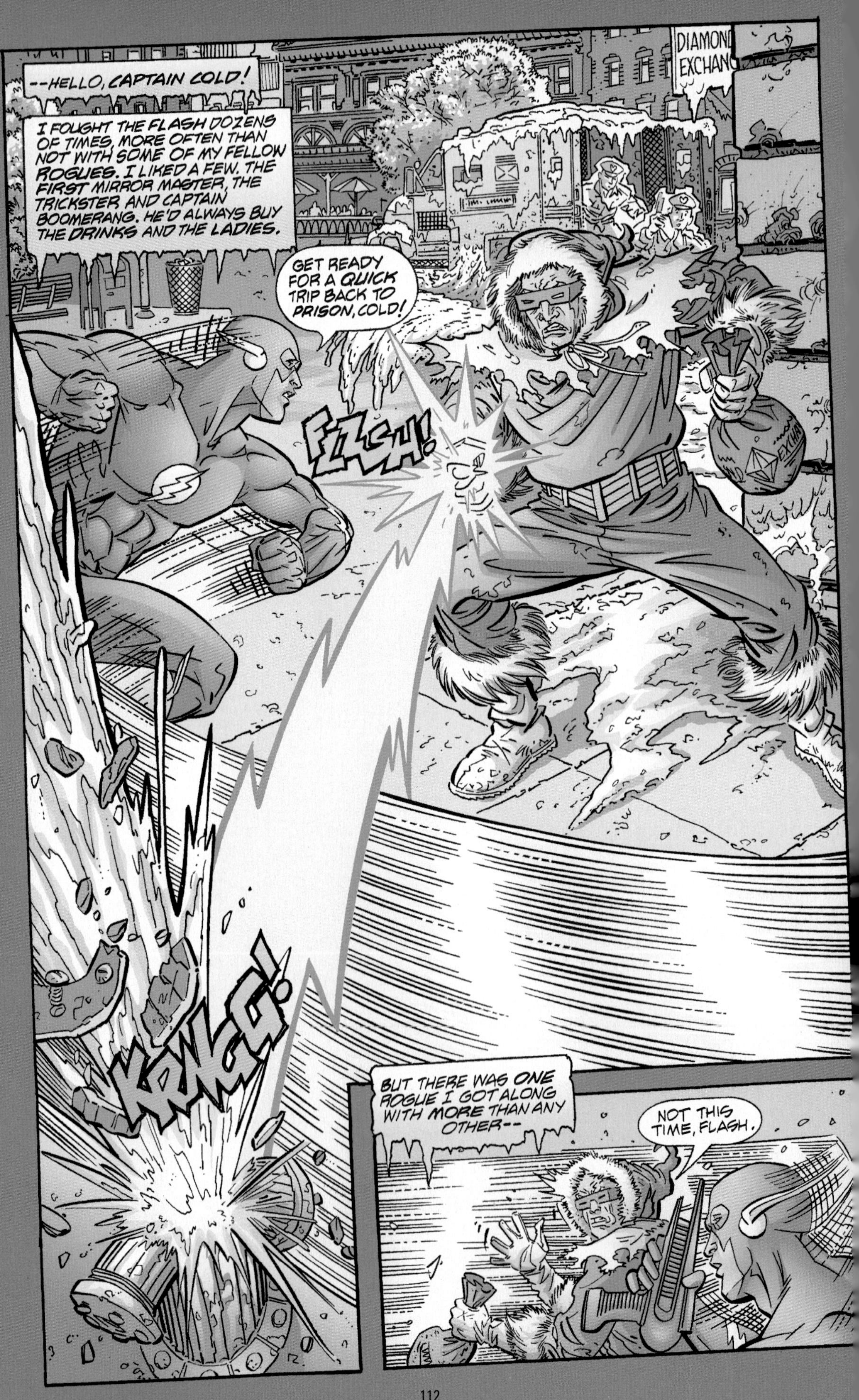
--HELLO, CAPTAIN COLD!
I FOUGHT THE FLASH DOZENS OF TIMES, MORE OFTEN THAN NOT WITH SOME OF MY FELLOW ROGUES. I LIKED A FEW. THE FIRST MIRROR MASTER, THE TRICKSTER AND CAPTAIN BOOMERANG. HE'D ALWAYS BUY THE DRINKS AND THE LADIES.
DIAMOND EXCHANG
GET READY FOR A QUICK TRIP BACK TO PRISON, COLD!
FZZSH!
KRACK!
BUT THERE WAS ONE ROGUE I GOT ALONG WITH MORE THAN ANY OTHER--
NOT THIS TIME, FLASH.

--MY SISTER.

SLSHH

ARR!

A NINE-POINT LANDING! WOULDN'T YOU AGREE, SPEEDY?

A FEW YEARS AFTER I TOOK UP MY COSTUMED IDENTITY, LISA CAME UP WITH HER OWN. THE GOLDEN GLIDER. ANOTHER OF MY FELLOW ROGUES, THE TOP, HAD BEEN KILLED IN A BATTLE WITH THE FLASH. THE TOP WAS DATING MY SISTER AT THE TIME. I GUESS LISA WAS LOOKING FOR REVENGE. LIKE ME.

THERE WAS ALWAYS SOME FRICTION BETWEEN US, ALL SISTERS AND BROTHERS HAVE IT, BUT I CAN'T REMEMBER A BETTER TIME IN MY LIFE.

--GOT TO INTRODUCE ME TO MIRROR MASTER. SO DAMN CUTE.

SILVER PORT

LISA...NOT THAT I DON'T LIKE YOU JOINING UP WITH THE ROGUES, BUT...

WHY'D YOU GIVE IT UP? YOU COULD'VE SKATED YOUR WAY TO THE OLYMPICS.

WHY DID I GIVE IT UP?

I WANTED TO BE LIKE MY BROTHER. WITH MY BROTHER.

I...I'M SORRY I LEFT.

I'M SORRY YOU DID TOO.

BUT WE'RE OUT NOW. AND THAT'S ALL THAT MATTERS.

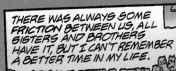

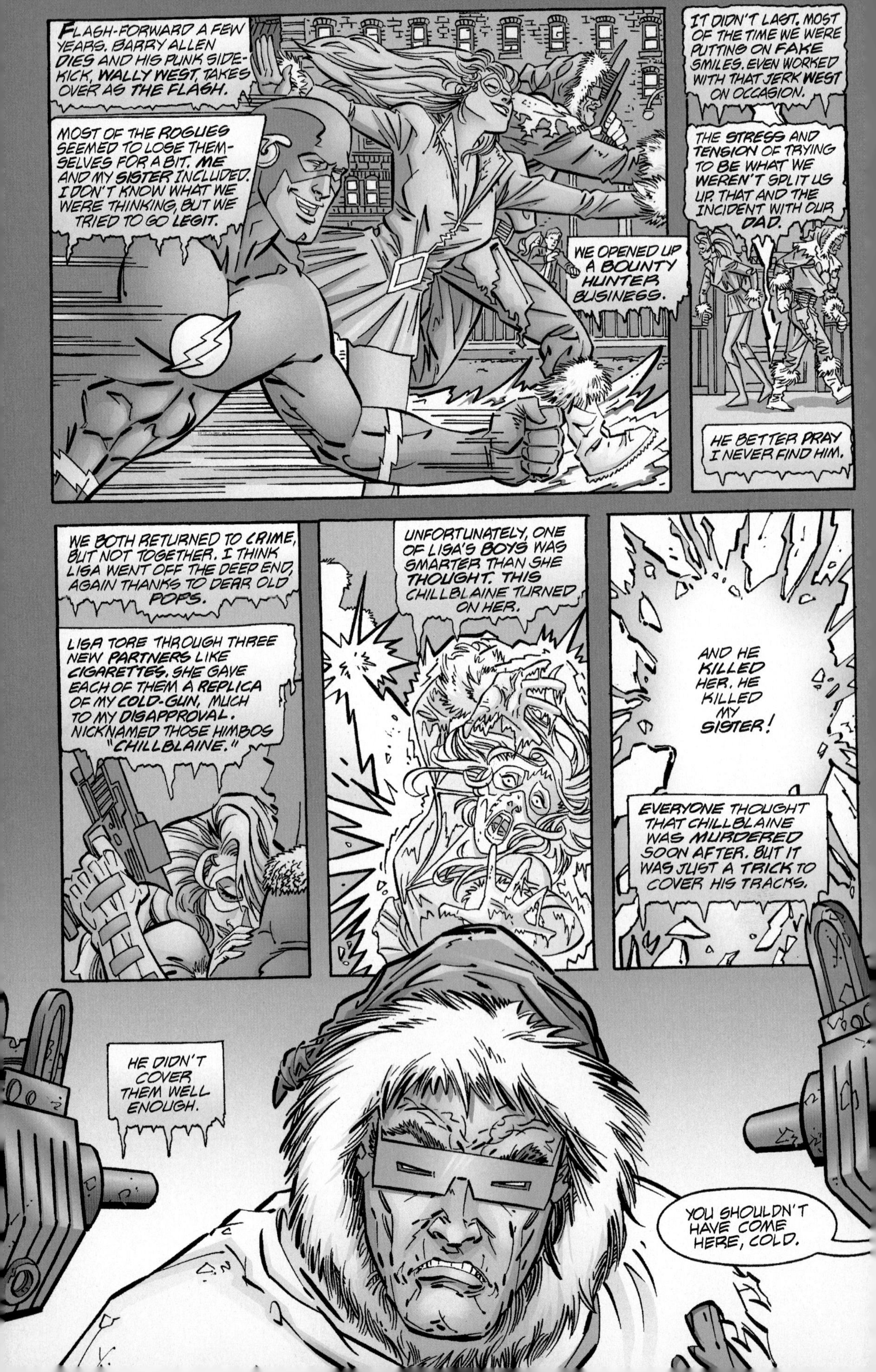
FLASH-FORWARD A FEW YEARS. BARRY ALLEN DIES AND HIS PUNK SIDE-KICK, WALLY WEST, TAKES OVER AS THE FLASH.
MOST OF THE ROGUES SEEMED TO LOSE THEMSELVES FOR A BIT, ME AND MY SISTER INCLUDED. I DON'T KNOW WHAT WE WERE THINKING, BUT WE TRIED TO GO LEGIT.
WE OPENED UP A BOUNTY HUNTER BUSINESS.
IT DIDN'T LAST. MOST OF THE TIME WE WERE PUTTING ON FAKE SMILES. EVEN WORKED WITH THAT JERK WEST ON OCCASION.
THE STRESS AND TENSION OF TRYING TO BE WHAT WE WEREN'T SPLIT US UP. THAT AND THE INCIDENT WITH OUR DAD.
HE BETTER PRAY I NEVER FIND HIM.
WE BOTH RETURNED TO CRIME, BUT NOT TOGETHER. I THINK LISA WENT OFF THE DEEP END, AGAIN THANKS TO DEAR OLD POPS.
LISA TORE THROUGH THREE NEW PARTNERS LIKE CIGARETTES. SHE GAVE EACH OF THEM A REPLICA OF MY COLD-GUN, MUCH TO MY DISAPPROVAL. NICKNAMED THOSE HIMBOS "CHILLBLAINE."
UNFORTUNATELY, ONE OF LISA'S BOYS WAS SMARTER THAN SHE THOUGHT. THIS CHILLBLAINE TURNED ON HER.
AND HE KILLED HER. HE KILLED MY SISTER!
EVERYONE THOUGHT THAT CHILLBLAINE WAS MURDERED SOON AFTER. BUT IT WAS JUST A TRICK TO COVER HIS TRACKS.
HE DIDN'T COVER THEM WELL ENOUGH.
YOU SHOULDN'T HAVE COME HERE, COLD.

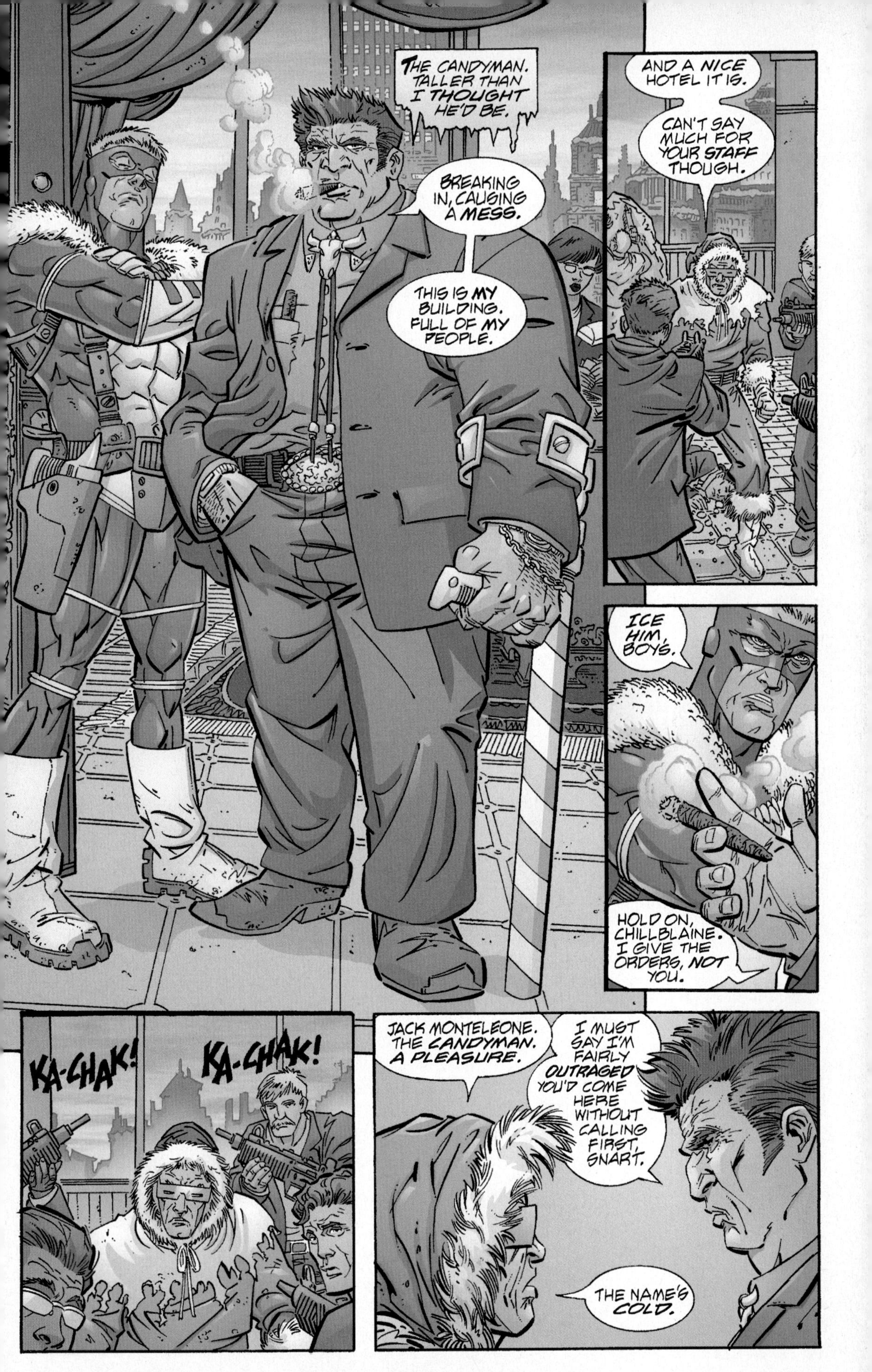
THE CANDYMAN. TALLER THAN I THOUGHT HE'D BE.
BREAKING IN, CAUSING A MESS.
THIS IS MY BUILDING. FULL OF MY PEOPLE.
AND A NICE HOTEL IT IS.
CAN'T SAY MUCH FOR YOUR STAFF THOUGH.
ICE HIM, BOYS.
HOLD ON, CHILLBLAINE. I GIVE THE ORDERS, NOT YOU.
KA-CHAK!
KA-CHAK!
JACK MONTELEONE. THE CANDYMAN. A PLEASURE.
I MUST SAY I'M FAIRLY OUTRAGED YOU'D COME HERE WITHOUT CALLING FIRST, SNART.
THE NAME'S COLD.

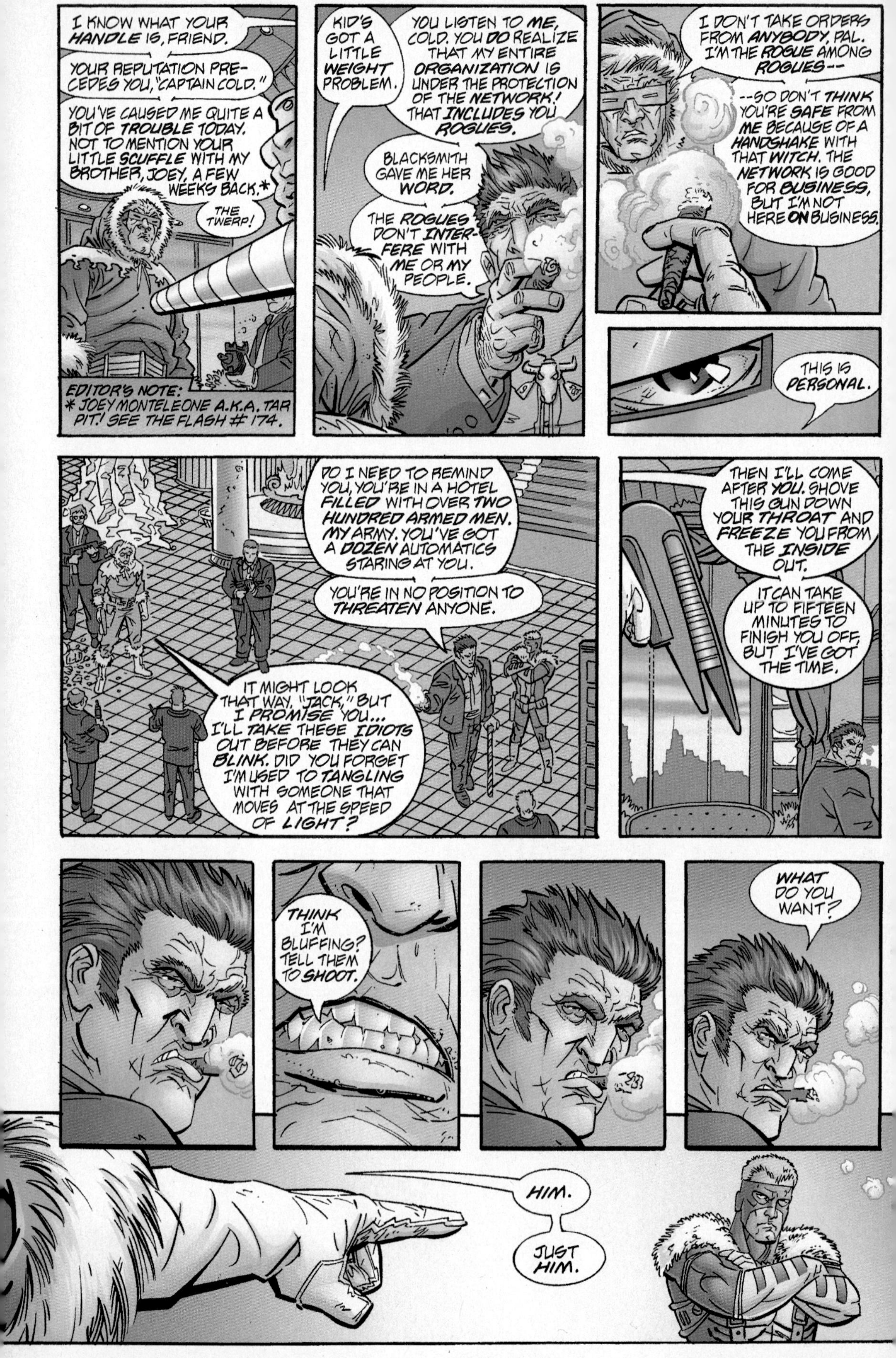
I KNOW WHAT YOUR HANDLE IS, FRIEND.
YOUR REPUTATION PRECEDES YOU, "CAPTAIN COLD."
YOU'VE CAUSED ME QUITE A BIT OF TROUBLE TODAY. NOT TO MENTION YOUR LITTLE SCUFFLE WITH MY BROTHER, JOEY, A FEW WEEKS BACK.*
THE TWERP!
EDITOR'S NOTE: * JOEY MONTELEONE A.K.A. TAR PIT! SEE THE FLASH # 174.
KID'S GOT A LITTLE WEIGHT PROBLEM.
YOU LISTEN TO ME, COLD. YOU DO REALIZE THAT MY ENTIRE ORGANIZATION IS UNDER THE PROTECTION OF THE NETWORK! THAT INCLUDES YOU ROGUES.
BLACKSMITH GAVE ME HER WORD.
THE ROGUES DON'T INTERFERE WITH ME OR MY PEOPLE.
I DON'T TAKE ORDERS FROM ANYBODY, PAL. I'M THE ROGUE AMONG ROGUES--
--SO DON'T THINK YOU'RE SAFE FROM ME BECAUSE OF A HANDSHAKE WITH THAT WITCH. THE NETWORK IS GOOD FOR BUSINESS, BUT I'M NOT HERE ON BUSINESS.
THIS IS PERSONAL.
DO I NEED TO REMIND YOU, YOU'RE IN A HOTEL FILLED WITH OVER TWO HUNDRED ARMED MEN. MY ARMY. YOU'VE GOT A DOZEN AUTOMATICS STARING AT YOU.
YOU'RE IN NO POSITION TO THREATEN ANYONE.
IT MIGHT LOOK THAT WAY, "JACK," BUT I PROMISE YOU... I'LL TAKE THESE IDIOTS OUT BEFORE THEY CAN BLINK. DID YOU FORGET I'M USED TO TANGLING WITH SOMEONE THAT MOVES AT THE SPEED OF LIGHT?
THEN I'LL COME AFTER YOU. SHOVE THIS GUN DOWN YOUR THROAT AND FREEZE YOU FROM THE INSIDE OUT.
IT CAN TAKE UP TO FIFTEEN MINUTES TO FINISH YOU OFF, BUT I'VE GOT THE TIME.
THINK I'M BLUFFING? TELL THEM TO SHOOT.
WHAT DO YOU WANT?
HIM.
JUST HIM.

YOU'RE ALWAYS SAYING YOU'RE THE BEST, CHILLBLAINE. *PROVE IT.*

WHAT?

LET'S GO, BOYS. LEAVE THE SNOWMEN TO THEIR GAME.

YOU MADE THE RIGHT *MOVE*, CANDYMAN.

NEVER STEP INSIDE MY HOME AGAIN, COLD. NEVER.

SLAMM!

KRNGGG

YOU'RE AN *ABSOLUTE ZERO!*

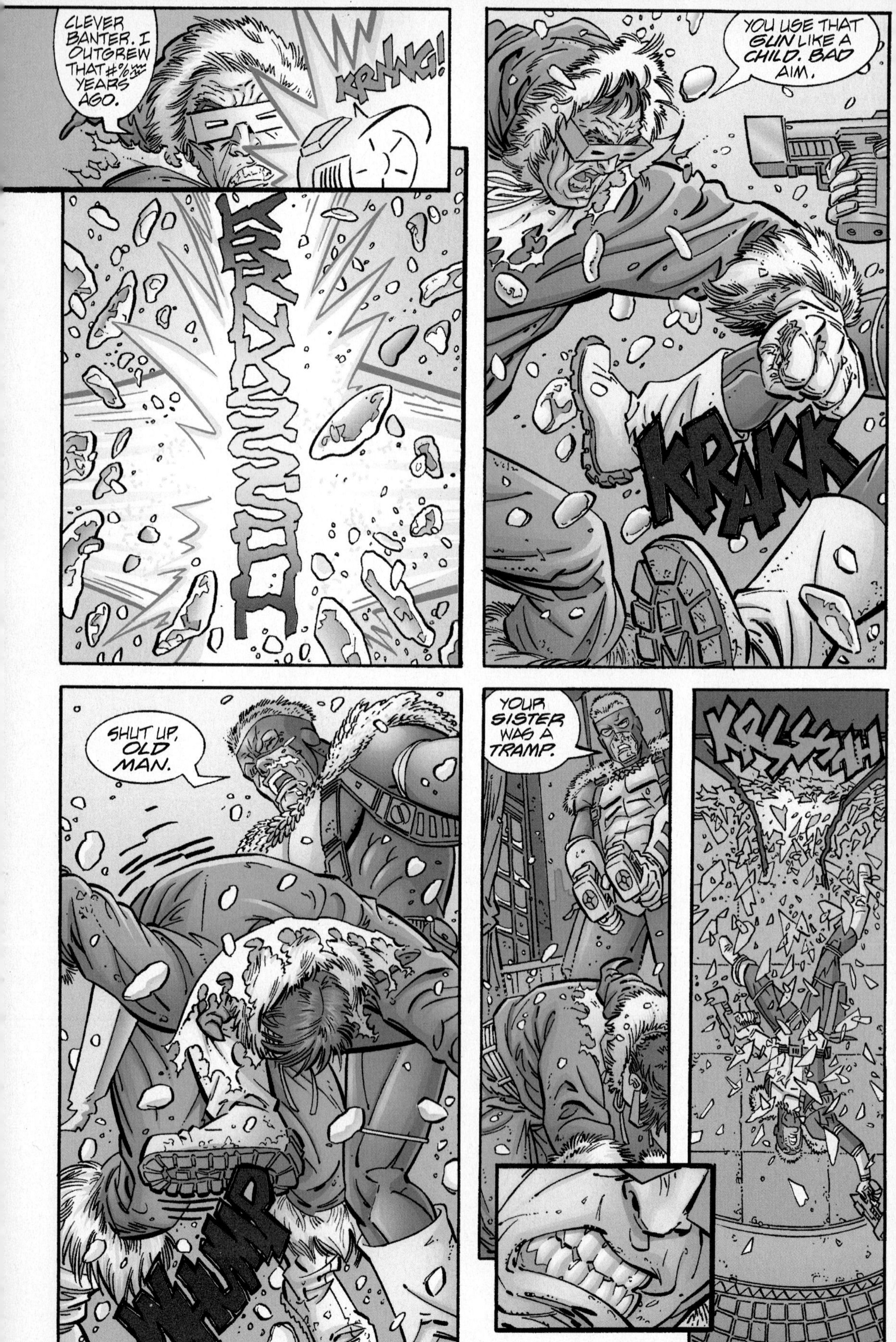
CLEVER BANTER. I OUTGREW THAT #% YEARS AGO.
KRANG!
YOU USE THAT GUN LIKE A CHILD. BAD AIM.
KRAKK
SHUT UP, OLD MAN.
WHUMP
YOUR SISTER WAS A TRAMP.

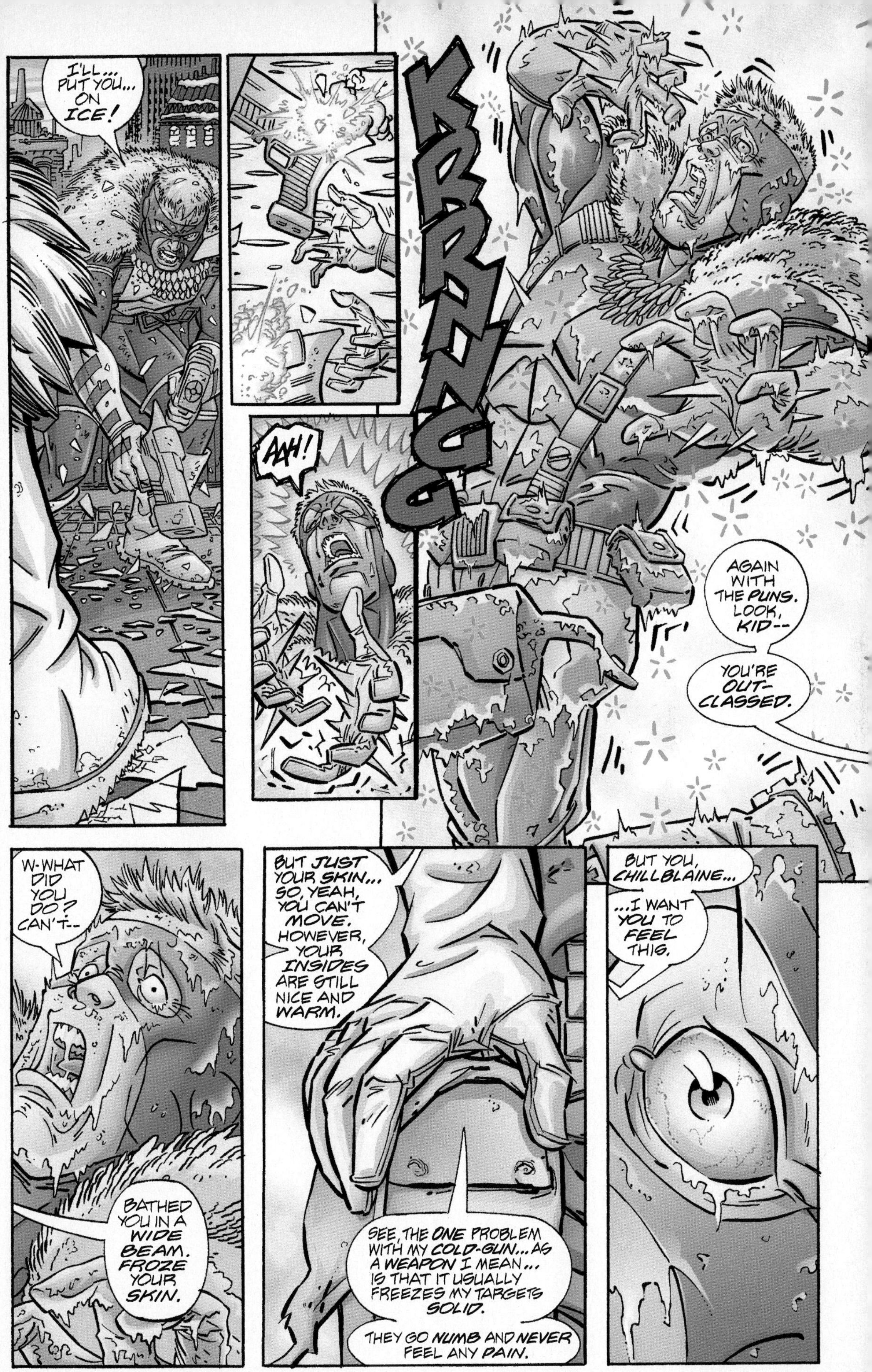
I'LL... PUT YOU... ON ICE!
KRRANG
AAH!
AGAIN WITH THE PUNS. LOOK, KID--
YOU'RE OUT-CLASSED.
W-WHAT DID YOU DO? CAN'T--
BATHED YOU IN A WIDE BEAM. FROZE YOUR SKIN.
BUT JUST YOUR SKIN... SO, YEAH, YOU CAN'T MOVE. HOWEVER, YOUR INSIDES ARE STILL NICE AND WARM.
SEE, THE ONE PROBLEM WITH MY COLD-GUN... AS A WEAPON I MEAN... IS THAT IT USUALLY FREEZES MY TARGETS SOLID.
THEY GO NUMB AND NEVER FEEL ANY PAIN.
BUT YOU, CHILLBLAINE...
...I WANT YOU TO FEEL THIS.

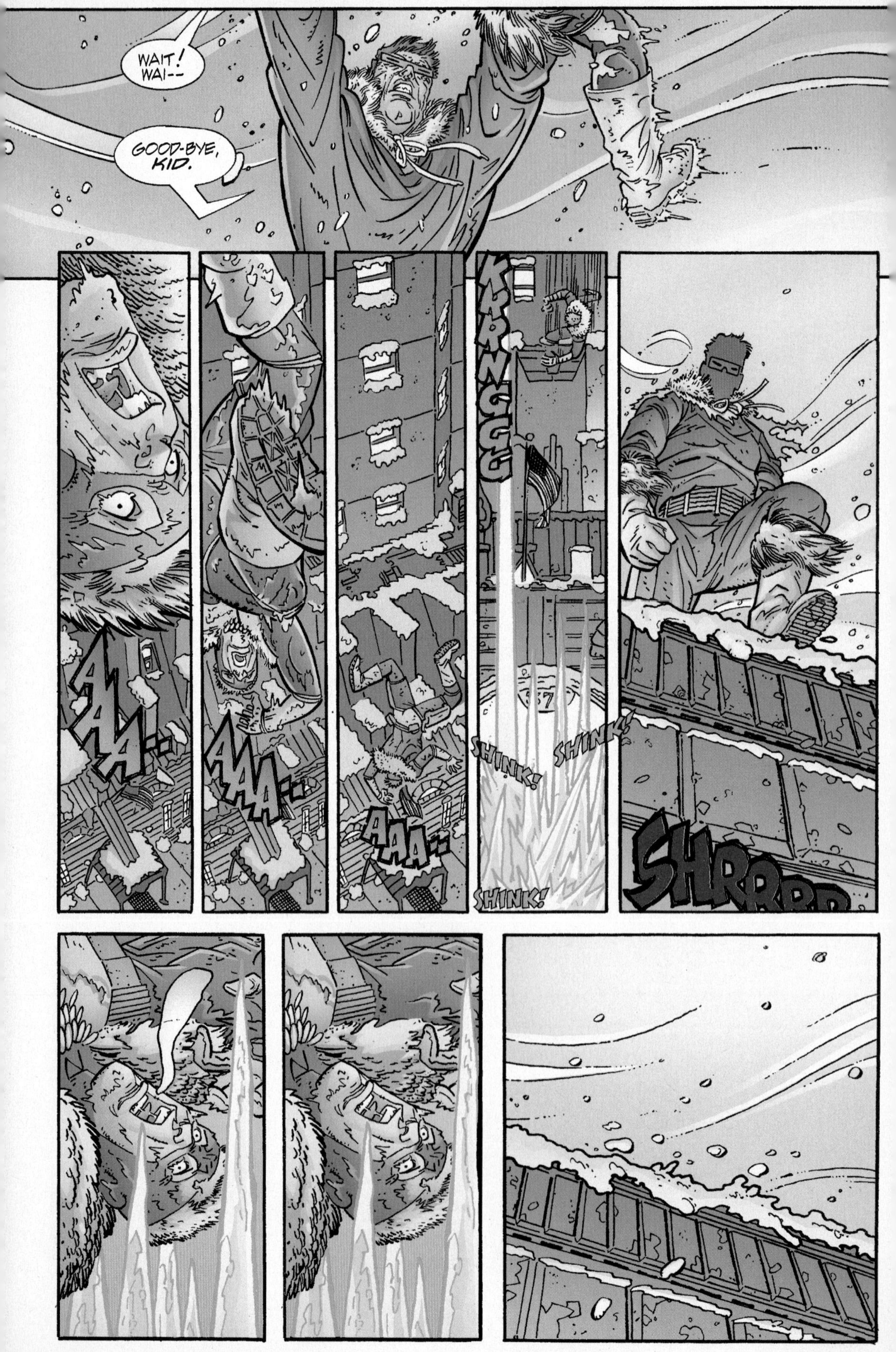
WAIT! WAI--
GOOD-BYE, KID.
AAA--
AAA--
AAA--
KARNGGG
SHINK!
SHINK!
SHINK!
SHRRRR

LENNY!? YOU THERE?

NOK! NOK!

JUST A SEC...

ANGIE. WHAT ARE YOU--?

IT'S WEDNESDAY, LENNY. ELEVEN. OUR USUAL "DATE."

NOT... NOT TONIGHT.

BUT, HONEY. I TURNED DOWN OTHER WORK FOR--

HERE, COME BACK NEXT WEEK.

YOU SURE YOU DON'T WANT... ANYTHING?

YEAH. SEE YOU LATER, OKAY?

YOUR MONEY. I'LL SEE YOU WEDNESDAY, SWEETIE.

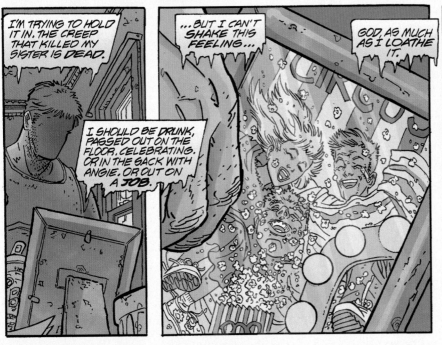

I'M TRYING TO HOLD IT IN. THE CREEP THAT KILLED MY SISTER IS DEAD.

I SHOULD BE DRUNK, PASSED OUT ON THE FLOOR, CELEBRATING. OR IN THE SACK WITH ANGIE. OR OUT ON A JOB.

...BUT I CAN'T SHAKE THIS FEELING...

GOD, AS MUCH AS I LOATHE IT.

AS MUCH AS I HATE IT--

121

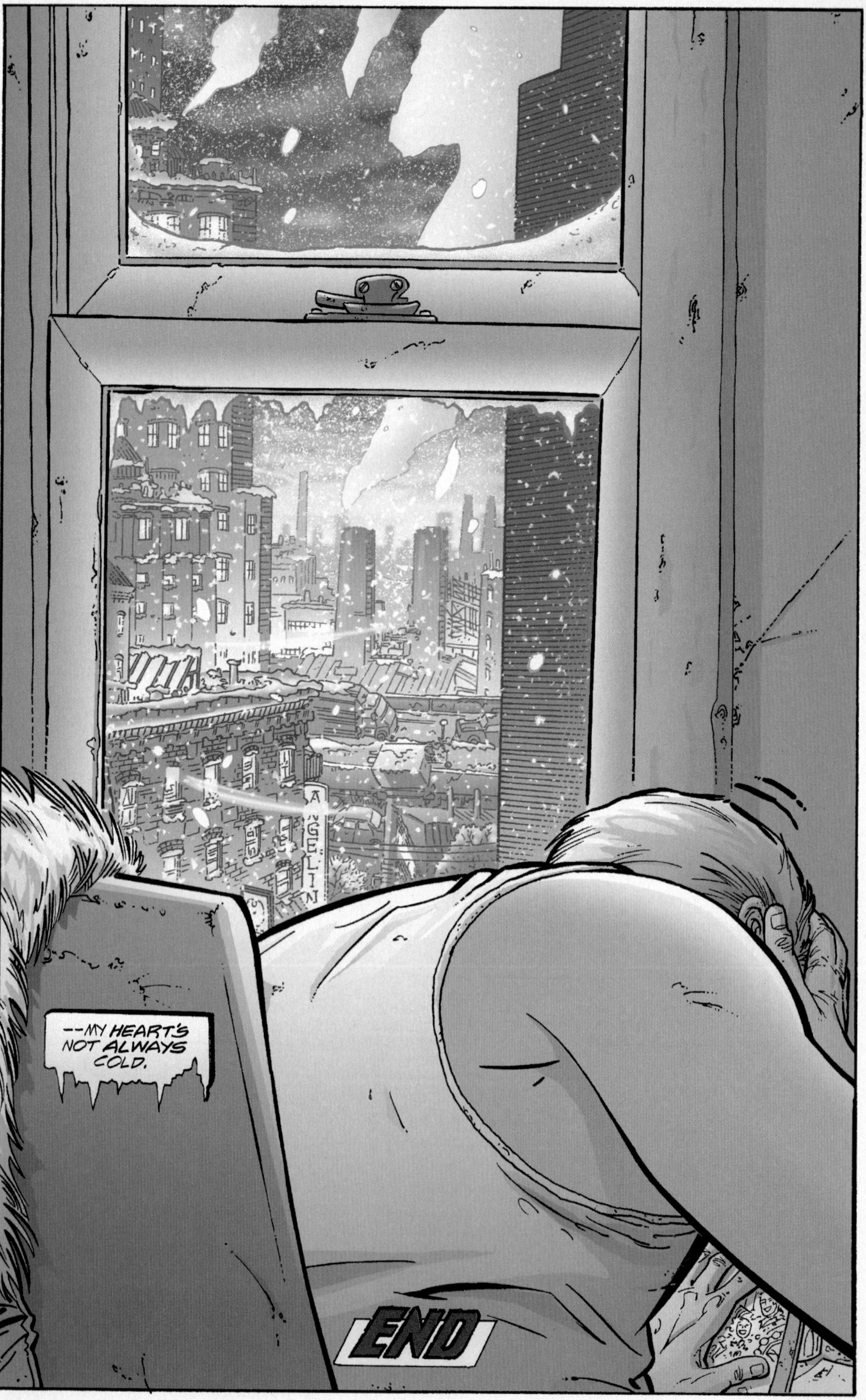
--MY HEART'S NOT ALWAYS COLD.
END

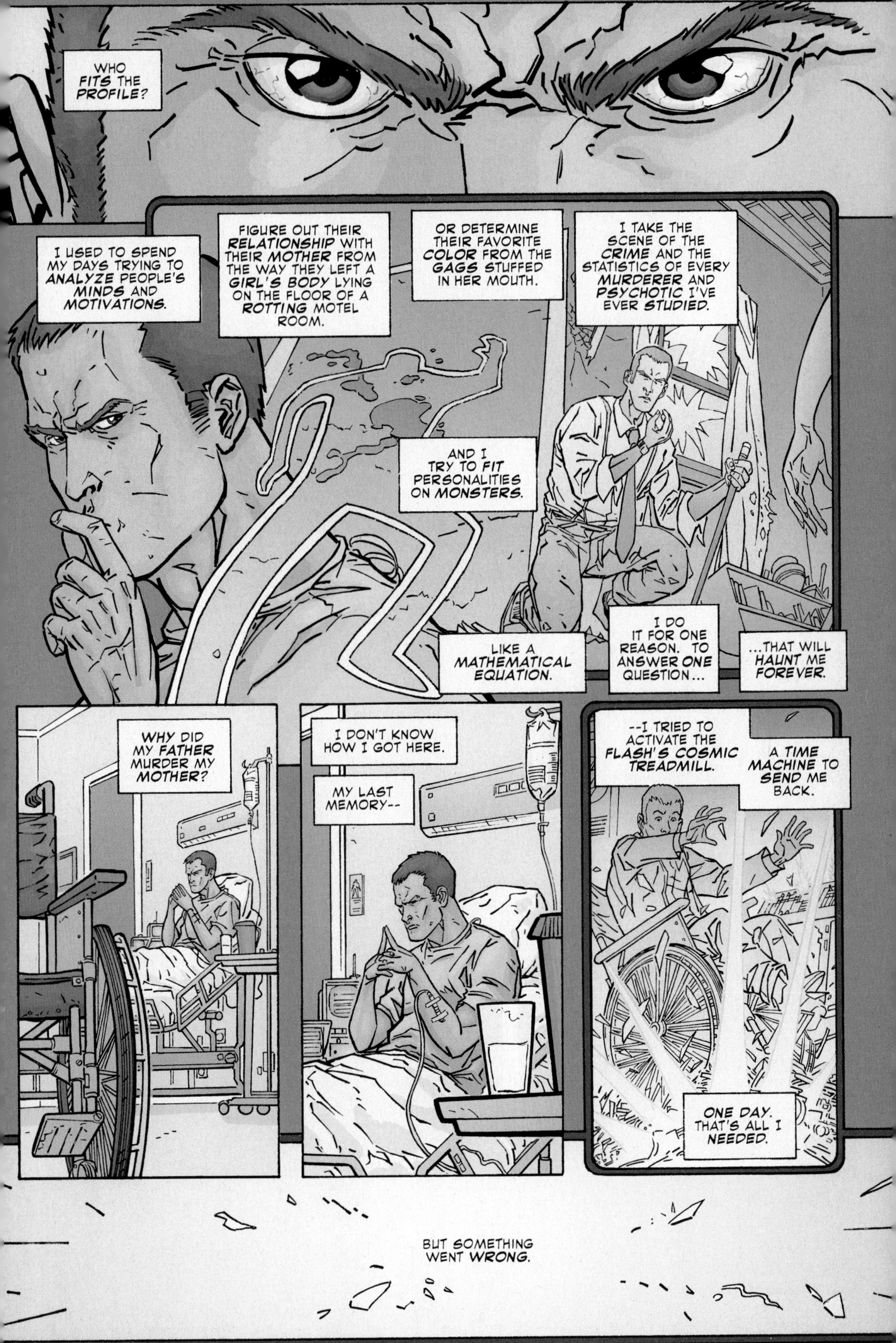
WHO FITS THE PROFILE?
I USED TO SPEND MY DAYS TRYING TO ANALYZE PEOPLE'S MINDS AND MOTIVATIONS.
FIGURE OUT THEIR RELATIONSHIP WITH THEIR MOTHER FROM THE WAY THEY LEFT A GIRL'S BODY LYING ON THE FLOOR OF A ROTTING MOTEL ROOM.
OR DETERMINE THEIR FAVORITE COLOR FROM THE GAGS STUFFED IN HER MOUTH.
I TAKE THE SCENE OF THE CRIME AND THE STATISTICS OF EVERY MURDERER AND PSYCHOTIC I'VE EVER STUDIED.
AND I TRY TO FIT PERSONALITIES ON MONSTERS.
LIKE A MATHEMATICAL EQUATION.
I DO IT FOR ONE REASON. TO ANSWER ONE QUESTION...
...THAT WILL HAUNT ME FOREVER.
WHY DID MY FATHER MURDER MY MOTHER?
I DON'T KNOW HOW I GOT HERE.
MY LAST MEMORY--
--I TRIED TO ACTIVATE THE FLASH'S COSMIC TREADMILL.
A TIME MACHINE TO SEND ME BACK.
ONE DAY. THAT'S ALL I NEEDED.
BUT SOMETHING WENT WRONG.

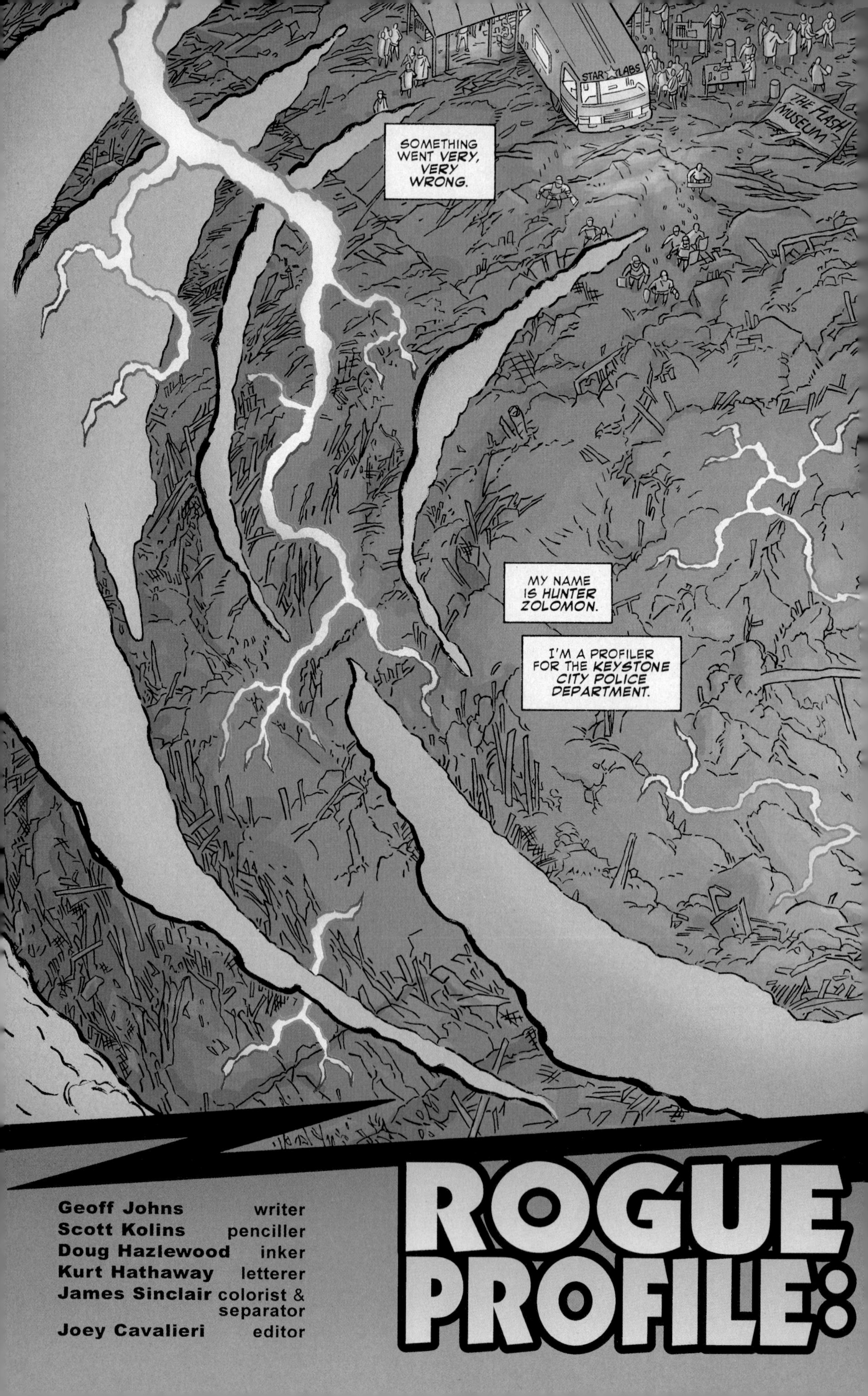
STAR LABS
THE FLASH MUSEUM
SOMETHING WENT VERY, VERY WRONG.
MY NAME IS HUNTER ZOLOMON.
I'M A PROFILER FOR THE KEYSTONE CITY POLICE DEPARTMENT.
ROGUE PROFILE:
Geoff Johns writer
Scott Kolins penciller
Doug Hazlewood inker
Kurt Hathaway letterer
James Sinclair colorist & separator
Joey Cavalieri editor

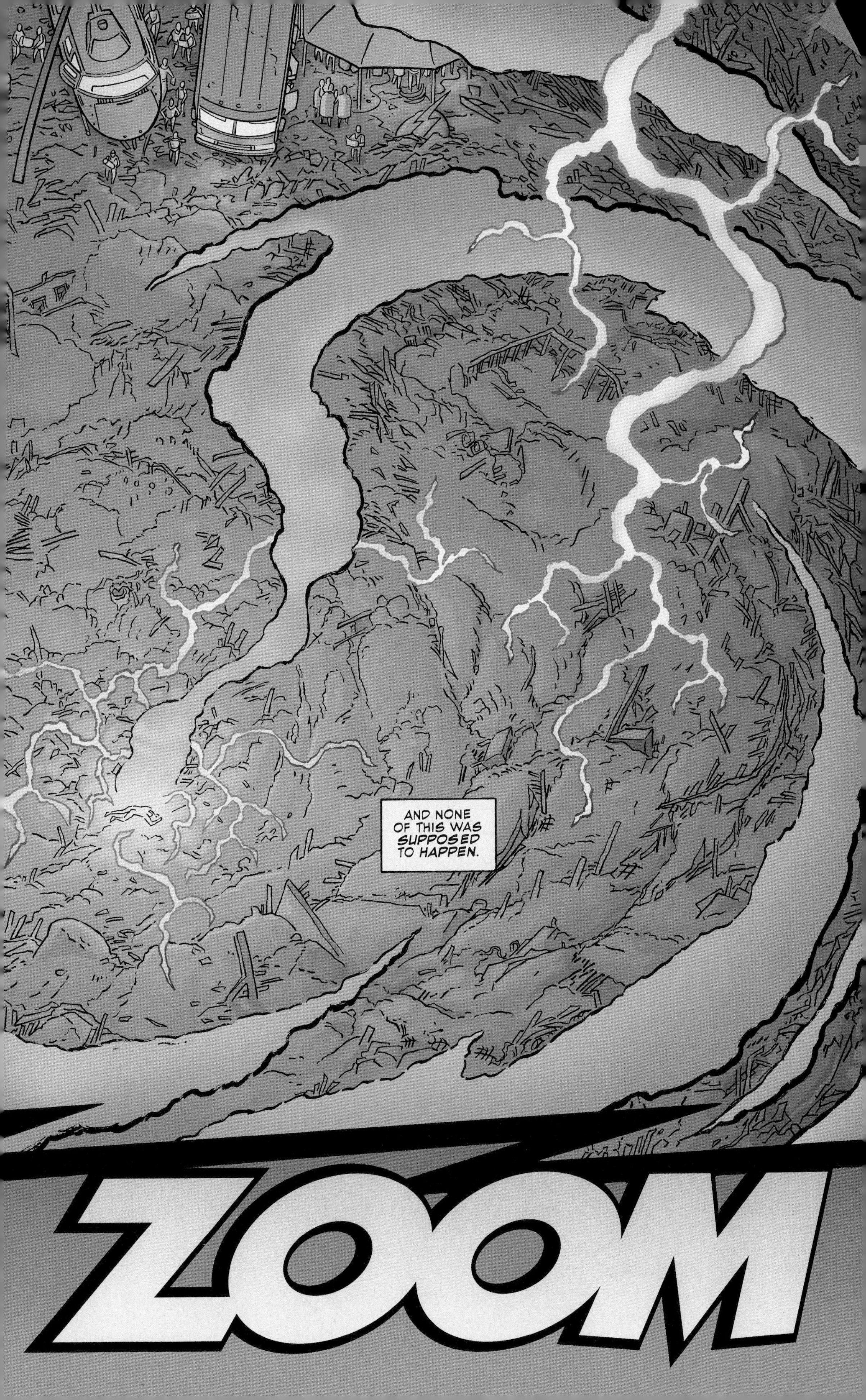
AND NONE OF THIS WAS SUPPOSED TO HAPPEN.
ZOOM

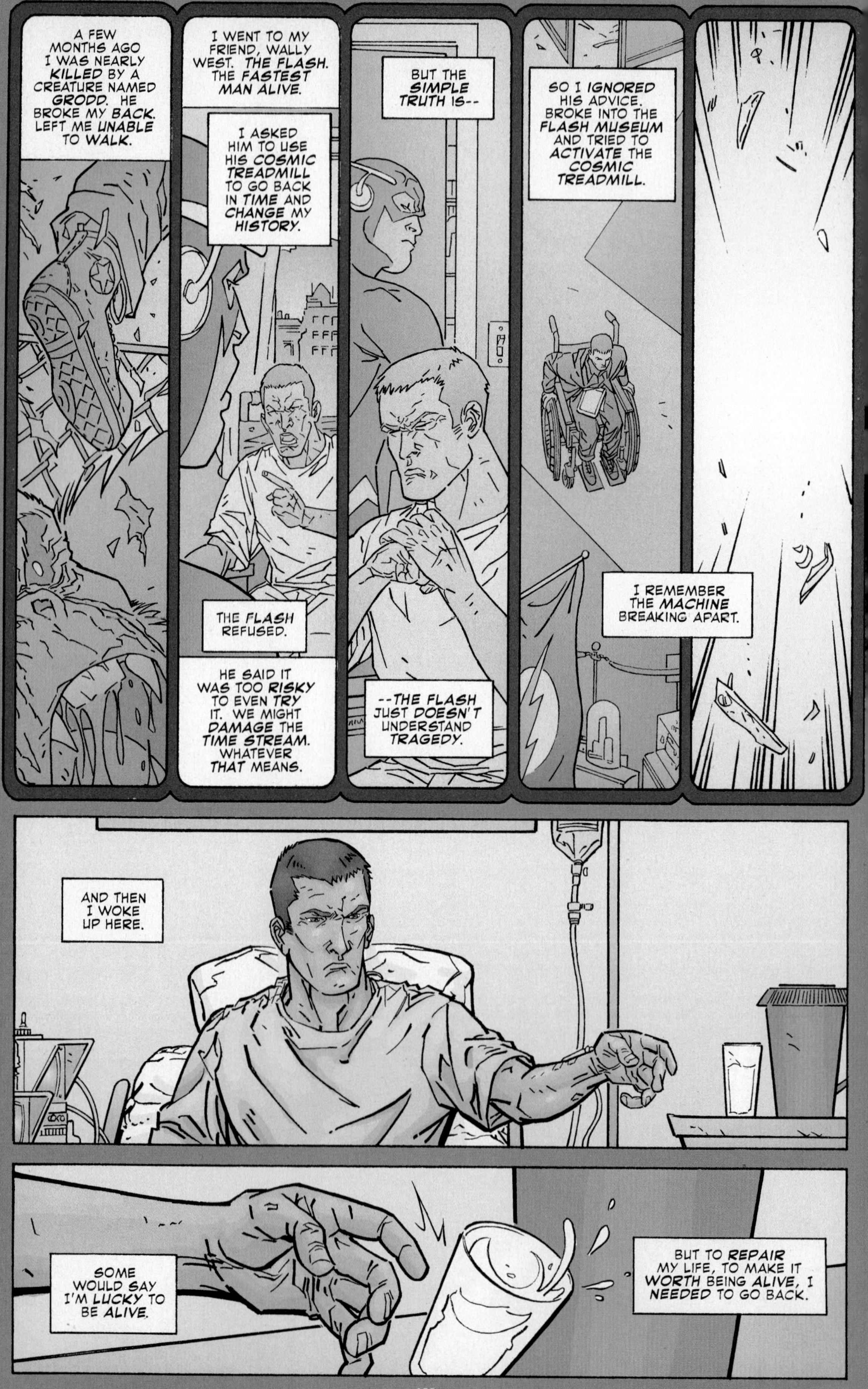
A FEW MONTHS AGO I WAS NEARLY KILLED BY A CREATURE NAMED GRODD. HE BROKE MY BACK. LEFT ME UNABLE TO WALK.
I WENT TO MY FRIEND, WALLY WEST. THE FLASH. THE FASTEST MAN ALIVE.
I ASKED HIM TO USE HIS COSMIC TREADMILL TO GO BACK IN TIME AND CHANGE MY HISTORY.
THE FLASH REFUSED.
HE SAID IT WAS TOO RISKY TO EVEN TRY IT. WE MIGHT DAMAGE THE TIME STREAM. WHATEVER THAT MEANS.
BUT THE SIMPLE TRUTH IS--
--THE FLASH JUST DOESN'T UNDERSTAND TRAGEDY.
SO I IGNORED HIS ADVICE. BROKE INTO THE FLASH MUSEUM AND TRIED TO ACTIVATE THE COSMIC TREADMILL.
I REMEMBER THE MACHINE BREAKING APART.
AND THEN I WOKE UP HERE.
SOME WOULD SAY I'M LUCKY TO BE ALIVE.
BUT TO REPAIR MY LIFE, TO MAKE IT WORTH BEING ALIVE, I NEEDED TO GO BACK.

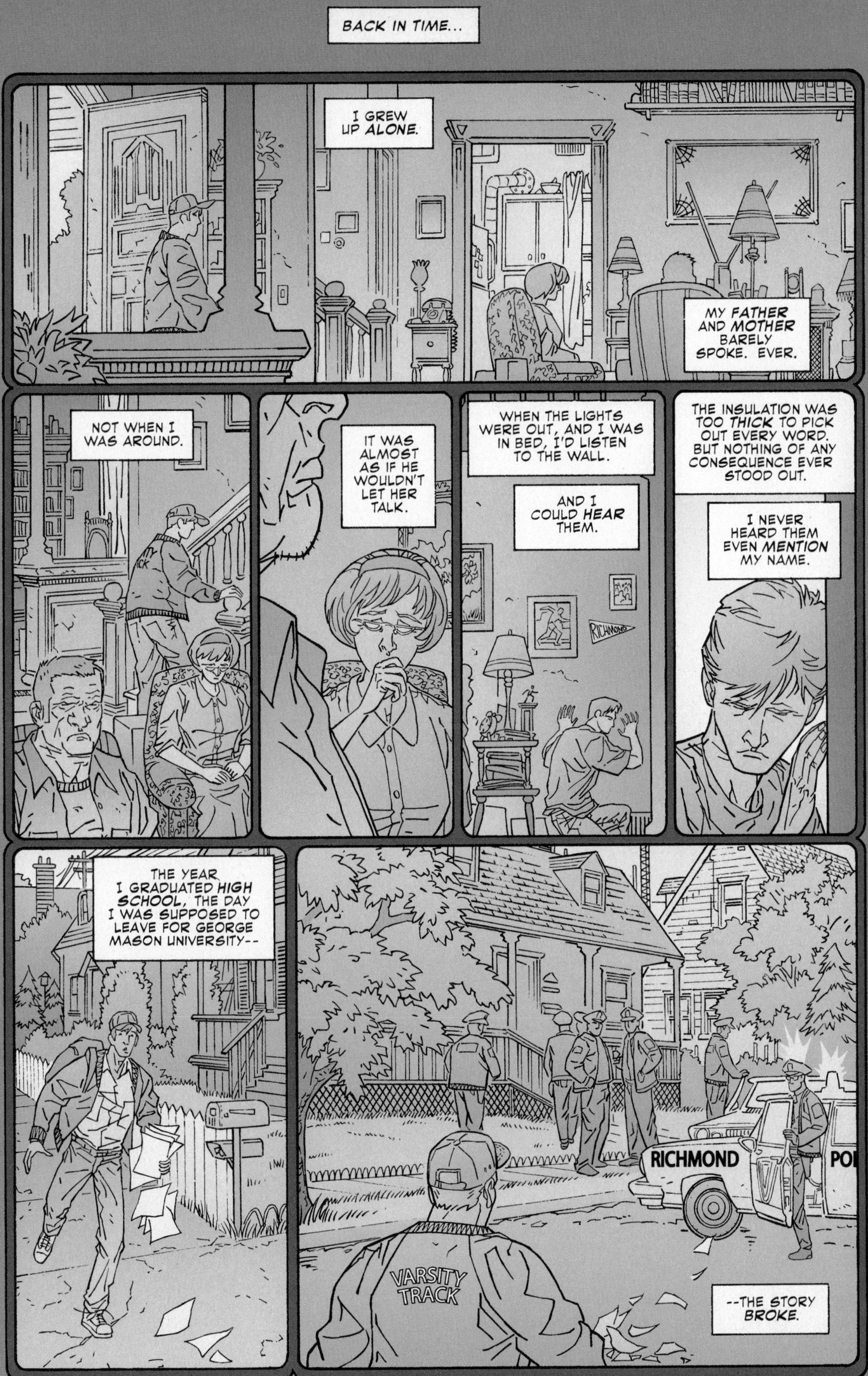
BACK IN TIME...
I GREW UP ALONE.
MY FATHER AND MOTHER BARELY SPOKE. EVER.
NOT WHEN I WAS AROUND.
IT WAS ALMOST AS IF HE WOULDN'T LET HER TALK.
WHEN THE LIGHTS WERE OUT, AND I WAS IN BED, I'D LISTEN TO THE WALL.
AND I COULD HEAR THEM.
RICHMOND
THE INSULATION WAS TOO THICK TO PICK OUT EVERY WORD. BUT NOTHING OF ANY CONSEQUENCE EVER STOOD OUT.
I NEVER HEARD THEM EVEN MENTION MY NAME.
THE YEAR I GRADUATED HIGH SCHOOL, THE DAY I WAS SUPPOSED TO LEAVE FOR GEORGE MASON UNIVERSITY--
RICHMOND
VARSITY TRACK
--THE STORY BROKE.

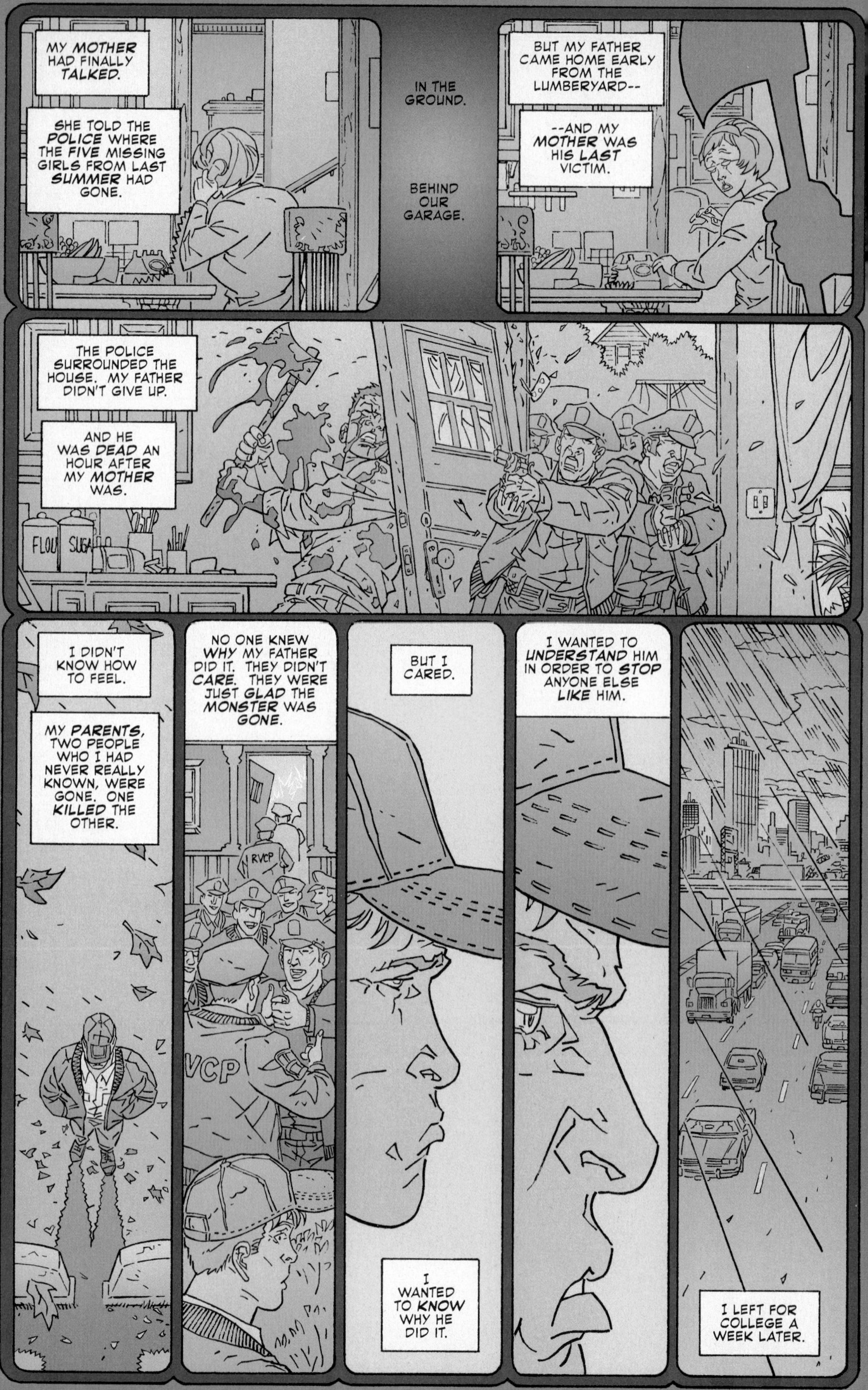

MY MOTHER HAD FINALLY TALKED.
SHE TOLD THE POLICE WHERE THE FIVE MISSING GIRLS FROM LAST SUMMER HAD GONE.
IN THE GROUND.
BEHIND OUR GARAGE.
BUT MY FATHER CAME HOME EARLY FROM THE LUMBERYARD--
--AND MY MOTHER WAS HIS LAST VICTIM.
THE POLICE SURROUNDED THE HOUSE. MY FATHER DIDN'T GIVE UP.
AND HE WAS DEAD AN HOUR AFTER MY MOTHER WAS.
I DIDN'T KNOW HOW TO FEEL.
MY PARENTS, TWO PEOPLE WHO I HAD NEVER REALLY KNOWN, WERE GONE. ONE KILLED THE OTHER.
NO ONE KNEW WHY MY FATHER DID IT. THEY DIDN'T CARE. THEY WERE JUST GLAD THE MONSTER WAS GONE.
RVCP
RVCP
BUT I CARED.
I WANTED TO KNOW WHY HE DID IT.
I WANTED TO UNDERSTAND HIM IN ORDER TO STOP ANYONE ELSE LIKE HIM.
I LEFT FOR COLLEGE A WEEK LATER.

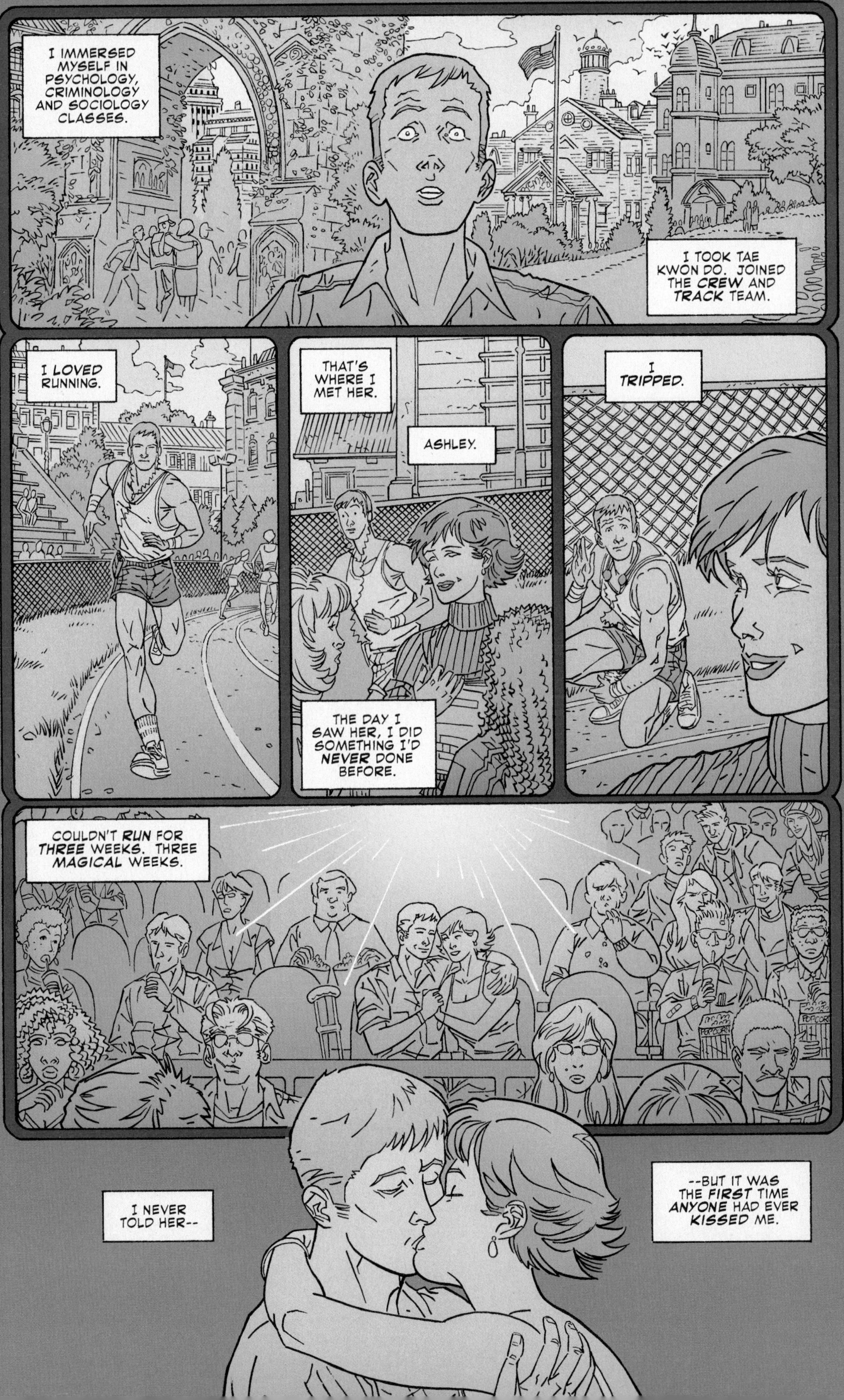
I IMMERSED MYSELF IN PSYCHOLOGY, CRIMINOLOGY AND SOCIOLOGY CLASSES.
I TOOK TAE KWON DO. JOINED THE CREW AND TRACK TEAM.
I LOVED RUNNING.
THAT'S WHERE I MET HER.
ASHLEY.
THE DAY I SAW HER, I DID SOMETHING I'D NEVER DONE BEFORE.
I TRIPPED.
COULDN'T RUN FOR THREE WEEKS. THREE MAGICAL WEEKS.
I NEVER TOLD HER--
--BUT IT WAS THE FIRST TIME ANYONE HAD EVER KISSED ME.

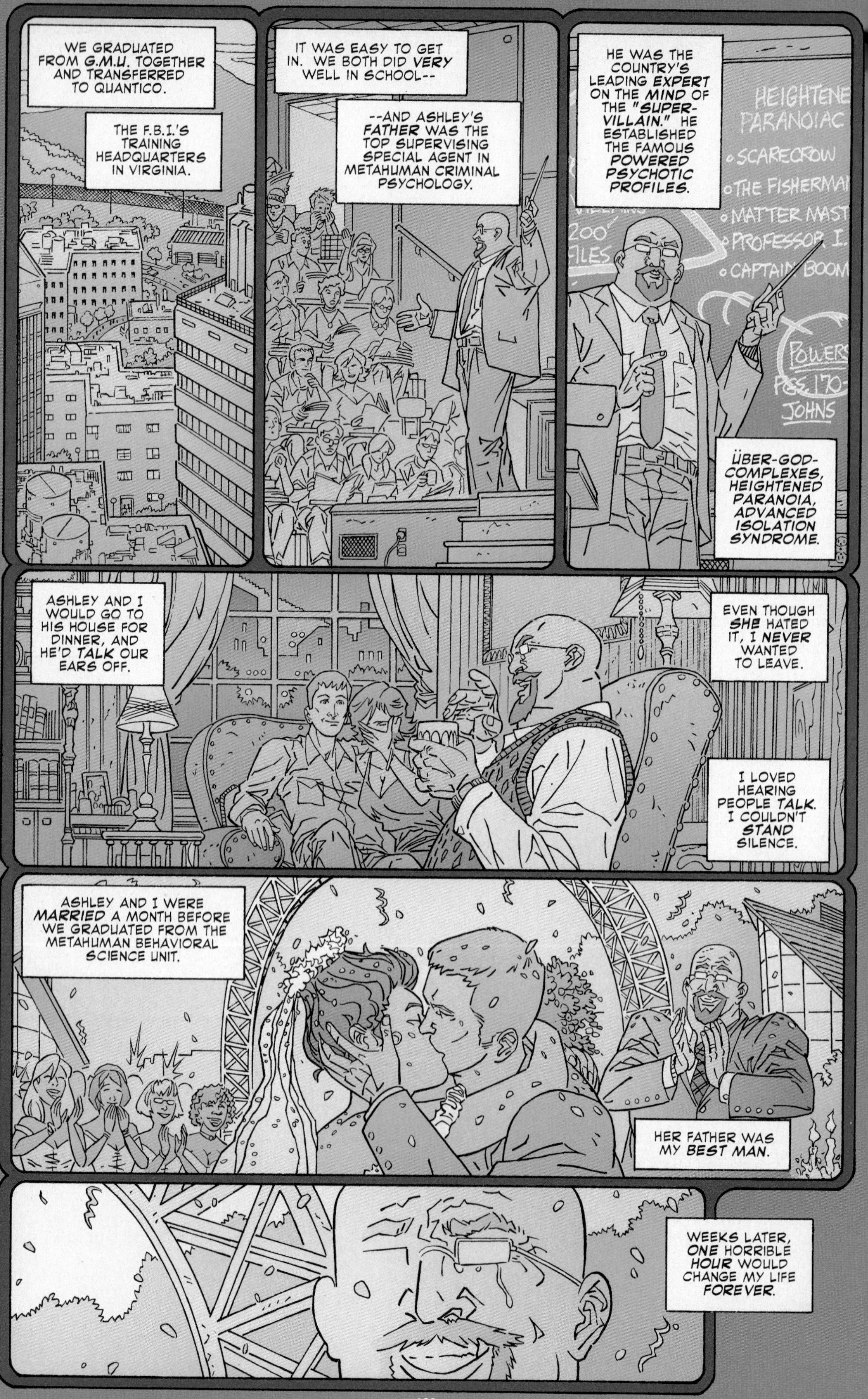
WE GRADUATED FROM G.M.U. TOGETHER AND TRANSFERRED TO QUANTICO.
THE F.B.I.'S TRAINING HEADQUARTERS IN VIRGINIA.
IT WAS EASY TO GET IN. WE BOTH DID VERY WELL IN SCHOOL--
--AND ASHLEY'S FATHER WAS THE TOP SUPERVISING SPECIAL AGENT IN METAHUMAN CRIMINAL PSYCHOLOGY.
HE WAS THE COUNTRY'S LEADING EXPERT ON THE MIND OF THE "SUPER-VILLAIN." HE ESTABLISHED THE FAMOUS POWERED PSYCHOTIC PROFILES.
HEIGHTENE
PARANOIAC
SCARECROW
THE FISHERMA
MATTER MAST
PROFESSOR I.
CAPTAIN BOOM
POWERS
PGS. 170-
JOHNS
ÜBER-GOD-COMPLEXES, HEIGHTENED PARANOIA, ADVANCED ISOLATION SYNDROME.
ASHLEY AND I WOULD GO TO HIS HOUSE FOR DINNER, AND HE'D TALK OUR EARS OFF.
EVEN THOUGH SHE HATED IT, I NEVER WANTED TO LEAVE.
I LOVED HEARING PEOPLE TALK. I COULDN'T STAND SILENCE.
ASHLEY AND I WERE MARRIED A MONTH BEFORE WE GRADUATED FROM THE METAHUMAN BEHAVIORAL SCIENCE UNIT.
HER FATHER WAS MY BEST MAN.
WEEKS LATER, ONE HORRIBLE HOUR WOULD CHANGE MY LIFE FOREVER.

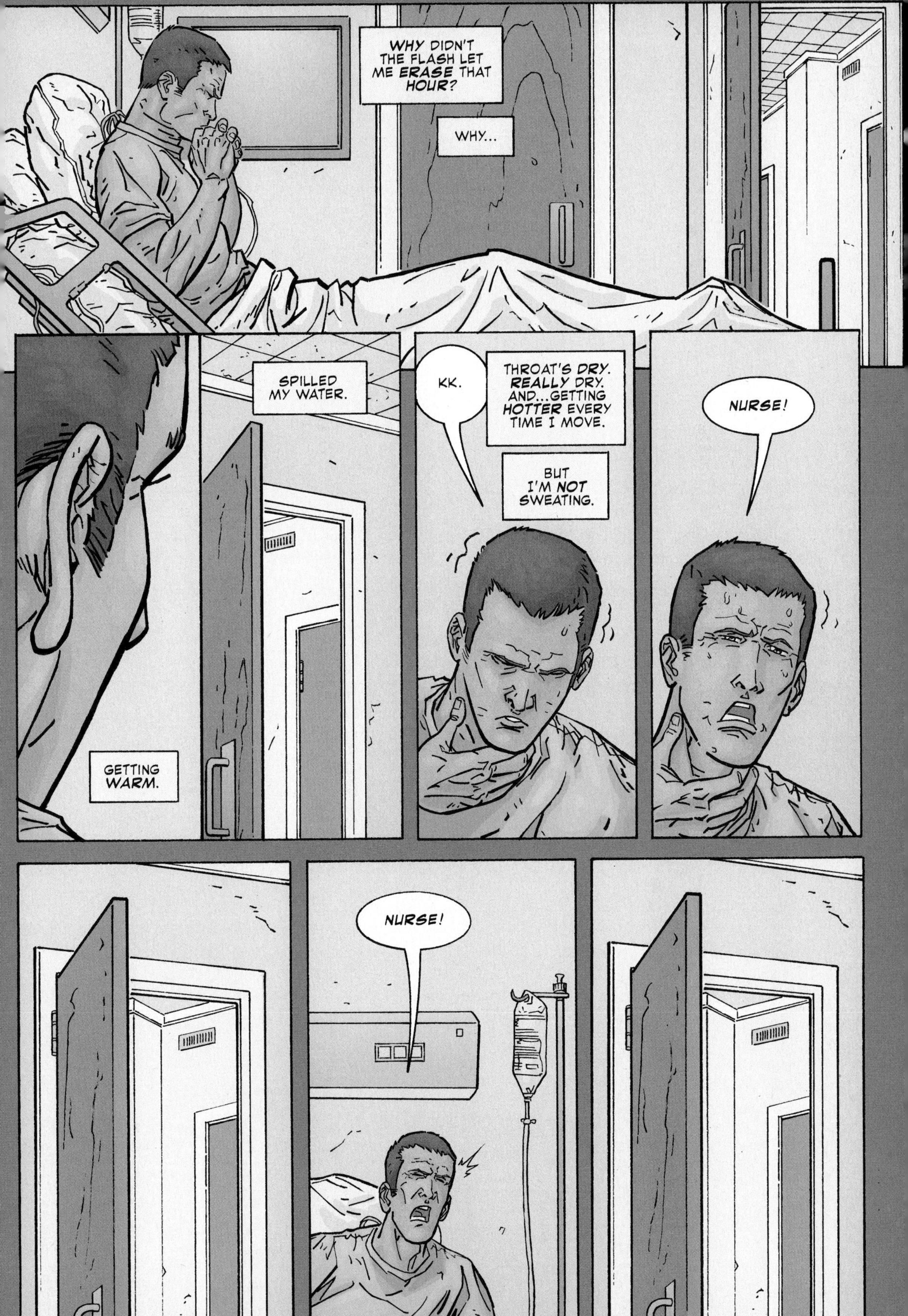
WHY DIDN'T THE FLASH LET ME ERASE THAT HOUR?
WHY...
GETTING WARM.
SPILLED MY WATER.
KK.
THROAT'S DRY. REALLY DRY. AND...GETTING HOTTER EVERY TIME I MOVE.
BUT I'M NOT SWEATING.
NURSE!
NURSE!

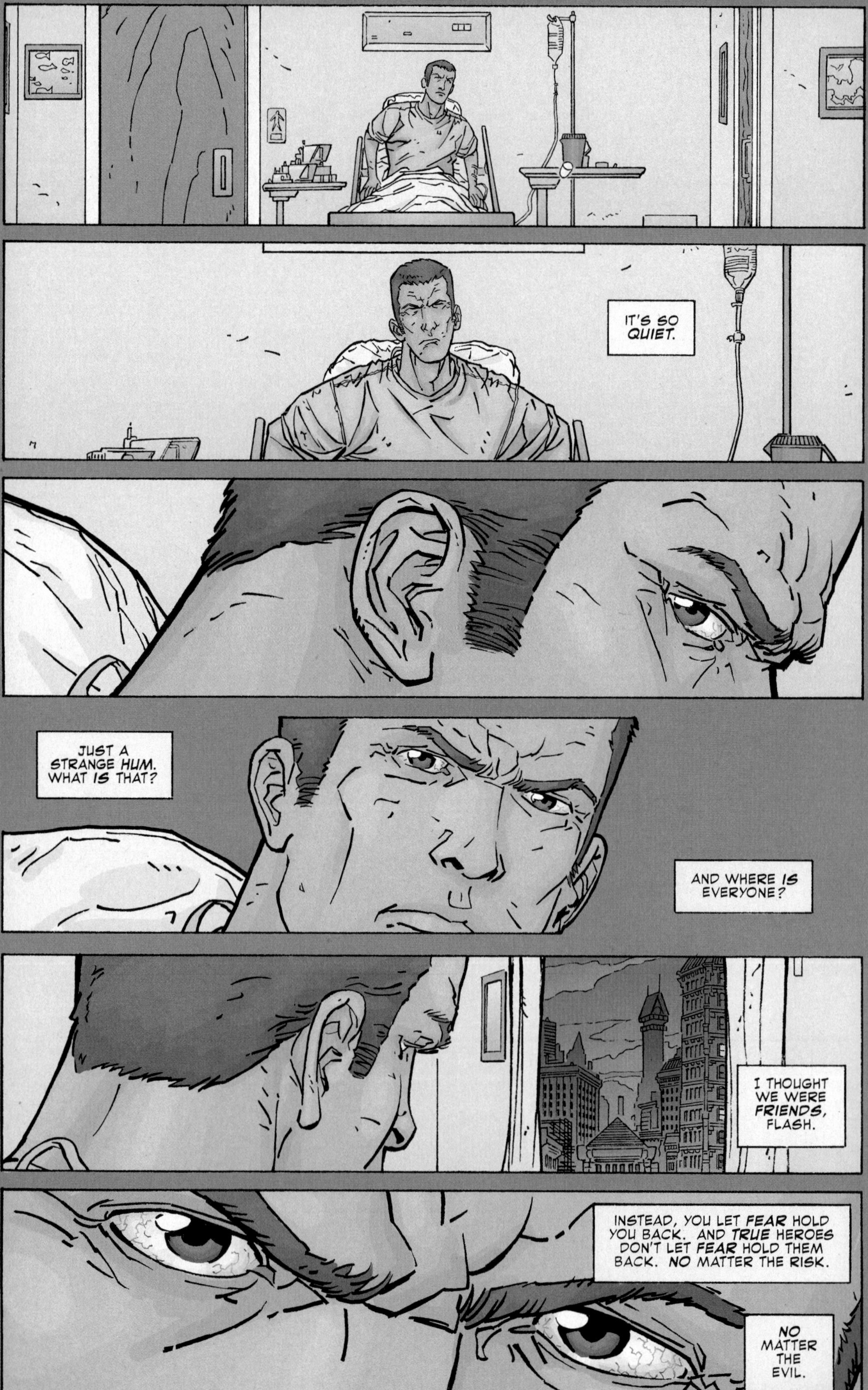
IT'S SO QUIET.
JUST A STRANGE HUM. WHAT IS THAT?
AND WHERE IS EVERYONE?
I THOUGHT WE WERE FRIENDS, FLASH.
INSTEAD, YOU LET FEAR HOLD YOU BACK. AND TRUE HEROES DON'T LET FEAR HOLD THEM BACK. NO MATTER THE RISK.
NO MATTER THE EVIL.

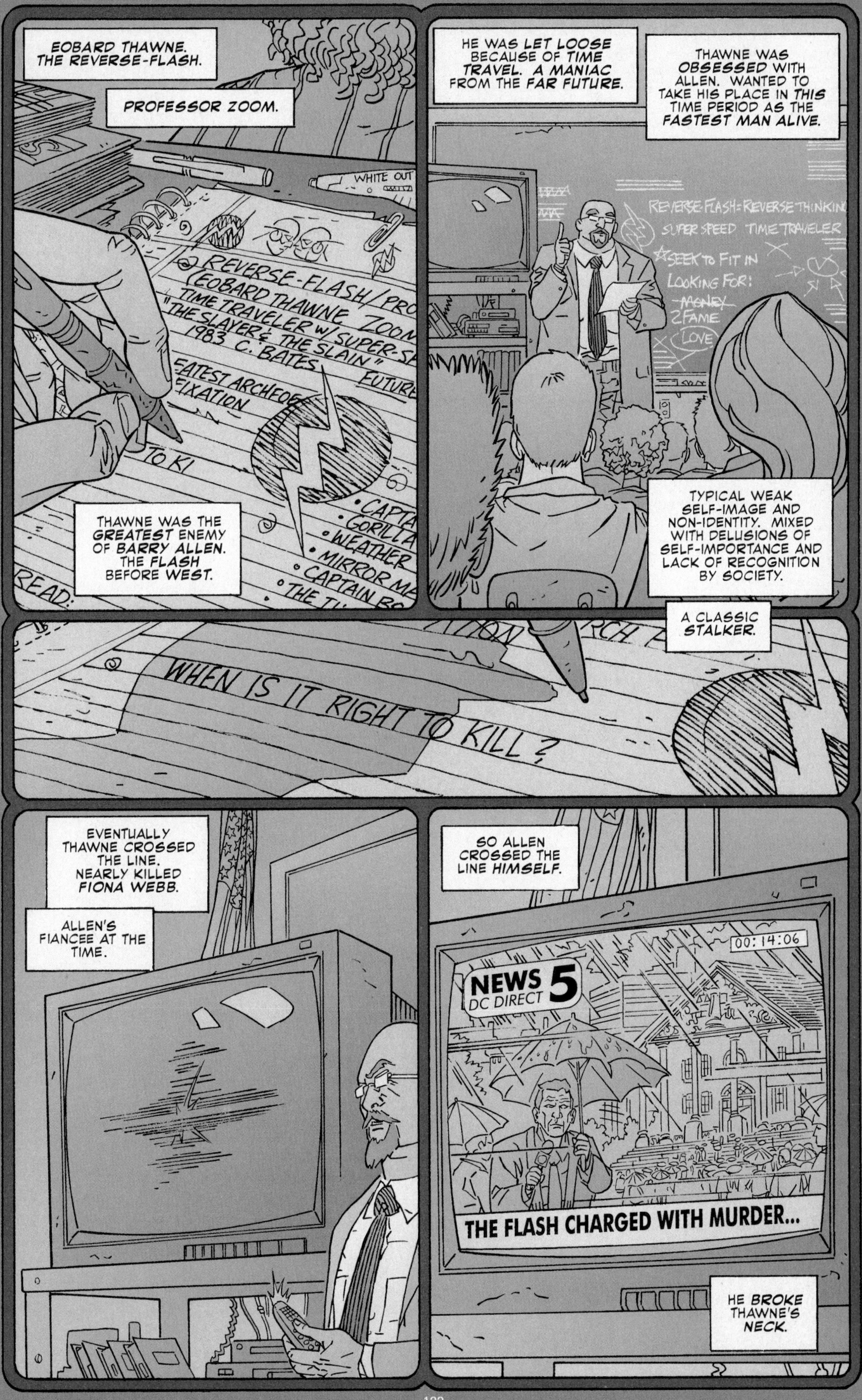
EOBARD THAWNE. THE REVERSE-FLASH.
PROFESSOR ZOOM.
WHITE OUT
REVERSE-FLASH/PRO
(EOBARD THAWNE ZOOM
TIME TRAVELER W/ SUPER-S
"THE SLAYER & THE SLAIN"
1983 C. BATES
FUTURE
FATEST ARCHFOE
FIXATION
TO KI
CAPTA
GORILLA
WEATHER
MIRROR MA
CAPTAIN BO
READ:
THAWNE WAS THE GREATEST ENEMY OF BARRY ALLEN. THE FLASH BEFORE WEST.
HE WAS LET LOOSE BECAUSE OF TIME TRAVEL. A MANIAC FROM THE FAR FUTURE.
THAWNE WAS OBSESSED WITH ALLEN. WANTED TO TAKE HIS PLACE IN THIS TIME PERIOD AS THE FASTEST MAN ALIVE.
REVERSE-FLASH = REVERSE THINKING
SUPER SPEED
TIME TRAVELER
SEEK TO FIT IN
LOOKING FOR:
MONEY
FAME
LOVE
TYPICAL WEAK SELF-IMAGE AND NON-IDENTITY. MIXED WITH DELUSIONS OF SELF-IMPORTANCE AND LACK OF RECOGNITION BY SOCIETY.
A CLASSIC STALKER.
WHEN IS IT RIGHT TO KILL?
EVENTUALLY THAWNE CROSSED THE LINE. NEARLY KILLED FIONA WEBB.
ALLEN'S FIANCEE AT THE TIME.
SO ALLEN CROSSED THE LINE HIMSELF.
00:14:06
NEWS 5
DC DIRECT
THE FLASH CHARGED WITH MURDER...
HE BROKE THAWNE'S NECK.

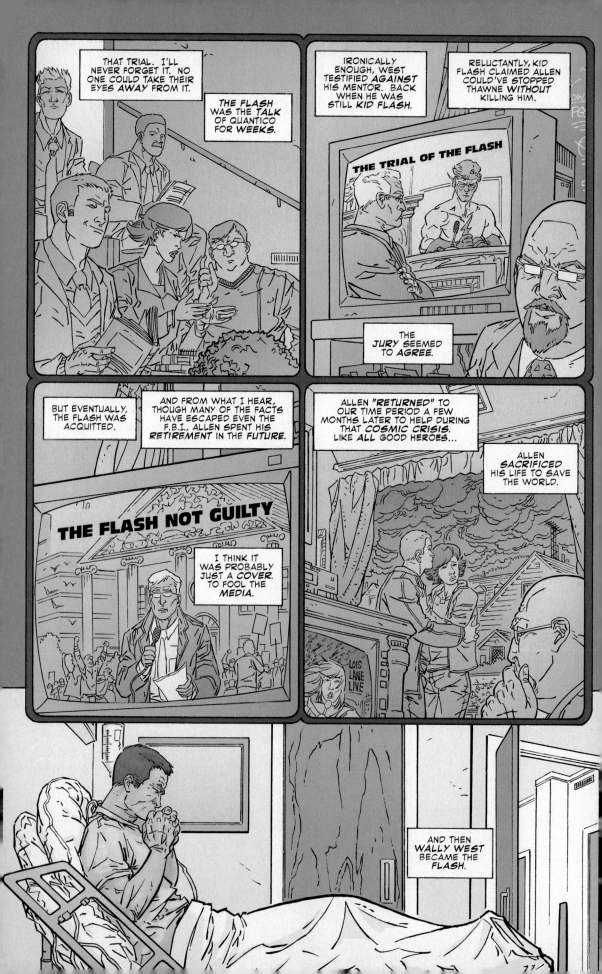

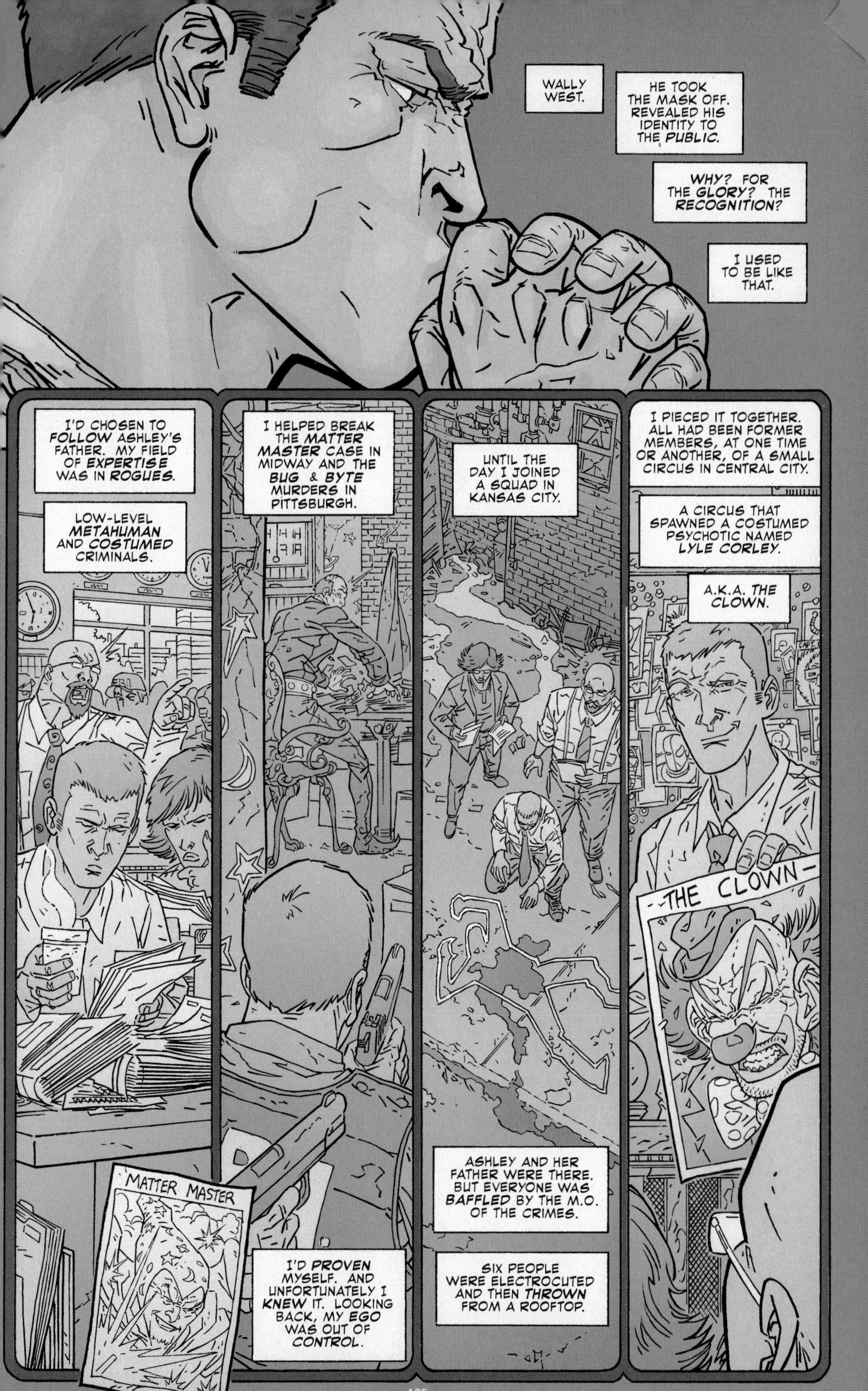
WALLY WEST.
HE TOOK THE MASK OFF. REVEALED HIS IDENTITY TO THE PUBLIC.
WHY? FOR THE GLORY? THE RECOGNITION?
I USED TO BE LIKE THAT.
I'D CHOSEN TO FOLLOW ASHLEY'S FATHER. MY FIELD OF EXPERTISE WAS IN ROGUES.
LOW-LEVEL METAHUMAN AND COSTUMED CRIMINALS.
MATTER MASTER
I HELPED BREAK THE MATTER MASTER CASE IN MIDWAY AND THE BUG & BYTE MURDERS IN PITTSBURGH.
I'D PROVEN MYSELF. AND UNFORTUNATELY I KNEW IT. LOOKING BACK, MY EGO WAS OUT OF CONTROL.
UNTIL THE DAY I JOINED A SQUAD IN KANSAS CITY.
ASHLEY AND HER FATHER WERE THERE. BUT EVERYONE WAS BAFFLED BY THE M.O. OF THE CRIMES.
SIX PEOPLE WERE ELECTROCUTED AND THEN THROWN FROM A ROOFTOP.
I PIECED IT TOGETHER. ALL HAD BEEN FORMER MEMBERS, AT ONE TIME OR ANOTHER, OF A SMALL CIRCUS IN CENTRAL CITY.
A CIRCUS THAT SPAWNED A COSTUMED PSYCHOTIC NAMED LYLE CORLEY.
A.K.A. THE CLOWN.
THE CLOWN

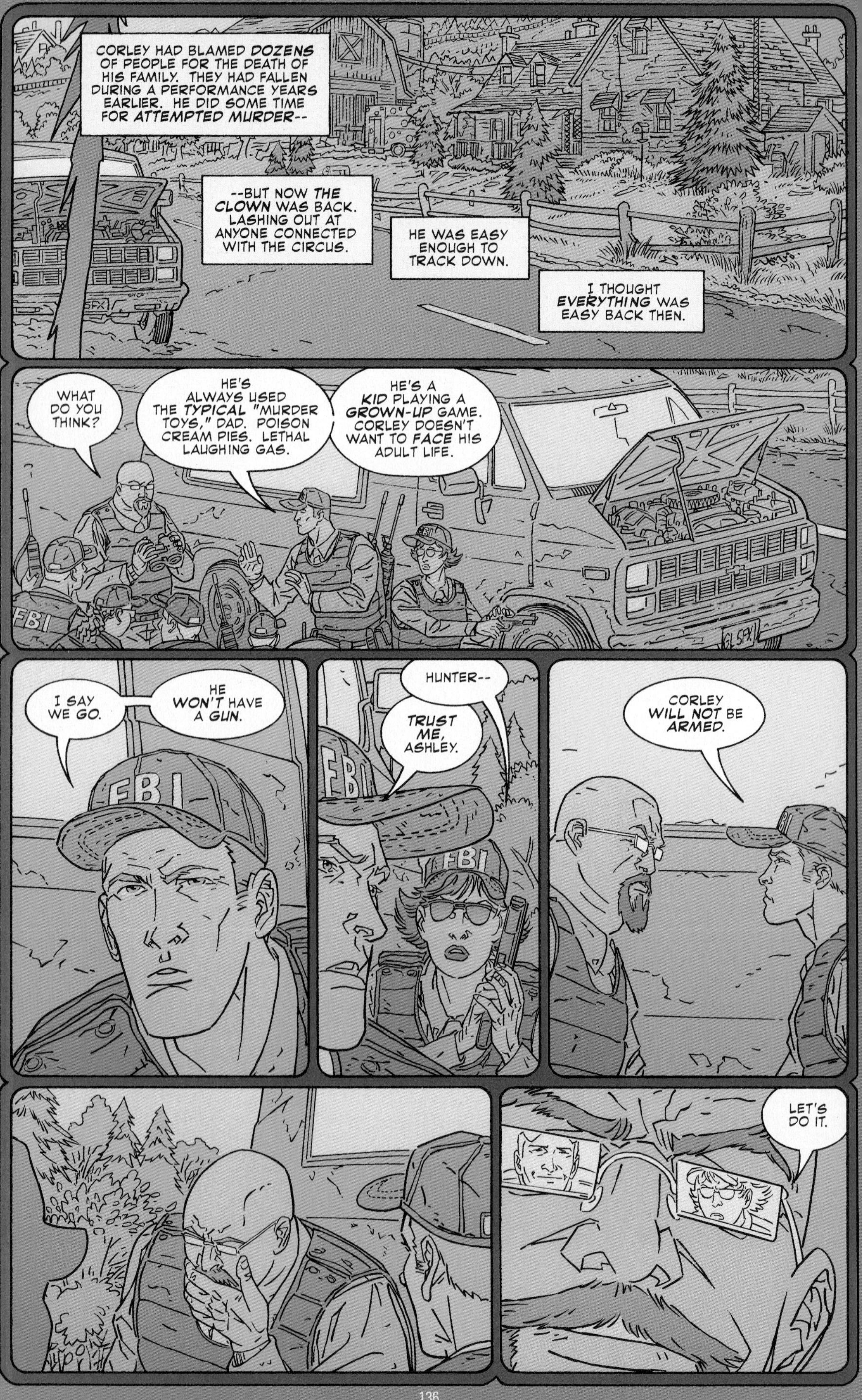
CORLEY HAD BLAMED DOZENS OF PEOPLE FOR THE DEATH OF HIS FAMILY. THEY HAD FALLEN DURING A PERFORMANCE YEARS EARLIER. HE DID SOME TIME FOR ATTEMPTED MURDER--
--BUT NOW THE CLOWN WAS BACK. LASHING OUT AT ANYONE CONNECTED WITH THE CIRCUS.
HE WAS EASY ENOUGH TO TRACK DOWN.
I THOUGHT EVERYTHING WAS EASY BACK THEN.
WHAT DO YOU THINK?
HE'S ALWAYS USED THE TYPICAL "MURDER TOYS," DAD. POISON CREAM PIES. LETHAL LAUGHING GAS.
HE'S A KID PLAYING A GROWN-UP GAME. CORLEY DOESN'T WANT TO FACE HIS ADULT LIFE.
FBI
I SAY WE GO.
HE WON'T HAVE A GUN.
HUNTER--
TRUST ME, ASHLEY.
CORLEY WILL NOT BE ARMED.
LET'S DO IT.

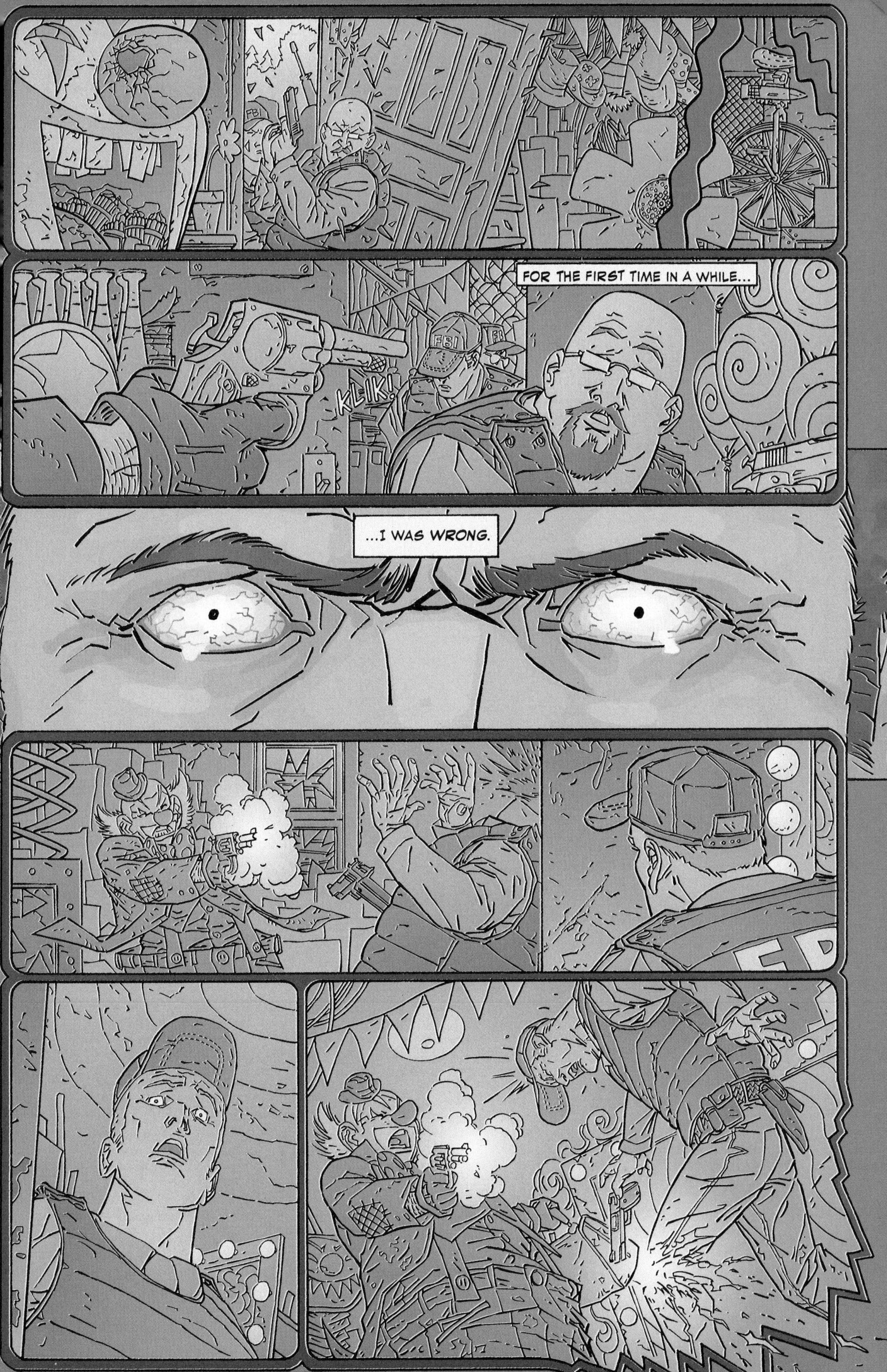
FOR THE FIRST TIME IN A WHILE...
KLIK!
...I WAS WRONG.

BLAM!

ASHLEY SHOT HIM DEAD. BUT I COULD STILL HEAR HIS *LAUGHTER.*

BOOM POW

NO ONE THERE EVER *FORGAVE* ME FOR WHAT HAPPENED.

THE BUREAU LET ME GO. ASHLEY FILED FOR *DIVORCE.*

WHEN THE KEYSTONE POLICE DEPARTMENT WENT LOOKING FOR A *PROFILER* TO HELP THEM WITH THEIR *INFESTED* CITY--

--IT WAS ALL I HAD.

UNTIL I MET THE FLASH.

THE FLASH.

AAAR!

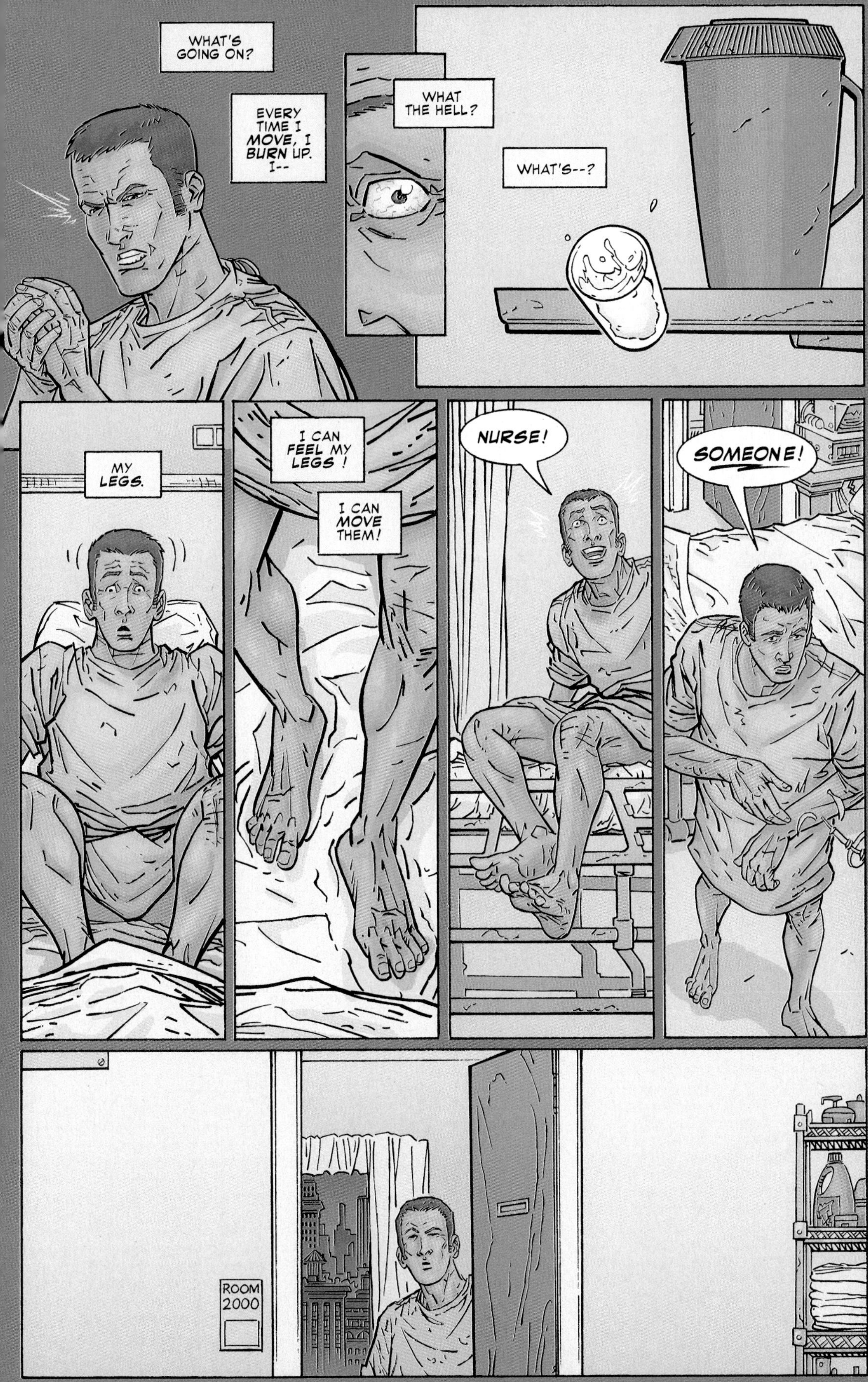
WHAT'S GOING ON?
EVERY TIME I MOVE, I BURN UP. I--
WHAT THE HELL?
WHAT'S--?
MY LEGS.
I CAN FEEL MY LEGS!
I CAN MOVE THEM!
NURSE!
SOMEONE!
ROOM 2000

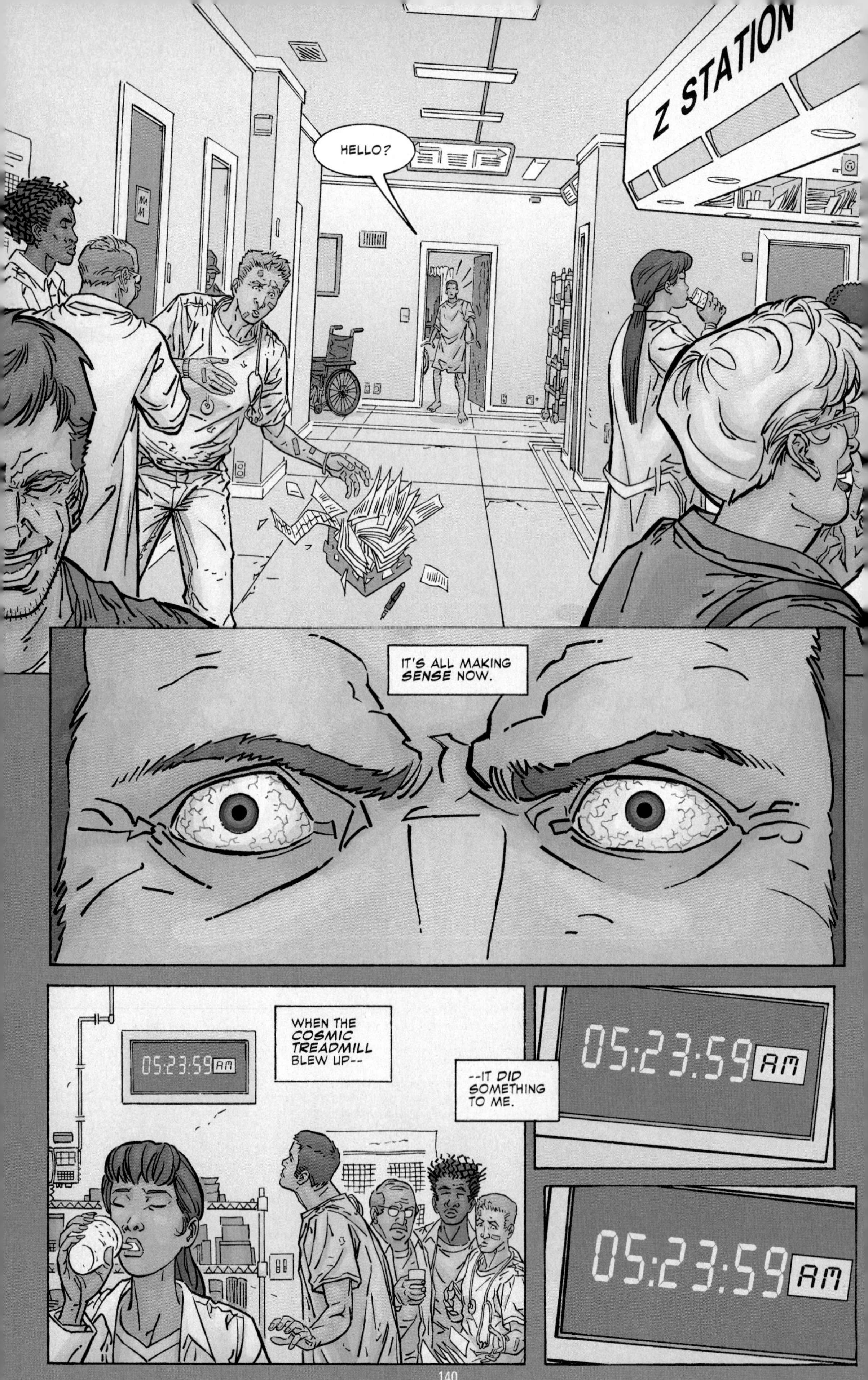
Z STATION
HELLO?
IT'S ALL MAKING *SENSE* NOW.
05:23:59 AM
WHEN THE *COSMIC TREADMILL* BLEW UP--
--IT *DID* SOMETHING TO ME.
05:23:59 AM
05:23:59 AM

THE *PEOPLE*. THE *GLASS* OF *WATER*. THE *HEAT* OF THE *FRICTION* ON MY *SKIN*.

AND THAT *HUMMING* SOUND.

IS *THIS* WHAT IT'S *LIKE*?

IS *THIS* WHAT IT'S LIKE TO BE THE *FLASH*?

THIS *SILENCE*...

MOTHER?

MY *THOUGHTS* ARE *JUMBLING* TOGETHER. JUMPING AROUND.

RUNNING.

WALKING.

FATHER.

ASHLEY.

FLASH.

IS IT THE *SPEED* OF MY *SYNAPSES* FIRING OFF? THE *EFFECT* OF *THINKING* THIS *FAST*?

OR HAS ALL OF THIS TAKEN ITS *TOLL* ON ME MORE THAN I EVER *REALIZED*?

HAS MY *GRASP* OF *REALITY* DETERIORATED SO MUCH THAT I CAN NO LONGER *FUNCTION* WITHIN IT?

IS IT THE *COSMIC TREADMILL* THAT'S DONE THIS TO ME--

Z STATION

--OR JUST MY MIND?

MY PSYCHIC COHESION IS *BREAKING* DOWN, ISN'T IT?

THE *THOUGHTS* IN MY HEAD AREN'T *RATIONAL.* THEY'RE *EMOTIONAL.*

IS THAT *RIGHT?* WHAT *MOTIVATES* THESE THOUGHTS? WHAT...

IF THIS REALLY *IS* HAPPENING... IT'S A *SIGN.*

I TRIED TO TELL THE FLASH BEFORE. THE *BEST* HEROES ARE THE HEROES WHO WILL TAKE *RISKS* TO HELP PEOPLE.

WHO HAVE *FACED* UNBELIEVABLE *TRAGEDY* AND *UNDERSTAND* WHY IT *MUST* BE PREVENTED.

AT *ANY* COST.

142

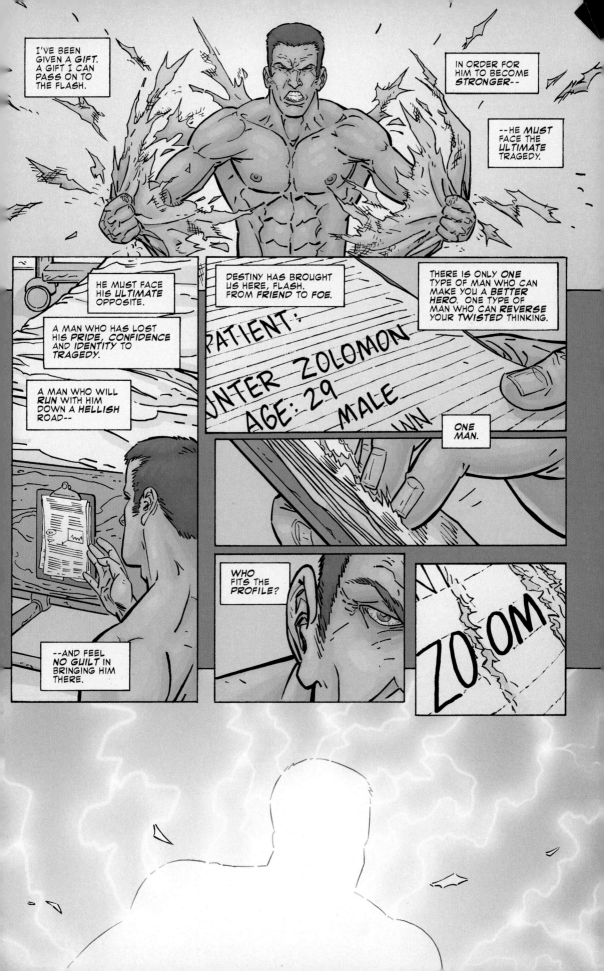

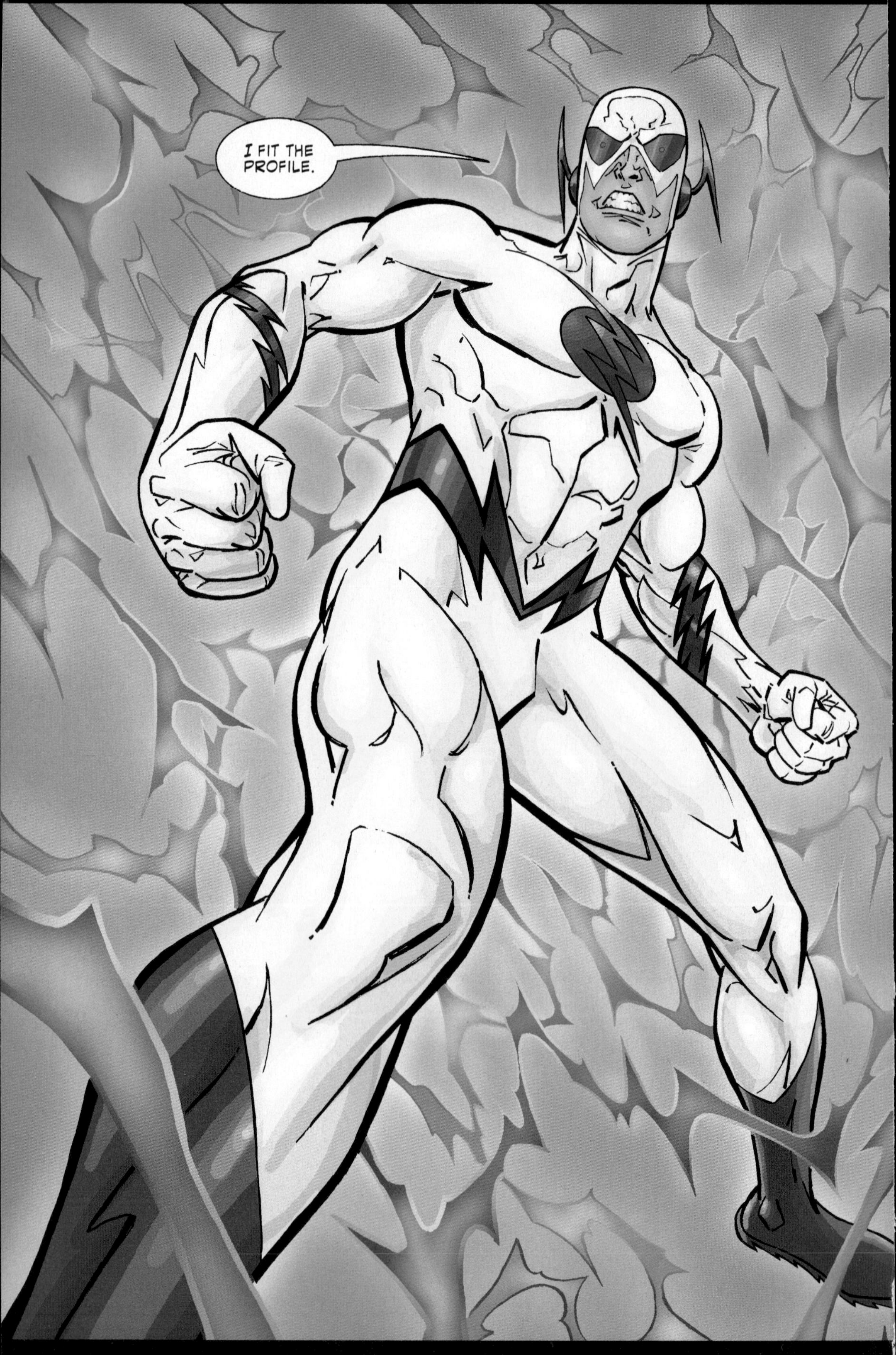
I FIT THE PROFILE.